The Hero of Panama

F. S. Brereton

[ZHINGOORA BOOKS]

This edition is published by
Zhingoora Books.

JIM RESCUES PHINEAS BARTON

Contents

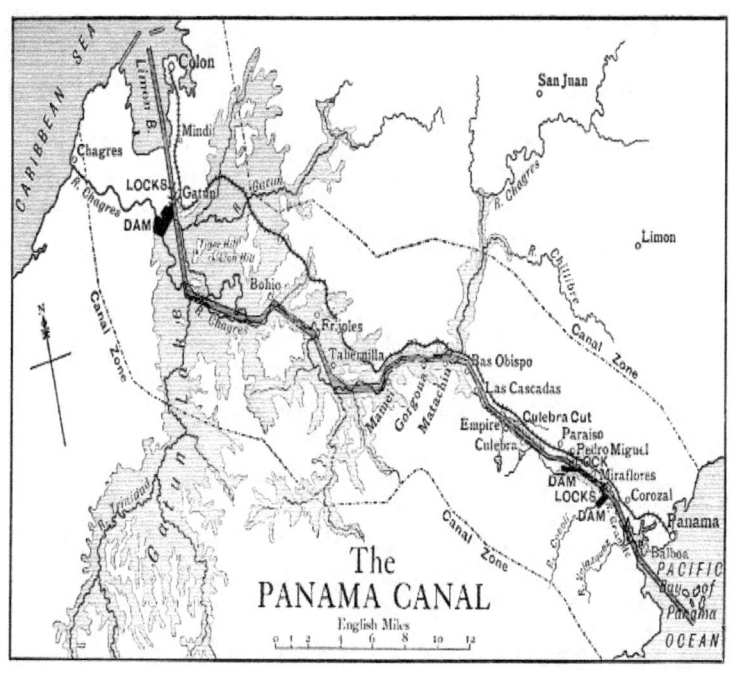

The
PANAMA CANAL

English Miles

CHAPTER I

A Post of Responsibility

It was one of those roasting days in the Caribbean, when, in spite of a steady trade wind, the air felt absolutely motionless, and the sea took on an oily surface from which the sun flashed in a thousand directions, in rays that seemed to have been lent some added fierceness by the reflection.

Squish! Squelsh! The ground surf, which was hardly perceptible from the coast, and scarcely so from the deck of a liner, was apparent enough from the old tub which wallowed in it. She rolled in a manner that was sickening to behold, until at times her scupper ports took in water, then a surge of the ocean would take her in a different direction; she would dive forward, dipping her nose in the oily sea till the hawser which had been passed out over her stern, secured to a large anchor, brought her up with a jerk and tumbled her backwards with her stern rail awash.

Ugh! It was enough to make a white man groan. Even a nigger would have been inclined to grumble. But the Chinamen aboard the tub seemed, if anything, rather to enjoy this rocking. One of them stood almost amidships, his feet wide apart to preserve his balance, while he gripped the handle of the pump he was working, and turned it over and over with a monotonous regularity that seemed to match with his surroundings.

The man, who was barefooted, boasted of the very lightest of clothing, and wore his pigtail rolled in a coil at the back of his head. Other protection against the roasting sun he had none. Indeed, to look at him, he hardly seemed to need it, while the hot blast which came from the adjacent land passed over him without any apparent effect. Ching Hu was in his element.

"Nicee place, missee," he sang out after a while. "Plenty nicee and warmee. Stay long? No? Velly solly."

On he went, turning the handle without a pause, while there crept into his slanting eyes just a trace of disappointment. He sighed ever so gently, then assumed his accustomed expression. Not the wisest man in all the world could have said whether Ching Hu were happy or otherwise.

Just about ten feet from him, sheltered beneath a narrow awning of dirty canvas, a girl stood on the deck of the small ship, or, rather, she occupied a projection which overhung the water. Had this vessel been a liner, one would have guessed that this projection was the gangway from which the ladder descended towards the water to enable passengers to come aboard. But here a rapid inspection proved it to be merely a platform built out from the side, and suspended some eight feet from the surface of the ocean. From it a clear view of the ship's side was to be obtained, and, in these wonderfully clear waters, of the sandy bottom of the lagoon at whose entrance the vessel was moored. And it was upon the latter, upon the bottom of this heaving ocean, that Sadie Partington's eyes were directed.

"Ching," she called out suddenly, turning towards him, "I think they'll be coming up right now. Call the boys."

"You sure, missee? Yes? Velly well."

Ching Hu raised his eyebrows quaintly as he asked the question, and on receiving a nod from the girl, who at once turned to stare into the water, he raised his voice and called aloud in a sing-song style which would have made a stranger laugh. "Tom, Tom!" he shouted. "You comee now wid Sam. Wanted plenty soon."

A black face popped instantly from the caboose leading to the cabin—a big, round face, the face of a negro of some thirty years of age. Then the shoulders came into view, and following them the whole figure of the man. He stood for a moment or two on the topmost step, balancing himself against the edge of the caboose, one hand gripping a plate, while the other vigorously polished it with a cloth. It gave one an opportunity of thoroughly inspecting this negro, and promptly one was filled with a feeling of pleasure. It was not because Tom was handsome, for he was the reverse of that. Nature had, indeed, liberally provided him with nose and lips, so much so that those two portions of his physiognomy were the most prominent at first sight. But if his nose were somewhat flattened and decidedly wide, and his lips undoubtedly big and prominent, Tom was possessed of other features which counterbalanced these detractions. His eyes seemed to attract attention at once. They seemed to smile at all and sundry on the instant, and flash a message to them. They were shining, honest eyes, which looked as if they could do nothing else but smile. Then the man's mouth completed his appearance of joviality; between the lips a gleaming double row of ivories were always to be seen, for Tom's smile was permanent. The smallest matter was sufficient to increase it, when the negro's ample face would be divided by a gaping chasm, a six-foot smile that could not be easily banished— the prelude to a roar of mirth and of deep-toned, spontaneous laughter. As for the rest of him, Tom was a monster. Six-feet-three in height, he was broad and thickset, and beside the dainty figure of Sadie Partington had the appearance of a veritable elephant.

"What you say, Chinaboy?" he asked, regarding the placid individual working the pump. "Come plenty soon, eh?"

"Ye-e-s. Missee say now."

"Den dinner be spoiled for sure. Taters boiled to rags ef I wait little minute. Stew no good ef left on fire for longer dan five minute. Missee, what you say dey doin'? They ain't gwine ter move yet?"

"Call Sam; you know as well as I do that the stew won't be spoiled. Come now, they're going to signal."

Sadie turned upon the negro with a frown, then again bent her eyes towards the bottom of the sea; for the girl was always ill at ease when the divers were working. Somehow or other, since her brothers had taken to this particular profession—and she had accompanied them upon their various trips—she had felt impelled to take upon herself the duty of watching them at work. She was only eleven now, though tall and old for her age, and for a year past she had almost daily taken her post on that tiny gangway to watch the two figures moving in the water below. For hours together she would be on the deck of this little boat, careless of the sun and heat, superintending the action of the pump and waiting for signals from the divers. And to Ching Hu, Tom, and the others her veriest nod was law. It was useless to argue with her: Sadie had a way of stamping her small foot which meant a great deal, and set all the men running to do her bidding. It was, therefore, with some show of alacrity that Tom prepared to follow his instructions.

"You Chinaboy," he commanded, grinning at a second Chinaman, who occupied the little galley down below, "yo make sure not boil de taters too much, and sniff dat stew. Not burn um, or, by de poker, Tom make yo smile. Yo comprenez what I say? Eh?"

He grinned one of his most expansive grins, and the Chinaman responded in a similar manner. He jerked his head in Tom's direction, thrusting it out of the galley door as he did so, and sending his pigtail flying. His little, pig-like eyes rolled while he brandished an enormous wooden spoon. "Ling knowee eberyting," he lisped. "See to dinner fine. Hab de stew beautiful."

"Den yo come along, yo Sam, lazy feller," shouted Tom at the pitch of his voice. "Whar yo got to, boy? I gives yo de biggest—oh, so yo dare!" he exclaimed, as a negro came from the after gangway, where a small ladder led to some of the men's quarters. "Yo's been sleepin'."

Tom held out an accusing finger, and gripped his comrade by the bare arm; for, without shadow of doubt, Sam's eyes were blinking. He had the appearance of a man who has just awakened. But the negro shook his head vigorously.

"Yo let go my arm, Tom, yo big elephant," he said, grinning widely. "I'se been down b'low fetchin' a bucket o' coal. What yo want?"

"Missie dar order us both; de boys is comin' up."

Tom still gripped the second negro, and playfully lifted him from off his feet as if he were merely a child, then he set him down against the ship's rail, while the two at once stared into the water. Truly they might have been described as brothers, so very alike were Tom and Sam in appearance. In fact, had their two heads been alone protruding from a window even Sadie would have been troubled to distinguish between them; but the similarity ended with the faces. Tom was huge, Sam was barely five feet in height, and slim in proportion; but he seemed to have inherited all the dignity which Tom had missed. Merry enough at all times, Sam was inclined to be a trifle pompous, and of a Sunday, when in port, his get-up generally was sufficient to open the eyes of everyone who beheld him. Now, however, his feet were bare, and he wore but a shirt and loose cotton trousers.

Let us join them at the rail and stare over into the water. Beneath the oily surface a wide stretch of yellowish-white sand was spread out on every hand, till it became a greenish tinge, and was finally lost in the blurr of the ocean; but directly beneath the ship it sparkled in the sun, while one could easily see the tiniest prominence, the few rocks existing here and there, and the deep shadow of the ship riding to her anchors. A derrick was rigged out over the rail, close to the platform occupied by Sadie, and from this was suspended a long wooden ladder, with ponderous weights attached to its lower end. Close at hand, through a sort of stirrup, passed a couple of ropes, while the piping conveying air to those below ran out over the gangway. It was there, too, that the smaller signal lines were attached.

As Tom and Sam looked over, their eyes caught the reflection from two metal objects down below, and very soon the latter became apparent as the helmets of the divers. They could see the two—for there were that number at work—seated on a huge boulder, side by side, while within some fifteen feet of them were the broken timbers and debris of what had once upon a time been a vessel.

"They've sat like that this past fifteen minutes," explained Sadie. "Seems that there's nothing to be found in the wreck. They'll be wanting to be hauled aboard in a minute. There's George moving."

As she spoke, one of the helmets swung slowly backwards, while the eyes inside peered aloft. Then there came a jerk at the life line. Sadie instantly responded.

"Coming up," she said. "Get a hold of the tackle, boys."

She still kept her place, superintending operations, while Tom and Sam together gripped the tackle, and, having pulled gently at first, began to haul lustily. In a little while one of the divers had reached the foot of the weighted ladder. At once the tackle was slacked off, while all watched the man slowly ascending from the depths, dipping deeper as the swell rolled the ship, and coming nearer the surface as she returned to an even keel. Then, with a squelch, the top of the shining helmet broke through the surface, the man reached the rail, and was lifted aboard. Sadie proceeded at once to loosen the screws securing the helmet to the rest of the dress, and lifted the huge metal globe from off the shoulders of the seated man.

"What luck, George?" she asked impetuously, staring anxiously into his face, and noticing how tired the man seemed, and how sallow he was. "You found something? It's going to pay?"

"Not if we work a year at it," came the answer in a dull, despondent tone of voice. "Help me to get this dress off, Sadie, my dear. I'm burning in it. I've felt smothered, so hot that I couldn't work down below. Jim's coming up at once."

The second diver was, in fact, already being hauled up, and anyone who happened to have watched the first make his ascent from the depths would at once have remarked the difference between the two. For the diver who now sat on a box on the swaying deck of the small vessel was bigger than he who was ascending; at the same time his movements had been far less active. The one now nearing the top of the ladder clambered up the rungs with the agility of a cat, in spite of the fact that every foot he rose made the weights he carried on his back and chest and on his boots all the heavier. His helmet shot out of the water with a burst, as the vessel rolled heavily, pulling the ladder up, only to throw it back at once.

"You hold on dar tight, yo, Massa Jim," shouted Tom, as he leaned over the rail. "Yo tink dis all a beanfeast. Not so when de ship roll so much. S'pose yo lose de hold. Buzz! Yo go right down to de bottom and stay dere fer good. Huh! Come in."

He gripped the extended hand of the diver, hauled the boy aboard, and promptly seated him on a second box. Three minutes later the helmet was off, and one had an opportunity of contrasting the young fellow who had appeared with the diver who had first of all ascended.

The latter was a young man of twenty-five perhaps, and, as we have said, was decidedly sallow and unhealthy-looking; in fact, natural good looks were marred not a little by his complexion. But with the one who had been addressed as Jim it was different. The young fellow was barely seventeen years of age, and his rosy cheeks displayed the fact that diving did not disagree with him.

11

Then, too, his voice was so different. It was crisp and laughing, and anything but despondent; while, when he had rid himself of his diving weights and of his heavy boots, and was on his feet, one saw that he was of a good height, held himself well, and moved with the quick step that one might have expected from having seen him clamber from the depths of the ocean. But there was concern in his face when Sadie called him.

"George don't feel over well, Jim," she called out. "He said a minute back that he was burning hot; now he's downright shivering."

"Fever," said Jim promptly, taking his brother's hand. "Tom, there, just leave Sam and Ching to haul in the tackle. I want you."

"Sah, what for? De master ill?"

Even his smile was almost gone as he looked at George with eyes which were startled and wide open, for the happy-go-lucky Tom, so unused to sorrow or sickness, could tell at a glance that his young employer was anything but himself.

"Get along and fetch a bed on deck," commanded Jim; "then rig a shelter over it. Best place it right aft; there's more room, and you'll be able to pull the awnings over better. George'll stay on deck; it's too hot down below."

Pulling his diving suit off hurriedly, he helped his sister to disrobe the sick man; then, with Tom at George's head and Jim at his feet, they carried him aft and laid him on the bed already prepared. Sadie at once took her seat beside him, armed with a fan, while the negro, Tom, hastened to fetch water from the big canvas sack in which it was placed every day to cool. A strong dose of quinine was given to the sick man, and thereafter there was little to do but to watch him and tend to his immediate needs.

"We'll get up anchor and make right off for Colon," said Jim, as he stood beside his sister, some little distance from the bed. "There's nothing down there to salve, and we're wasting time and money. Better get back and see if there isn't another job to be had. This salvage work ain't paying us at all. We're losing heavily. Guess we'll have to get back on to the land."

Even he was a little despondent as he spoke, for matters had indeed not been going well for George, Jim, and Sadie. Americans born, one only of the three could remember their mother; for she had died shortly after Sadie's birth. But their father was a constant and pleasant memory to them all, for he had been with them till six months previously. A diver by profession, Mr. Silas Partington had managed to save a few dollars, and had bought up a salvage plant, with which for a while he had done excellent business. Then he had met with a grave misfortune. He and those whom he employed had worked for weeks at the salving of a sunken steamer, and had actually brought her to the surface and commenced to tow her into shallow water, when an accident had happened. The bulkhead which they had bolted across the huge rent made in the ship's side by a collision that had sent her to the bottom had, for some unforeseen reason, blown out. The air which had been forced into the vessel, and which had expelled nearly all the water in her, thus bringing her to the surface, had escaped at once, and down she had gone under the ocean; but on that occasion she had found her bed in a deep hollow, where diving was impossible.

"It just broke Father," said George, when describing the thing to Jim. "He lost heavily. There were weeks of work paid for, besides valuable plant lost. It brought him down to this."

"This" was the purchase of an old vessel, and the seeking of salvage jobs along the Caribbean coast. Silas had brought his children with him—George because he was already a partner, Jim and Sadie because he could not afford to keep them on the mainland. The cruise along the coast of Mexico had proved disastrous, for Silas had been blown overboard during one of those terrible tornadoes which occasionally sweep the gulf, and George was left to fend for the family—an undertaking he found none too easy. Jobs were few and far between, and that wretched Caribbean swell, together with a shifting, sandy bottom, made salvage work extremely difficult. The coffers of the Partington family were, indeed, already very empty, and the time was at hand when the ship must be sold to pay wages. And now George was down with fever.

"It's this hole of a place," growled Jim, as he thought the matter out that evening. "A man can't work off this fever-stricken coast and escape it. We'll get back to America. Somehow or other we'll manage to get work."

Early that evening George again was in a high, burning fever, and needed careful watching; but as the night wore on he quietened down. During the first hours of the morning the terrible burning again seized the sick man, and in a moment, as it seemed, he awoke in a frenzy and leaped from his bed. Dashing Jim aside as if he were a child, and knocking Sam to the deck, he leaped over the rail and splashed into the water. In the dim light they watched him striking out for the shore, and as they followed in the dinghy they saw him clamber on to the mud banks and enter the forest. But though Jim searched high and low, and lay off that pestilential part for a solid week, often repeating his search in the forest, there was never any trace of his brother. The sick man was utterly swallowed up by the jungle.

"Dead?" asked Sadie sorrowfully, her young cheeks hollowed by the trouble.

Jim nodded. "Sure," he said, with emphasis. "Dropped in some corner and never rose again. There's no manner of use searching further. Sadie dear, we've got to get ashore and set up somewhere for ourselves. I've got to be father and brother and everything to you."

That, indeed, was the position of affairs. Sadie was too young to look to her own fortunes, while Jim was none too old. But an American lad can make as good a struggle as anyone: Jim swore that he would. He had long since tried to remember friends of his father's, but had given the matter up as hopeless. There were only Ching, Tom, and Sam, all three of whom had been employed on the salvage plant, and were old servants.

"Too poor to help us, anyway," he thought. "They'll easily get employment, and will go their own way. I'll have to hunt out a job in New York. I'll take anything that'll give me enough to feed and give a roof to Sadie. Besides, there's the boat; there'll be a little left for her when all the wages are paid."

"And I ain't gwine ter be dismissed, not nohow," said Tom, when Jim told the jolly negro of his plans. "Me and Sam and Ching's been doin' a jaw. We're a-goin' to hold on to you and missie. We're all a-goin' ter get work together till you've made a pile fer yerself and can give us employment. Yo ain't no right ter order us away."

Thus it happened that Jim, having sold the boat and effects at Colon, went aboard a coaster bound for New York, Sadie and Tom and Sam, with the Chinaman, accompanying him.

"There's five hundred dollars in this bag," he told his sister. "That'll keep the wolf away till we've had time to look round. Don't you fear, Sadie; we'll land upon something good yet, and, who knows, one of these days, perhaps, I'll make that pile that Tom's always talking about. But guess it'll want a heap of doing."

CHAPTER II

En route for New York

"Wanted, hands to help in building construction down town, New York."
The advertisement caught Jim's eye as soon as he looked at the newspaper which happened to be aboard the coaster on which he and Sadie and the others were voyaging to New York, and fascinated him.
"See here, Sadie," he said. "It'll be just the thing. There must be heaps of jobs which I could do, even though I have no knowledge of building. Carrying bricks and so on, you know. There will be good wages, and the money will keep us going while I look round. Eh?"
"And perhaps there'll be a firm working in the docks round New York," ventured the wise Sadie. "Then you'd be able to get a job at diving. I shouldn't mind there; it isn't as dangerous. This building work would give Tom and Sam and Ching jobs too."
"Sure!" exclaimed Jim, beginning at once to feel less despondent. Not that this young American was apt to be downcast for long. But we must tell the whole truth concerning him. The heavy responsibilities so suddenly cast upon his shoulders, and the persistent ill fortune of the family, had somewhat upset his nerves, and robbed him of a little of his accustomed jollity. Still, with five hundred dollars behind him, and this advertisement before his eyes, he felt that the far future might be left to take care of itself; for the immediate prospects were brightening.
"We'll take the job, the whole lot of us," he said, as they sat on the deck in the dusk discussing matters. "We'll take a little tenement down in the working quarters. You'll housekeep, Sadie, and we four will go and earn dollars. Gee! There's no frightening me. This thing was beginning to get on top of me, and bear me down; but now, not a bit of it. I'll win out; one of these days I'll own a salvage plant of my own."
It is better to face difficulties brightly and with full courage than tackle them half-heartedly. Jim felt all the stronger for his courage, and paced the deck alone that night with hopes raised, and with full assurance for the future.
"I'll get a widow woman, or someone respectable like that, to come and help Sadie keep house," he said to himself. "It'll be company for her while I'm away. And of course there's her education: she'll have to have more schooling. We've

rather forgotten that she's still only a child, for she behaves as if she were grown up."

That was, indeed, one of the pathetic items in the history of Jim's family. His father, Silas, had been pressed as it were into a course of action which meant a sudden cessation of all home life for Sadie, and which brought the child amongst grown-up men when she should have been at school, with some of her own sex about her, and playmates to romp with. Circumstances had, in fact, acted adversely both for Silas and his daughter.

"But we'll alter all that," Jim told himself. "Heigho! I'm for turning in."

He paced the deck once or twice more, then crept down the companion. He was nearing the bottom, when his progress was suddenly arrested by a shout.

"What's that?" he wondered. "Came from right forward."

Curiosity caused him to run nimbly up the steps again. His head was just emerging from the opening when the shout was repeated, while it was taken up instantly by men above his head, on the bridge of the ship. At the same moment there came the tinkle of the engine telegraph.

"Port! Port your helm! Hard a port!" he heard the lookout shout from his post on the forecastle. "Ship ahead! Port your helm!"

"Hard astern, Mr. Dingle! hard astern!" came in steady but sharp tones from the bridge, then there followed once more the tinkle of the telegraph. Jim felt the tremble and throb of the engines suddenly die down; indistinct shouts came to him from somewhere in the interior of the coaster. Then the engine throbs recurred furiously, as if the ship were making a frantic effort. Crash!

He was thrown hard against the combing of the gangway, his head striking the woodwork heavily, so that he was partially stunned. That and the succeeding jar, as the coaster came end on into the bows of another steamer, toppled Jim over. He lost his foothold, and rolled down the steps into the gangway down below. Then he picked himself up, feeling dazed and giddy, and for a moment held tight to a pillar supporting the deck.

"A collision," he told himself. "A bad one too—full tilt into one another. It's shaken the electric light out. Lucky they keep an emergency oil lamp going."

The temptation to dash up on deck was strong within him, and had he been alone on the vessel, with none to care for, no doubt he would have obeyed the inclination. But there was Sadie; Jim was her protector. He dashed at once towards her cabin, and came upon her at the doorway, looking frightened.

"There's been a collision, Sadie, dear," he said, endeavouring to keep his voice quiet. "Guess we may have to move; let me come in and fix you."

The child was not undressed, fortunately, and Jim at once pushed into the cabin, groped for one of the cork life preservers which are placed in overhead racks, and adjusted it to her body.

"Now," he said, "bring a warm coat, and leave the other things. Ah, here's Tom!"

"Sah; me here, right enough. You's not hurt, nor missie?"

"Not a scratch, Tom. Just take Sadie right up on deck and stand beside her. That Sam?"

In the dusk outside there was a second figure, and behind that another. The faithful negroes, and Ching Hu, the Chinaman, had rallied at once to their youthful master.

"Me, in course," cried the little Sam. "Guess this here's a collision. But we ain't got no cause to mind; not at all, not at all, missie."

"Get life belts, put them on, and then go on deck," said Jim shortly. "Sadie, take charge of this bag of dollars. I'm going up to see what's happened."

Conscious that he had done all that was possible, and that Sadie was now in excellent hands, he turned and made for the companion, directing Tom to take the whole party on deck, and wait for him near the companion. With a few active steps he was there himself, and able to look about him. There was a slight sea fog enveloping the ship, through which, a hundred yards away, shone the lights of a steamer. Shouts came from her deck, while her siren was blowing frantically. On board the craft on which he himself stood there was also considerable noise and confusion. A couple of lights were swaying right forward, and running there Jim saw that a man was being slung over the bows in a rope's end. Right aft, where were quarters for steerage passengers, there was the sound of many voices, shouts, and hoarse cries of alarm, and once the shrill shriek of a woman.

"How'd it happen?" he asked one of the deck hands standing near him.

"How do most of these here things happen, siree?" came the answer. "This here fog did it. The lookouts war bright enough; but reckon the two ships jest bumped clean into the same course, and didn't see one another till their bows was touchin'. We're holed badly, I'm thinking. You take my advice, and get hold of your traps."

Jim leaned over the rail, and stared at the man swinging in the rope's end. The lantern he carried showed a huge rent in the bows of the ship, while the sound of rushing water came to his ears.

"Six feet by five, down under the water line, mostly," came from the man. "You'd better be slinging me over a sailcloth or something, or else the water'll fill her."

"They'll never do it," thought Jim, staring at the rent. "I've been enough on board ships to know what this means. I'll get back and see that Sadie's safe."

He ran back to the companion, where he discovered his friends seated on the hatchway.

"Tom," he said, "come along below with me. We shall have to take to the boats, and the sooner we've food with us the better. Lead along to the galley."

"Purser's store, sah; I knows very well. You say we gwine ter leave de ship."

"She's holed badly; she's bound to founder, I guess."

"Den de Lor' help us!" groaned Tom. "You listen here, sah. Forty Spaniard workmen living aft. Dey play de dickens. Dey fight for de boats. Not like dat at all. Tom say dat dere be trouble."

The mention of the men who had taken passage aft caused Jim some amount of perturbation. He had noticed them as he came aboard, and it was because of their presence on the ship that he had taken passage for himself and Sadie amidships.

"I'd have gone steerage with her had it not been for those dagoes," he had told himself. "There's little enough money to spare nowadays for luxuries; but they're a rough crowd, and I wouldn't like Sadie to be amongst them."

It had followed that he and Sadie had taken berths amidships, while Tom and Sam and Ching had, as a natural course, got places aft. Jim realized, now that Tom reminded him of the fact, that the Spaniards on the ship might prove a greater danger to them than the foundering of the vessel.

"Guess they're a rough crowd, and likely to lose their heads," he said aloud. "Let's get some food quick, Tom, and then see what's happening. We'll keep close together."

They ran along the alley way towards the purser's store, and, finding the door closed, Tom burst it in with a mighty heave from his shoulder. Jim snatched one of the hanging oil lanterns, and together they made a hurried survey of the contents.

"Here's a sack; hold it open, Tom," commanded Jim.

He ran his eyes round the shelves, then, without hesitation, pitched tins of preserved beef, of milk, and of other foodstuffs into the sack. In little more than a minute it was full to the neck.

"Get ahead," said Jim promptly. "I'll bring along this cask."

He stuffed a metal cup into one pocket, and hoisted a small cask of beer on to his shoulder. Had he been able to make a careful selection he would have sought for water; but in an emergency beer would do as well as anything, and already he knew that time was very limited. Indeed the ship had already a bad list on her; she leaned so much to one side that walking was difficult, while she was down at the head so that his return to the companion was made uphill. But in a little while the two arrived, panting, at the top of the companion, Tom bearing the lantern with him.

"Holy poker! but dere's the duce of a row aft, massa," sang out Sam, seeing them arrive. "I tink dem men is trying to put out de boats."

"How many are there?" asked Jim quickly.

"Seven, I tink. One just here; the others aft. Not like de noise dem scum make."

Jim had never been aboard a vessel under similar circumstances, and had therefore never experienced the confusion which follows a collision. He had read of such affairs, and had marvelled at the wonderful coolness and discipline maintained in some cases. Then he had heard of very opposite results, where men had lost their heads, and where they had fought, each for his own individual safety, as if they were wild beasts. Remembering the class of individual who had taken passage aboard this coaster, he could not help but wonder whether discipline would be maintained on this occasion. The shouts, the babel of sounds coming from the stern, seemed to indicate the opposite.

"See here, Tom," he said, when he had listened for a while. "You and Ching will stay right here by this boat, taking care of Sadie. Just give a look to the tackle, swing her out, and put all the grub on board. Best put Sadie there also. Sam and I'll get along right now to see what's being done. The captain maybe'll want some help. Those fellows along there appear to be fighting like demons."

"Den you git along, sah. Me and Sadie'll be all right. Ching Hu, yo Chinaboy, jest you hoist dat cask aboard, and mind yo don't let um tumble."

That was the best of the huge negro; he could be depended upon to keep his head, while his devotion to Sadie was without question. Jim felt no qualms as to his sister's security as he dashed forward again, Sam close at his heels. A minute later he met a little group coming towards him swiftly. It was the captain of the vessel, with his two officers, and some half-dozen men.

"It's a case with us," Jim heard him say as the group came to a halt.

"She'll be down in half an hour, and that don't give us too much time to get ready. Mr. Jarvis, jest hop down to the engine room and tell 'em all to come up. Quartermaster, guess you'd best make a round of all the cabins; there's time for that, and we want to see that no one's left. You others had best come along with me: we've got to fix those fellows aft. They tell me they're fighting like rats to get the boats out. We'll have to stop 'em. Glad I am there's so few women aboard. What about the young lady amidships?"

"She's safe, Captain," broke in Jim at once. "I've put her in charge of one of my negroes and the Chinaman. She's been placed in the boat by the companion, and we've got food and drink there also. I'm ready to come along and help you aft."

There was a lantern swinging in the captain's hand. He lifted it coolly, for there was no trace of flurry about this solid-looking man, and closely scrutinized Jim's features.

"Gee!" he exclaimed, reaching out to shake his hand. "You're the sort of chap a skipper's glad to know. You've seen to the safety of the sister, as is only right, and now you come along shoulder to shoulder with us. Guess there'll be bad trouble back there."

"Guess there will," answered Jim. "They're fighting, if one can judge by the noise."

"Jest like tigers, and they'll take some quelling. Look here; get a hold of anything handy and don't stand no nonsense. We can't afford to take lip from any of those Spaniards. Ef a man shows a knife, lay him flat on the deck. Come along."

He led the way swiftly along the deck, and the handful of men with him followed closely, picking up any likely weapon as they went. Jim possessed himself of an axe handle. It was long, and moderately heavy, while sufficiently tough to withstand any blow. He swung it up over his shoulder and took his place beside the captain and his mate. In a minute they had arrived at the rail from which one overlooked the small waist of the vessel, where the steerage passengers were accommodated. An oil lamp hung from the boom, which was housed in its crutches over the waist, and the feeble rays served to show what was happening. There were a couple of boats on either side of the deck, and about these a seething mass of men fought. Without knowledge of the sea, having no idea how to swing the boats out, and no order or method, the result of the frantic efforts of these foreign workmen had been disastrous in one case at least. One of the boats hung suspended from the tackles, while its stern washed in the water below, spars and oars and sails having been tumbled out of it. The other three still hung in their davits, and had been hoisted by the tackles from the crutches placed between their keels and the decks. As the captain and his men arrived, some of the men below were tugging at the tackles, while others were cutting the canvas covers of the boats adrift with their knives. In one corner of the waist of the ship three women were huddled, two men being engaged in a desperate fight within three feet of them.

"Down below there!" bellowed the captain. "Stand away from those boats."

"STAND AWAY FROM THOSE
BOATS"

He might have spoken to a party of dead men for all the effect his words had. The frantic individuals down below seemed not to have heard them. They still went on with the work of preparing the boats, though it was clear to everyone that, what with their eagerness and their utter selfishness, the hoisting out, if left to them, would end only in disaster.

"Down below there, you dogs!" shouted the captain. "Stand away there! Fall in in the centre of the deck."

He repeated his words in Spanish, for a skipper who sails those seas soon acquires a considerable vocabulary; but his orders fell upon deaf ears only, and all the while time was flying, the ship was settling, the moment when she would founder was drawing dangerously nearer.

"Guess we've got to fix 'em in our own way," said the captain, turning on his little party. "See here, we'll get down this port ladder, beat the men back from the two boats there, and then tackle the others. Jest keep close together, and ef there's opposition don't be too gentle. This ain't the time for gentleness; they'll understand hard knocks when there ain't anything else that'll knock sense into their silly heads."

He led the way promptly, looking in the feeble rays of his own lantern, and that suspended from the boom, a regular commander. With his clear-cut but anxious features, his peaked beard and short moustaches, this skipper gave one the impression of power, of coolness, and of courage. Indeed he was just the sort of man required in such an emergency, for he inspired his followers with confidence, and took his post at their head as a matter of course. The mate slid down the ladder immediately on his heels and Jim took the whole flight in one bound.

"Now," said the captain.

"Lummy! Dis someting like, dis am," murmured Sam, his eager little face looking up into Jim's. The diminutive negro had armed himself with an enormous stake which he had discovered in some odd corner, and he flourished it. There was a little grin on his face, while his sharp teeth flashed. In fact, in one brief moment, the negro, who had always worked so well and so quietly, who had never displayed any pugnacity or traces of excitement, had become an altered individual. There was a something about him which seemed to say that fighting was a pursuit which pleased him, that he was longing for the fray. But by now the whole party was gathered in the waist. The captain led them to the port boats, flinging aside all who stood in his path. In fact, to clear the Spaniards into the centre of the deck was no difficult matter. They were so absorbed in their task that they were taken by surprise. But a moment or two later, when they found a group of resolute-looking men lined up between them and the boats, which seemed to be their only hope of safety, the frantic people became furious and desperate.

"Two of you men just see that the tackles are free and all ready for hoisting," said the captain, his eye on the passengers. "We've got trouble to meet here, and when it's over we shall want to get the boats out precious slippy. Ah, you would, would you?"

In the short space of time which had elapsed since he had come to the waist the fury of the Spaniards had risen perceptibly. It wanted only a maddened leader now to turn the whole pack upon the captain and his men; and, in a trice, the man made his appearance. A huge fellow, with glittering ear-rings, whipped something from his belt and snarled at the captain. Then, with a shout as if he were a maddened beast, he dashed forward, a huge dagger held before him.

"I've got more of that for the likes of you," said the captain, stepping swiftly forward and meeting the man with a terrific blow from his fist. Indeed the Spaniard turned a half-somersault, and landed with a thud on the deck. But his mates were too desperate to notice his discomfiture; they came at the little band in a mob, and in a moment Jim and his comrades were fully engaged. A little active man bent low and ran in at our hero, while the latter caught the glint of something bright in his hand. Crash! The staff with which he had provided himself fell on the Spaniard's head and sent him sprawling. Bang! Sam's ponderous weapon missed the mark at which it was aimed and struck the deck heavily. Next instant the negro was locked in the arms of one of the attackers and was rolling with him on the decks.

But Jim had no time to watch him, nor opportunity of assisting, for the horde of men threw themselves on him and his comrades furiously. One managed to come to close quarters with him and struck with his knife; but the blade did not reach his person. A quick leap to one side saved him. Then the staff swung downwards and the man collapsed.

"A rare blow, lad. A rare one!" shouted the captain. "Boys, we'll be moving forward."

But the command was easier to give than to obey. Not all the efforts of the little party could make an impression. It seemed as if the captain would be defeated in his efforts to control the boats. But suddenly others arrived on the scene. It was the engine hands, headed by an enormous negro. Was it wonderful that Tom should itch to join in the fray? He had seen his mistress into a place of safety and had left Ching to guard her. Then, realizing that instant victory in this struggle could alone save everyone on board, he had led the engineering staff down the companion.

"By de poker! not stand quiet and 'low boats to be hoisted out," he bellowed, forcing his way to the front. "Not 'bey de captain and help when de ship sinkin'. By de poker, but dis not go on! Yo, what yo doin'?"

He seized a man who rushed at him, as if he were merely a child, twisted him round till his feet were in the air, and threw him back at his comrades. Then, smiling all the while, he rushed at the attackers, regardless of their knives, striking them down in all directions.

"Hooray! Now, boys," shouted the captain, "that darkie's done it for us fine. Beat 'em back; there's still time to mend matters."

Bunched together, and led by Tom, the little party threw themselves upon the Spaniards, striking right and left remorselessly. And in the space of a few seconds they had borne them back as far as the bulkhead, above which was the poop.

"If some of you men don't drop those knives precious quick I'll know why," commanded the skipper.

"By de poker—yes! Tom know why, yo bet!"

The huge negro strode in front of all, his big fists doubled, his head thrust forward as if he were a bull about to charge. His eye fell upon the rascal who had begun the attack, and who, meanwhile, had recovered his senses. There was a dagger in the villain's hand, and Tom did not fail to see it. In a trice he had pounced upon the man.

"What yo not obey for?" he demanded wrathfully. "Yo not hear de cap'n say yo to drop all knives? By de poker, but in two seconds yo sorry yo ever born! Yo drop that knife."

There was no disobeying such an order. Tom seized the Spaniard, gripped him with both powerful hands, and shook him till the man's head threatened to fall from his shoulders. Then he turned and grinned at the captain.

"Ready now to do as yo order, Cap'n," he smiled. "S'pose yo say fall in half here and half dere, get ready to haul on tackle. Dey ready to do as yo say."

"George, you're a real treasure! You're a brave man, Tom. Jest get 'em ranged up in order, and quick with it. Young sir, I'll be obliged ef you'll help him."

He nodded to Jim, left three of the men to stand by him, and at once turned to the boats. As for the Spaniards, Tom's huge frame and the prowess he had already displayed seemed to cow them. They obeyed his orders with alacrity, and were soon ranged up in two lines. By then their aid was wanted.

"Yo jest get to dem tackles yo in dat row," commanded Tom. "Haul when you told. If one ob yo try to get into de boats before I say yo can, me carve yo into little pieces—so."

He brandished an enormous knife, which he had picked up from the deck, and showed his teeth. The result might have been anticipated, for the passengers who had been fighting like a pack of beasts but a few moments before were absolutely cowed. They would rather face drowning than the anger of this terrible negro. It followed, therefore, that, now that they were helping in the task, the boats were swiftly swung out.

"Put the women aboard this one," said the captain. "We'll lower them with the boat. The others can go down by a rope ladder; it's smooth, thank goodness, or things would be worse. Now, lads, quick with it; she won't swim much longer."

Riot and fury had now been replaced by order and calm method. One by one the boats were lowered, passengers entered, and a crew was placed aboard. Moreover the purser and his men found time to make a raid on the stores, so that each boat was victualled. As for Sadie, she and Ching sat in the boat lowered from amidships, and waited anxiously for her brother and the others. Presently they came, the captain being the last to step over the rail. By then the decks forward were awash, while the stern of the vessel was pitched high in the air. Her propeller was plainly visible, lifted clear of the water.

"She'll plunge in a few moments. Best get clear away," said the captain. "The other ship, I hear, is foundering also. We'll have to stand by till morning. Is everyone with us?"

The answer had hardly left the mate's lips when there came a cry from Sadie. Her finger shot out, and in a moment all saw the object which had attracted her attention. It was the figure of a man standing on the sinking steamer. Instantly a groan escaped the captain.

"Couldn't risk going back for him," he said; "he must swim for it."

"But he's disabled; he's the man with a broken arm," sang out Jim. "He couldn't swim if you paid him to."

"Can't help it; I've the boat's crew to think of," declared the captain, shaking his head sadly. "That ship's on the point of diving; we're too close as it is. If I go nearer we risk the lives of all, your sister's into the bargain."

"A fact," cried the mate emphatically. "The skipper's saying only what's true."

"Ah! I thought she was going then!" shouted one of the crew aboard the boat, seeing the steamer lurch suddenly. "'Tain't more'n a matter of seconds."

"Then I'll chance being in time; I'm going for him."

Jim tore off his coat, and kicked his shoes away. Before they realized his intentions he had stepped on to the gunwale, and had plunged head foremost into the sea.

CHAPTER III

Jim Partington shows his Mettle

"Come back, lad," shouted the captain, as Jim's heels disappeared beneath the surface of the ocean. Then he rose quickly to his feet, and, gripping the gunwale of the rocking boat with both hands, he stared through the gloom at the sinking ship, and at the solitary figure now clinging to the rail amidships. Indeed the unhappy individual who had been accidentally left on the foundering vessel showed that he was in almost as frantic a condition as had been the Spanish workmen, when fighting in the waist for possession of the boats. He was waving the one arm which was uninjured vigorously, and as Jim set out in his direction he was seen to throw one leg over the rail, to clamber with difficulty upon it, then to sit there holding desperately, and looking as though every movement of the ship would cast him into the water.

"She's a going! Gee! did yer see her lurch then? My, I thought she was under!"
The deck hand who had shouted the words threw up his hands in the direction of the steamer, and turned a pair of startled, staring eyes upon her. There was good reason for his alarming observation, for at that moment the foundering vessel rolled heavily from side to side, as if she found her position irksome. Then she dipped her nose still deeper into the ocean, kicking her stern clear of the water till ten feet of her dripping keel were visible, and until her decks were at such a steep angle that none but an acrobat could have retained his position on them. Indeed the unfortunate individual clinging to the rail was swung from his insecure seat, and, falling backwards, crashed on to the deck and slithered down it till one of the bridge pillars arrested his progress.

"Holy poker, but dat near shave, I guess! Massa Jim, what yo doin' dat for? Yo's mad! Yo's goin' to drown yo'self!" shouted Tom, rising to his feet so rapidly that his huge bulk set the ship's boat rocking dangerously.

"Drown himself! He's jest committing suicide! I tell you, he's bound to go under," growled the captain, who, if the truth had only been known, felt himself so strongly impelled to leap into the sea and help in this foolhardy but gallant effort at rescue that it was only by exercising the greatest self-control that he was able to hold himself in check.

"If I wasn't skipper I'd do it," he cried. "But it would be a fool's game. Besides, I've got to remember that I'm in charge of this expedition."

Meanwhile Jim's head had burst from the surface of the water, and the plucky lad was forcing his way towards the sinking vessel with powerful strokes. He gave no heed to the shouts and calls of those behind him, not even when Sadie, beside herself with anxiety, rose from her seat in the stern of the boat and shrieked to him to return instantly.

"I'll do it, or go under," he told himself grimly. "A sinking ship ain't going to frighten me. Guess a chap couldn't float out there in safety and see a man drowned before his eyes, especially a man that's unable to fend for himself."

Though the water dripped into his eyes from his hair, and made seeing difficult, he, too, had observed the terrific lurch which the foundering vessel had just given; and if he had had any doubts as to her true condition they were instantly set aside by the mass of her stern elevated in such an ungainly manner into the air.

"Aboard there!" he shouted; "jump over into the water. She is going down."

Thanks to an oil lantern which still hung amidships, below the bridge, he could see the man for whose rescue he was striving, and as he thrust his way strenuously through the water he watched the injured passenger pick himself up on hand and knees and struggle towards the rail. He wedged his feet against a stanchion supporting the latter, and as Jim arrived within a few yards of the vessel, the man was again endeavouring to clamber over the rail.

Then there came, of a sudden, another sluggish lurch. The ship appeared to shiver throughout her framework, and rolled heavily from side to side. A moment later her bows rose rapidly from the ocean in which they had been submerged, while the stern regained almost its normal position. It looked, in fact, as if she were making one last gallant effort to float upon the surface. But again she rolled heavily from side to side, till her decks were slanting at a sickening angle, greater indeed than that to which Jim and his mates had become accustomed when cruising to the south along the Caribbean coast.

"By de power, but dat terrific, dat 'nough to shake de life out of anybody," muttered Tom, whose eyes all this while had been staring into the gloom, endeavouring to follow every movement of his young American master. Indeed, so acute was the vision of the dusky giant that details were visible to him, and to Sam, his diminutive brother, which others aboard the boat had no idea of. "Lummy, but Tom not like to see dat ship shake herself so! She go down with a bust in one little moment, and den—and den, what happen to Massa Jim?"

The very thought of the disaster which would follow drove the negro into a condition almost of frenzy. His eyes bulged from their sockets and looked as though they would tumble from his head. A whimper from Sadie set Tom's honest heart throbbing and palpitating. It was real pain to the fine fellow to know that his little mistress was in trouble. That and his own courageous, impetuous nature made it impossible to stay any longer inactive in the boat. Every muscle in his body trembled, while his breath came quick and deep.

"I's goin' ter help!" he shouted. "Nebber yo fear, missie; soon hab Massa Jim back safe and sound."

With that he floundered overboard, causing the boat to rock once more till her gunwale dipped beneath the oily surface of the ocean, a mass of water flooding the interior instantly. His head had hardly bobbed up in view again when there came a sudden exclamation from Sam, and a moment later the little fellow had slipped away to help his dusky brother in his gallant task.

"Jemima! But if that don't take it!" bellowed one of the crew of the boat, looking himself as if he were about to follow. "Every mother's son of 'em'll go down. That ship'll suck 'em under sure. Ain't we going nearer?"

In his eagerness he seized an oar, banged it into the rowlock, and proceeded to bear upon it; but a stern order from the captain at once arrested the movement.

"Belay there!" he cried sharply. "I ain't going to risk the lives of all aboard for those in the water. We're too close to that ship by a long way, much too close to my liking. Drop another oar in there, Macdougal, and pull us away a bit. Harvey, jest get to at bailing; she's taken a bit of water aboard. Miss Sadie, it's the right thing we're doing. It'll help them best in the end."

But there was mutiny in the eye of Macdougal. In the excitement of the moment the eager fellow could not in his own mind differentiate between the safety of those aboard the boat and those who had plunged into the water.

"What's that?" he growled. "Go farther away! Desert them as is wanting our help! Wall, if I ain't jiggered! We calls ourselves white men, and——"

"Stop!" commanded the skipper sternly. "Get down on that seat and pull, Macdougal. You're a fool, I'm thinking. Jest remember that I'm your skipper still, and taking orders from no one. I'm working in the interest of all."

"Aye, aye, sir. Macdougal, get to at it!" growled the mate, scowling at the sailor, and clenching a pair of brawny fists. Not that this officer was really angry with Macdougal. In his heart of hearts he rather admired the man; but discipline was discipline, and the skipper had many a time proved his own courage and discretion. Still, even his persuasion did not make of the sailor a willing man; for the moment Macdougal was obedient, though mutiny and smouldering anger flashed from his eyes.

Meanwhile the sinking vessel had displayed another series of erratic movements. That sickening roll from side to side had been replaced by a gentle pitching fore and aft, and as the seconds fled swiftly by, the pitching had become slowly and almost imperceptibly greater. Then, suddenly, the vessel tossed her bows into the air till her watermarks were visible to those swimming in the ocean. But it was only for a little while. The bows came down again with a heave, which sent her forecastle beneath the surface, till she looked as though she were in the act of plunging to the bottom. Up she came again, displacing a huge mass of water, and raising a wave which spread quickly across the sea till it reached the boat hovering at a distance and rocked it. She canted heavily to port, showing the whole of her length of deck, and with such a violent movement that the passenger aboard was flung clear of the rail right out into the water. Then souse went her bows once more, raising the stern like a pinnacle into the gloom which surrounded everything.

"Yo grip him and get away back, quick as yo can," bellowed Tom, his mouth almost submerged, his powerful arms bearing him swiftly to help in the rescue. "I's close behind yo, Massa Jim."

But he might have shouted to a log of wood for all the use his words were. Jim heard not a syllable of his warning, for his eyes and all his attention were fixed upon the injured man who had been thrown from the vessel. He reached him in the course of a few seconds, and turning him upon his back supported his head.

"I'm fine," he heard the man say faintly. "This arm of mine don't give me no more than a dog's chance of swimming. You clear off, young chap. You've the right stuff in you, there ain't a doubt; but I'm fine. Don't you get worrying."

The last words were almost cut off by water lapping into his mouth. The huge wave raised by the sudden lifting of the vessel caught them both, and for a moment the two were hidden from sight by a mass of surging green foam. Jim kicked frantically, bearing himself and the man to the surface. Something struck hard against his chest, and, gripping at it with the one hand he had free, he swiftly realized that fortune had been good to him, for it was a buoy, cast loose by the injured passenger himself but a little while before, and now swept to hand at a most opportune moment. He looped his arm over it, and, slipping the other deeper down, hugged the man closer, drawing his head well up on to his own shoulder.

It was as well that he had made this hasty preparation, for, of a sudden, the ship beside which they floated soused her bows deep again, and slid farther beneath the surface. She seemed to hesitate, to make one other effort. There came a loud explosion, accompanied by the sound of splintering and rending wood. Air gushed from a mighty aperture which had made its appearance at the point where but a little while before the Spanish passengers had been fighting so frantically; then she plunged to her bed in the ocean. Swift as a dart she shot beneath the surface, leaving in her wake a swirling whirlpool, a twisting vortex into which everything—splinters of wood, spars, and human beings—were sucked with alarming swiftness, and with such force that none could resist it. So it happened that Jim and the passenger once more disappeared from the ken of those who were watching so eagerly.

How frantically Jim kicked; how desperately he clung to the buoy and to the man at whose rescue he aimed. The swirling water bearing them both down beneath the surface of the Caribbean in the wake of the vessel almost tore them apart in the course of that desperate struggle.

At one moment the pull on the buoy was so intense that he felt as if his arm would be dragged from its socket. An instant later a recoil of the waters swept it back against his face with such violence that his jaw was all but broken.

"Done for," he thought. "I can't stand much more of this. My lungs are bursting, my head feels as if it will explode."

The sound of seething, gushing water deafened him at first, but when he had been a little while immersed the thunderous notes, so distressing a moment ago, seemed to become lessened in intensity. The buzzing was now, if anything, rather pleasant, while his mind, acutely active but a second before, became blissfully content, as if absorbed in paying attention to that curious singing in his ears. But if he himself were unconscious of other things, nature still urged him to struggle on for existence. Jim had no idea of the frantic kicks he gave, of the grim force with which he clung to the man and to the buoy. Then something revived his senses and caused his wandering wits to take notice of his surroundings. A breeze blew in his face, while someone shouted in his ear. He opened his eyes, and in the gloom that pervaded everything made out the grinning features of Tom.

"Yo's dere, den; yo's safe," he heard the negro exclaim. "By lummy, but dat extra near squeak, so I tell yo! Let go ob de man. Me take him for de moment. Yo puffed, blowin' like an engine."

Jim was exhausted; his breath was coming in quick, painful gasps. He could not spare any for an answer, and, indeed, had so little strength left in him that he did not even resent Tom's movement to take the injured passenger from his care. Instead, he clung to the buoy, fighting for air, wondering vaguely exactly what had happened.

"Yo hang dere quiet and easy," said Tom, one hand on the buoy and his muscular arm about the half-drowned man. "Yo puffin' like a grampus now, but in a little bit yo be better, not make such a noise, have plenty strength again. Den take de man and swim back with him. Tom only come to look on and see dat all well."

It was like the gallant fellow to make light of his own adventure, to stand aside now that he was sure that Jim was safe, so as not to rob him of the honour which would follow. Tom was indeed a very honest negro, a man with a wide, big heart, which held a large corner for Jim and his sister. He grinned in Jim's face, then suddenly turned and looked over his shoulder.

"By de poker, but here someone else!" he muttered. "Who dar? We's safe and sound. Yo hab no cause to worry."

"And I ain't worryin'," came a well-known voice through the darkness. "I comed along here jest to see what's happenin'. Is Massa Jim right and well?"

A growl burst from Tom's lips as he recognized the voice, and at once he turned a pair of blazing eyes upon the culprit who had dared to follow him.

"Dat yo, Sam?" he demanded. "Den what fo yo dare to leave de missie? Yo get back right now, or by de poker, me knock you into twenty cocked hat! What fo yo jump overboard and risk gettin' drowned?"

The question brought a gurgle from the jolly little Sam. He laughed outright beneath the nose of the irate Tom, and, reaching the buoy, clung to it for a moment or so before he deigned to reply.

"Yo's one great big donkey, yo am, Tom," he roared, shaking with laughter. "Yo tinks yo de only man allowed to jump into de water; but dat not so. De young massa place yo in charge of de missie, and yo no right to leave. Me knows dat; me comes along right out here to haul yo back. Yo one great big blackguard."

To the astonishment of Tom and Jim the little fellow burst into violent sobs, though his words had conveyed anything but an idea of sorrow. Sam shook from the top of his woolly head to his shoeless toes, and set the buoy rocking. Big tears coursed down his cheeks, though the water dripping from his hair almost cloaked them, and when he tried to speak again he gulped at the words and failed to express them. It was, in fact, a strange if comical procedure, and for the moment Jim's muddled condition did not help him to arrive at the meaning. But he grasped the truth a moment later, for Tom helped him.

"Yo—yo one little rascal, yo!" he heard the huge fellow exclaim, though there was no anger in his voice, no resentment for the words which Sam had hurled at him. Rather there was a strange trembling which denoted friendly feeling, accompanied by a sudden gripping of hands between the two darkies which seemed to say that they were perfectly agreed. Then Jim gathered the full meaning of Sam's tears, of Tom's magnanimous action. It was joy for his, Jim's, safety that had set Sam howling, and the tears coursing down his cheeks. It was that same feeling which induced Tom to overlook the high-flown language of his small brother and grip his hand so warmly.

31

"You're just two great grown-up babies," he laughed across at them. "You seem to imagine that no one can do anything without you, that I'm like a piece of china, liable to break on the smallest occasion. See here, Tom and Sam, shake hands. Guess you're both of you white right away through from head to toe. I owe you both a heap for coming out after me; but mind what I've said—I ain't a piece of china. Guess I'm old enough and ugly enough to look after myself."

Tom grinned back at his young master and hung to the buoy for a while, still clinging to the hand he had offered. Then he dropped it, moved to the farther side, as if to place himself in a position of safety, and presently made his reply.

"Sah," he said, "p'raps you old enough, as yo say, p'raps no. Ugly 'nough: yes, I tink so. Yo's ugly 'nough to do one ob de stupidest tings as ever I seed. What fo yo jump into de sea like dat and swim toward a ship dat was sinking? S'pose she drag yo down? S'pose yo neber come up agin. Who den take care of missie?"

Even behind his fun there was a deal of truth. Who indeed would be left to care for the sister? But Jim had come up again, and, feeling better, he promptly made his presence felt.

"Jest swim back quick," he commanded Sam, "and tell 'em we're all right. Tell 'em to come along. We'll hang to the buoy. Now, Tom, set to splashing with your legs. There'll be sharks about here, and they're extra fond of darkies."

Tom paled for a moment under his dark skin and looked the reverse of comfortable. Then he laughed uproariously, shouted to Sam to hurry his departure, and promptly did as Jim had ordered. For it was as well to be cautious: both knew that sharks abounded in that corner of the Caribbean Sea, and some of the brutes might very well be in the vicinity. They kicked continuously, therefore, till the boat came up with a rush, and they and the injured man were lifted aboard.

"Young man, you can jest give me a grip of yer hand," cried the skipper of the foundered vessel when all were safely in the boat, stretching across to the triumphant Jim. "I guessed when you came up alongside us on the ship, telling me that you had fixed matters for your sister, and were ready to help us out with the trouble those Spaniards were giving, that you had got stuff behind you—the right sort of stuff, too. Then you tackled the hounds in proper style, so that I knew I had a man with me; a man, siree, not jest a boy. But this last thing's better than all. Guess this gentleman owes you a life. Guess he'll be for ever in your debt. Young man, I'm pleased to have met you."

It was a glowing tribute to our hero's courage, and he went crimson from the top of his dripping head to his stockinged toes as he listened to the words. Not that anyone could tell, for the gloom shrouded everything. However, Sadie, sitting beside him, clinging to his arm as if loath to part again with her protector, guessed his pleasure, while her own courageous little heart felt as if it would burst with pride.

"I'm glad you did it, Jim," she whispered, "though I was terrified. And Tom and Sam were really brave; they are so devoted. Can you believe, I had the greatest difficulty to keep Ching with me? He hates swimming, as you know, but he was very nearly following."

"Brave, honest fellows!" answered Jim with a gulp, for such devotion touched him. "They are, indeed, true friends to us."

However, he had no time for further conversation; for now that the captain had given his decision on events so recent, the mate and crew of the boat were determined to make their own voices heard.

"A right proper thing to have done: wish you was my own son," declared the former. "Shake, young man. It's a treat to meet one who's a true American."

"One of the very right sort," growled Macdougal, still trembling with excitement. "See here, young feller, I've nigh lost a job through you. I was for kicking up a rumpus direct against the old man's orders. Chief, I'm main sorry for them words and looks; but there's a time when a man has to kick. I thought you was funking."

"Funking!" exploded the mate, though the captain sat rigidly in his place, making no response. "Him funking! The man you and I have sailed with these past three years and never known to fail us. You guessed that the chief who led us against those Spaniards was funking! Gee! I've a mind to smash your head in with this oar."

There was real anger in the voice. The mate was furious, and his huge doubled fists showed that he was ready for anything; but the skipper quickly quietened him.

"Belay there, Mr. Jarvis," he said in his ordinary tones. "Macdougal's a fool, as I've already told him; and if he never knew it before he does now. I'm not afraid of anyone's criticisms. There's a motto I'm always a believer in. It runs: 'By their works shalt thou know them'. Guess I've never done a thing to allow any man to think I was funking. Macdougal was too excited to be responsible for his thoughts; it's just the man's bluntness which has made him tell us so honestly. But take the lesson to heart, Macdougal; keep a clear, steady head always and it'll carry you through heaps of difficulties. Watch the men you work with, and get to know all about them: moments of excitement aren't the times for coming to conclusions. Now let's get on to other matters. How's that gentleman?"

33

"Fine," came in shaky tones from the bows of the boat in which the rescued passenger had been laid. "Guess I know everything. I've been lying here these last few minutes wondering whether I was alive or dead, and what had been happening. Is that the skipper?"

"It is, sir."

"Then allow me to say that you've as fine a crew as ever I set eyes on. It wasn't their fault that I was left aboard the ship. The collision knocked me silly, and guess I lay away there on the decks out of sight; but I never reckoned you'd have men aboard ready to take such risks to rescue a passenger. That young chap who swam out for me wellnigh went down with the vessel. I held my breath as we went under till I thought I should bust. And all the time I could feel him holding tighter to me and kicking. Gee, he's a full-blooded lad! He's got pluck if you like. And those coloured men come close after him. When I'm feeling better, guess I'd like to take a grip of their hands."

It was evident that he considered Jim to be one of the crew, and his gallant action undertaken in the course of duty; but the captain undeceived him.

"That young chap's a passenger like yourself, sir," he said. "And the darkies are ditto. I allow that you have every reason to want to thank them; you owe them your life. But let us see to the other vessel; this affair has taken her wellnigh out of my head."

The oars were dipped in the water, and the boat was slowly rowed in the direction of the twinkling lights which showed the position of the other steamer. She had sheered off to some distance, but as the boat approached her it became clear that her condition was not so desperate as had been imagined.

"She's listing badly to port and is down at the head. You can tell that easily," declared the experienced captain. "We'll row right alongside and I'll go aboard. You come too, Mr. Jarvis, and we'll take that young man there."

He motioned to Jim, and, having put his helm over, so directing the boat alongside the steamer, he called to one of the hands in the bows to hold to the companion ladder which had been dropped over her side. Casting his eyes about him, Jim was able to pierce the gloom to some extent, and became aware of the fact that a number of small boats were also lying off the vessel. In fact there were at least seven of them. Another remarkable fact was the silence which pervaded everything. A little while before there had been a deal of shouting, and some amount of confusion, no doubt; but now everything was orderly.

"Fine discipline," remarked the skipper. "The chief of this boat got his passengers away first of all, and then set to work to repair damages. Guess he hadn't mad Spaniards to fight. Come along, please."

He scrambled on to the companion and ran nimbly up the steps. A tall man met him when he reached the deck, and introduced himself as the captain.

"You're chief of the ship that's foundered?" he asked.

"I am," came the rejoinder. "We were badly holed, and there wasn't a chance from the very first. Then we had a horde of mad Spaniards to fight: the hounds lost their heads and struggled for the boats. After that we found, when it was too late to go near the ship, that one passenger had been left aboard; but we saved him, thanks to the pluck of a passenger. Now, sir, I'm sorry for this collision. We'll not discuss it now; the courts ashore will deal with the evidence. I've come along to see how you fared."

"And thanks for the kind thought, sir," came the answer. "Reckon the question of who's to blame can be dealt with as you say. I congratulate you on the way you managed to come out of a difficulty. I'd have sent along; but then, you see, I wasn't sure that we weren't foundering too. There's a hole as big as three rum casks punched in our bows, and you can see that we've shipped no end of water; but our water-tight bulkheads were closed right away and that's saved us. We've the carpenters at work this instant, and as soon as they've plugged the gap with planks and oakum we'll be able to put matters a little more shipshape. Our pumps are just holding the water now; when the gap is plugged we shall gain on it. I reckon to have my passengers aboard in half an hour; you'll bring yours along, and welcome."

Half an hour later, in fact, found Jim and his friends, together with all the passengers and crew of the sunken steamer, aboard; while some twenty-four hours later the port of Colon had been reached.

"And here we have to start right off again," said Jim, discussing affairs with his sister. "That five hundred dollars will have to be drawn upon for clothes and other things, seeing that we lost everything with the ship. It'll mean I shall have to be quicker in getting a job when we reach New York. But don't you fear, Sadie; somehow I've a notion that our fortune is about to improve. Things are looking brighter."

They watched the steamer slowly berthed, and then made for the gangway. Bidding farewell to the skipper and the crew, with whom they had become most friendly, they were about to make their way ashore when the man whom Jim had rescued accosted them.

"I've fixed rooms for you all," he said. "You'll not disappoint me, will you? I've a house away up on the hill, and there's heaps of room."

"But—but we're going on direct for New York," cried Jim, astonished at the proposal.

"No doubt, sir; no doubt. But then there don't happen to be a steamer for a week, and Colon's a bad place to rest in. You'll oblige me by coming. I ain't had a chance, so far, of thanking you and the others for what you did. You'll surely give me a chance to get to know you better. Come and stay for a week till the steamer puts into port."

It may be imagined that Jim eagerly accepted the invitation, and, accompanied by Sadie, Tom, Sam, and Ching, took up his quarters with this new friend. Not for a moment did he guess that this week's delay would make a vast change in his future. His eye at the moment was fixed on New York, where he hoped to make that fortune of which he had laughingly spoken. He never imagined for one instant that the Isthmus of Panama would detain him, and that there he would join his compatriots, the Americans, and with them would take his share in that gigantic undertaking, the Panama Canal.

CHAPTER IV

Relating to Phineas Barton

Phineas B. Barton was in his own way an extremely pleasant and jolly man, but he required a great deal of knowing. He was moderately tall, clean shaven, as is the typical American of to-day, fairly good-looking, and about forty years of age. When he liked he could be voluble enough, but as a general rule his conversation was chiefly noteworthy by its absence; for Phineas was undoubtedly prone to silence and taciturnity.

"It's like this," he explained to Jim; "I'm boss at the present time of the foreign labour we employ on the Panama Canal works, and guess I have to talk most all the day when I'm at work. So a fellow gets used to keeping his mouth shut at other times, so as to rest his jaw. Glad you're coming out to my quarters."

He had thanked Jim quietly and with apparently little feeling for his action in plunging into the sea to save him when the steamer foundered, and after that had said not a word. But that did not imply that Phineas was ungrateful. It was not in his nature to employ many words; he had decided to show his gratitude in other ways. It was for that reason, no doubt, that he had invited our hero to his house. And, now that the whole party had disembarked, he proceeded to lead the way.

"Got any traps?" he asked.

"Not a stick," Jim answered. "We're here as we stand up."

"Then transport isn't a difficulty. It's nine miles to my quarters, and the railway will take us there quick. There's cars going one way or the other most always; come along to the terminus."

Jim and his comrades had no idea of the work which was going on on this narrow isthmus of Panama, therefore the reader may imagine that he was intensely surprised, once he and his friends had left the one-storied dwellings of Colon, to find human beings seething everywhere. Bands of labourers of every colour were working along the route where the canal would open into the Caribbean, while heavy smoke and the rattle of machinery came from another spot farther on.

"Where we're getting to work to cut our locks," explained Phineas, nursing his broken arm. "It's there that I broke this arm of mine two weeks ago. I was fool enough to get in the way of a dirt train, and of course, not having eyes itself, it shunted me off the track with a bang. That's why I was on my way back to the States; but guess that holiday'll have to wait. I'm keen to get back to work."

From the open car in which the party was accommodated he pointed out the various features of the isthmus, and in particular the works of the canal. And gradually Jim gathered the fact that this undertaking upon which his country had set its heart was gigantic, to say the least of it.

"No one knows what we're doing save those who've been here," said Phineas, a note of pride in his voice. "Back home there's folks ready enough to criticize and shout that things aren't being done right; but they ought to come right out here before opening their mouths. You've got an idea of the canal, of course?"

Jim reddened. To be truthful, his own struggle to make a way in this world had occupied most of his attention. He was naturally interested in all that concerned his own country, but even though so near to the isthmus he had never been farther than Colon when the ship put into port, and whilst there had merely observed rather a large number of policemen, both white and black. Of the huge army of workmen engaged in the canal enterprise he had not caught a glimpse.

"It's an eye-opener, this," he admitted. "I had no idea there were so many men, or so much machinery, though if I had thought for a little I could have guessed that there must be a bustle. As to the scheme of the canal, I haven't more than the vaguest idea."

"And I can't give you much information here. We'll want to get aboard an inspection car and run right through. That'll be a job for to-morrow. We'll have the inspector's car, and run along to the other side. But, see here, this canal's the biggest thing in canals that's ever been thought of. The Suez Canal don't hold a candle to it. The Kiel Canal is an infant when compared with what this will be when it's finished. There's fifty miles, or thereabouts, of solid dirt between Colon and Panama, and America has decided to get to at that dirt and cut a way clear through it, a way not only big enough to take ships of to-day, but to take ships of to-morrow, ships that'll make the world open its eyes and exclaim."

The very mention of the work made Jim gasp. He asked for particulars promptly. "It'll take a heap of time, I expect," he said. "Reckon a canal a mile long and fifty feet wide by thirty deep isn't dug in a day."

"Nor hardly in a year. But we're not digging all the way," explained Phineas. "America has selected what is known as the high-level canal; that is, she's not just digging a track clear through from Atlantic to Pacific, a tide-level canal as you might call it, for there are difficulties against such a scheme. To begin with, there's a tide to be reckoned with at Panama, while this Atlantic end has none; which means your water level at the Pacific side is different from that at the Atlantic. Then there's river water to be contended with. This isthmus gets a full share of rain, particularly near the Atlantic, and the rivers get packed with water in a matter of a few hours. Well, you've got to do something, or that flood will swamp your canal, wash away your works, and do other damage."

"Then the high level has fewer difficulties?" asked Jim.

"You may say so, though the job is big enough in all conscience. Shortly put, it's this. We begin the canal by dredging in Limon Bay, right here beside Colon, and cut our dirt away, in all for a matter of just over seven miles. Then we build three tiers of double locks, which will take any vessel, and which will float them up in steps to the 85-foot level. Once up there the ship steams into a huge lake where there's dry land to-day. We get that lake by damming the Chagres River right there before us, at Gatun, throwing the water back into a long natural hollow, and when the work is finished we shall have a body of water there four-fifths the size of Lake Geneva. Anyway, it'll allow a steamer to get along under her own power till she arrives at the other end of the lake at Obispo. Even then she uses her own power, though she has to slow down. She enters what we call the Culebra cut, just nine miles long, where we are burrowing our way through the hills. That's one of the biggest of our jobs. You'll be interested when you see it. We've a small army of men at work, and rock drills and steam shovels are going all day, while dirt trains travel to and fro more often than electrics in the New York subway. Then comes a lock at Pedro Miguel, and another at Milaflores, which let our ships down to Pacific level. Way down at that end we've a lot of dredging to do to clear the below-sea track of the canal."

Indeed it was no wonder that Phineas found it a matter of impossibility to describe the gigantic, herculean task which America has undertaken. Moreover, it may be forgiven our hero if he failed, in such a short space of time, fully to comprehend what was being done. A canal was being fashioned, that he knew well enough, and now Phineas had given him a rough idea of its direction, and of the methods to be employed to obtain a waterway from one ocean to the other. The rest had necessarily to be left to the imagination, and to the moment when clear plans of the works could be studied.

"But you know a bit about it, and that's good for the present," said Phineas. "I'm not going to give you a bad headache right off by throwing more particulars at you, though I fancy you'd be interested to know just one or two items."

"And those?" asked Jim, by no means bored with the description. In fact, like any healthy youngster, he was intensely interested in this canal, and was burning with impatience to see all the machinery employed, the methods used by the engineers and their staff to bring about the various works. "I'd give something to see the lake," he admitted. "Almost as big as that of Geneva? Gee! That's a whopper."

"You may say so," agreed Phineas, again a tinge of pride in his voice. "There'll be somewhere about 160 square miles of water in that lake, and a fleet will be able to lie to in it. Those locks at Gatun, which are to be double—one for steamers going up, and the other for ships coming down—will each give a usable length of 1100 feet, which is a good 300 feet longer than any ship yet afloat. They'll be 110 feet wide, and have a minimum depth of 41 feet. Put that all together, and remember that when the gates of the locks are shut, and water allowed to come down, the biggest battleship yet heard of will be lifted solid just about 32 feet, and then warped on into another lock as like the last as two peas. In less than an hour we'll raise a ship up to our high-level canal from the Atlantic, and we'll do it, sir, as easy as you lift rowing boats down on the rivers."

Phineas went hot at the thought of the undertaking, and, looking at him, Jim could see that the man was filled with a huge pride, with a tremendous fixity of purpose, the courage and tenacity to push on with a labour which his country had begun, and which the honour of the nation demanded should be brought to a satisfactory conclusion. And in a little while Jim understood that there was not a white employee engaged on the isthmus who did not dream of the day when the canal would be opened, when their own countrymen, some of whom at this moment were ready to discount their labours, would be amongst the keenest admirers of the finished task.

"But guess it's time we thought of the house," said Phineas, dragging his attention away from the works before him. "I've a shanty way up the hill there, with a housekeeper to look to it for me. She'll take care of Miss Sadie."

They descended from the car and slowly trudged up the hill. Then Phineas gave them a welcome to his home.

"Looks cool and nice; don't it?" he remarked, as they ascended a flight of steps leading on to a wide veranda. "I can see you looking at my windows, young man. Well, we don't have any out here. A chap gets to live without them easily enough. There's just copper gauze right round the veranda, and the same over the window openings. Most days it's so hot one doesn't think of their absence. And if a cold spell comes, one can easily put on something warmer. Now we'll get along in and feed. Ha, Mrs. Jones, that's you again! You didn't think to see me back so soon, till I telephoned from Colon. This is Miss Sadie, and this is Jim, the young man who rescued me. We're just hungry, so we'll come right in if things are ready, and Tom here, and Sam, and Ching can get round to the kitchen. You'll find 'em useful boys."

40

The widow who looked to Phineas's affairs was a pleasant woman, and gave our hero and his sister a real welcome. As to the negroes, though she looked at them askance at first, she rapidly found them a blessing. For Tom installed himself as butler unasked, while Sam carried dishes to and fro. Ching settled down to the work of washing up the things as if he had been brought to the isthmus for that very purpose.

"All of which just makes things slide along as if they were oiled," said Phineas with a glad smile, as he lolled on his veranda afterwards.

"See here, Jim, them boys of yours can go along helping Mrs. Jones while you're here; but of course, if they were at work on the canal, they would have their own quarters along with the other coloured men. Pity you're not staying. Where do you go after New York?"

It was a leading question, and Jim explained his position frankly.

"I don't complain," he said, "but we certainly have had our share of ill fortune. First Father lost his money, then his life. Afterwards my brother went off his head with fever, and was lost in the forest way down there below Colon. I've got to find work other than diving."

"You've done a bit of that, then?" asked Phineas.

Jim nodded. "A lot," he said. "But I'm not really skilled."

"You've handled tools and machinery?"

"Many a time; Father made me learn from the very beginning."

"See here!" cried Phineas suddenly; "you're after a job, and look to earn dollars. Well, there are dollars to earn here for a good man. Try a spell on the canal works. We've vacancies almost all the while, for men get tired of the job, while others fall sick. Then there's every sort of work, to suit the knowledge of everyone. Of course white men have the pick. They're skilled men, and naturally enough they get posts of responsibility. Some drive steam navvies, others rock drills, while some are powder men, and place the charges which we fire every night after five. At the locks there's pile driving and concrete laying, with white men to run the engines or supervise. As to diving—well, there may be some of that, but it's the land we're chiefly engaged with."

The temptation to accept the proposal right off was strong, and Jim found it difficult to keep from answering. Then he suddenly asked a question.

"There's my sister," he said. "I suppose Tom and the others could easily get work, and so stay here; but this place hasn't the best of reputations for health. I must look after her."

"And she'll be as well looked after here as anywhere," said Phineas eagerly. "We're high up out of the valley, the house has lately been built, while that yarn about the health of the isthmus is old history. We've changed all that. An

American army surgeon, with others to help him, discovered that yellow fever was given by a particular form of mosquito. Well, he set to work to find where that mosquito lived and bred. Then he formed a sanitary corps, drainage was looked to, scrub cut down, windows barred by copper gauze. And we've fixed that mosquito. Yellow fever is now unheard of on the isthmus, while there's very little malarial fever. The canal zone, particularly in these high parts, is as healthy as New York. Come now."

"I agree to stop if she cares to do so," cried Jim suddenly, for there was an eagerness about the man before him which captivated him. It was clear, in fact, that Phineas was anxious that Jim should stay; and since he promised work, and stated that no harm could come to Sadie from residence there, why, if matters could be arranged, Jim made up his mind he would stay. Perhaps here he would find the means to cut the first steps in that flight which was to lead to a revival of his fortunes.

"Then here's a plan," said Phineas. "I'm real glad you'll stay on here, for I want a companion. I lost my wife five years ago, and by rights should be living way over there in one of the hotels the American Government has built for its employees. But I chose to have a house alone, and at times it's lonesome. You'll stay along with me, and Sadie'll have Mrs. Jones to look after her. There's a Government school a quarter of a mile away, with plenty of boys and girls going. As for the darkies and the Chinaman, I can't promise anything at present. Depends on the work they have to do; but I've an idea I could make that fellow Tom extra useful."

Exactly what was in the mind of this American official Jim could not guess. He went to bed that night with a feeling of exultation to which he had been a stranger for a long while, for Sadie had taken to Mrs. Jones, and was delighted at the thought of remaining.

"Why trouble to go along to New York?" she asked him, in her wise little way, when he asked her what she would like. "This place is glorious. The view from the house is really magnificent, and there's no loneliness anywhere. Look at the works going on, with thousands of men. Then Mrs. Jones tells me that there are a number of boys and girls, so that I am sure to have companions. You can earn good wages here, Jim, and perhaps rise to a position of responsibility."

"Rise! that I will!" our hero told himself, for he was bubbling over with enthusiasm. "I've myself alone to look to, and I'll work and make those in authority over me see that I'm trustworthy. I'll show 'em I'm not a skulker. Wonder what job I'll get?"

It was at an early hour on the following morning that he was up and out, only to find Phineas abroad before him.

"That you, youngster?" he sang out cheerily, seeing Jim. "I've been down to the office of the Commission doctor, who's fixed this arm for me. The man who saw to it aboard the ship that brought us in hadn't too much time, for there were others who'd been injured by some of those Spaniards who'd been fighting. In consequence I had a bit of pain last night; but I'm easy now. Let's get some breakfast, then you and I'll be off."

An hour later found the two down at the point where the dirt trains were already dumping their contents, and just where the huge Gatun dam was to be erected, so, standing on an eminence, Jim was able, with the help of his friend, to follow in a logical manner the plans of the American engineers. For he could look into the long, winding hollow along which at that moment flowed the tributaries of the Chagres River.

"It's just as clear as daylight," said Phineas, his face aglow, for anything to do with the Panama Canal warmed him, so great was his enthusiasm. "Away there below us, where you see two rivers coming together to form what is known as the Chagres River, you may take it that the level of the land is just a trifle above that of the sea, and of course the water on this isthmus has found the lowest level possible. It could not get away to the east because of the hill, and west here, where we are, there's another. So that water just flows out between them, the hills themselves forming, as it were, the neck of a bottle. Well, we're just putting a cork into that neck. We're erecting a dam across the valley between these two hills which will be 7700 feet in length, measured across the top, while its base measurement will be 2060 feet."

"Enormous!" exclaimed Jim. "But surely such a tremendous mass is hardly necessary?"

"What! with 164 miles of water behind it? Young sir, let me tell you that there'll be a clear depth of water of 80 feet all along this end of the lake we're forming. A body of water like that exerts terrific pressure, and to make that dam really secure against a fracture, to make an engineering job of it, as we should say, the dam ought to be constructed of masonry built right into solid rock. But there ain't no rock, more's the pity."

"None?" asked Jim. "Then you won't be able to use masonry?"

"Right, siree! But we're going to fix the business, and reckon, when the dam's finished, nothing'll move it. Listen here, and jest look away where I'm pointing. There's an army of niggers and European spademen at work along the line the dam's to follow. They're working a trench right across, 40 feet down into the soil. Those engines you can see smoking along there are driving sheet piling of 4-inch timbers 40 feet down below the bottom of that trench. When they have finished the job of piling, the trench'll be filled chuck up with a puddled core of clay that'll act like a sheet anchor."

"And so hold the dam in position," suggested Jim.

"Just what I thought you'd say. No doubt that puddled core will help to hold the huge mass of earth that we're going to dump around it. But we're working that piling in and making the core for another purpose also. With a huge body of water in this hollow there'll be a certain amount of soaking into the subsoil—seepage we call it. It might loosen the ground underneath our dam, and so cause the thing to burst; but with a 40-foot trench, filled with a puddled core which'll stop any water, and this extra 40 feet of piling—just 80 feet of material altogether—we stop that seepage, and at the same time kind of fix a tooth into the ground that'll hold the weight of New York city."

The whole thing was gigantic, or, rather, the scheme of it all; for the reader must realize that Jim and his friend were looking down upon an unfinished undertaking. But those smoking engines and the army of men at work were an indication of the enormous labour and skill required in the erection of this Gatun dam, itself only one item in the numerous works of the canal, though, to be sure, one of the vastest. In fact, When Jim learned that from base to summit the dam would measure no less than 135 feet, and would be 50 feet above the level of the water in Gatun Lake, there was no wonder that he gasped.

"It just makes a man scratch his head," laughed Phineas. "And sometimes it makes one inclined to swear, for there's folks in the States who can't cotton to what we're doing here, and who wonder why there are so many men employed and so much money being spent. They seem to think that the canal ought to be finished in a matter of three or four years."

"Then the sooner they come out here and see for themselves what is happening the better for everyone," cried Jim indignantly. "That dam alone will take a vast amount of time, I imagine."

"Then you come along down here, sir, and I'll show you a work that's just as gigantic."

Phineas took our hero to the western end of the trench across which the dam would lie, and there caused him more astonishment. For here another army of labourers was employed in delving, while enormous steam diggers tore huge mouthfuls of earth and rock away from the sides of the cutting that was being made to accommodate the double line of three locks which, when America has completed her self-imposed undertaking, will raise the biggest vessel ever thought of to the surface of the lake above, or will drop her with equal facility down on to the bosom of the Atlantic.

"There's those steam navvies," observed Phineas, halting in front of one and surveying it reflectively. "A man who runs a machine like that can earn good dollars, and there's competition for the post. Say, Jim, how'd you care to try your hand at it?"

The very suggestion caused our hero to hold his breath. It was not that he was frightened by the mass of machinery; it was merely the novelty of the work. He stepped a pace or two nearer before he answered, and watched closely what happened. A young American, only a few years older than himself, sat on a seat beside the gigantic main beam of the digger, his head within a few inches of the flying gear wheels which transmitted movement, while right beside him, fixed to the base of the steel-girded beam, was the engine. One hand was on the throttle, while the other operated a lever. Down came the huge bucket attached to the secondary beam, the chains which supported it clanking over their stout metal pulleys; then the hand operating the lever moved ever so little, the chains tautened, and the hardened-steel cutting lip of the digger bit into the bank which was being excavated. Deeper and deeper it went. Glug! glug! glug! the machine grunted, while the tip of the main steel girder, where the hauling chains passed over it, bent downwards ever so little. A shower of broken earth burst over the edge of the digger, a faint column of dust blew into the air, while the engine gave forth another discordant glug. Then up came the huge bucket, crammed to the very top with debris, the whole machine shuddering as the strain was suddenly taken off it. But the man remained as composed as ever. He touched another lever, causing the apparatus to swing round on its axis. Almost instantly a movement from his other hand released the trigger holding the bottom of the huge earth receptacle in place, so that, before the machine had actually finished swinging, the huge mouth of this wonderful invention was disgorging its contents into a dirt car alongside.

"Fine!" cried Jim delightedly. "That's a job I should like immensely, but I guess it requires a little training."

"Practice, just practice," smiled Phineas. "See here, Jim; this arm of mine has started in aching again. How'd you care to stay along here and have a lesson? That young chap's a friend of mine, so there'll be no difficulty about the matter."

It may be imagined that Jim eagerly accepted the offer. He was keen enough to accompany Phineas on his promised trip right along the canal works, but already the sight of all that was happening round about Gatun had been sufficient for one day, while the huge machine before him and its cool and unruffled operator fascinated him.

"Gee! nothing I'd like better," he cried.

45

"Then come along." Phineas at once went close up to the machine, and at a signal from him the operator brought it to a rest.

"Howdy?" asked the young fellow. "Getting in at it, Mr. Barton?"

Under the tan which covered face and arms there was a sudden flush of pride which an ordinary individual might well have passed unnoticed. But Jim was slowly beginning to understand and realize something of the spirit that seemed to pervade every member of the whole staff engaged on the isthmus. For there was no doubt that the completion of the canal was a pet object to them one and all, an undertaking the gradual progress of which filled them with an all-absorbing interest. Each mouthful of dirt, for instance, which this steam digger tore from the ground and shot from its capacious maw into the earth trains was a little more progress, something further attained towards that grand and final completion to which all were sworn.

"Howdy? Say, Harry boy, this here's Jim. You've heard of that little business we had on the way to New York?"

The young man nodded, and regarded Jim critically. "Wall?" he asked curtly.

"He's the lad that came along after me when I was left aboard the foundering vessel."

The one who had been addressed as Harry dropped his hands from the levers, swung round on his seat the better to gaze at our hero, and, still with his eyes on Jim, replied to Phineas.

"I read it in the paper," he admitted. "How did it happen?"

Phineas promptly gave him the narrative, Harry meanwhile keeping his eyes on Jim. Then, when he learned that our hero had decided to stay on the isthmus, and seek work there, he climbed out of the narrow cab bolted to the side of the digger, dropped lightly to the ground, and, walking straight up to Jim, held out his hand.

"It's men we want here," he said pleasantly. "Guess you're one. Glad to shake hands with an American who's done a good turn for my friend Phineas. What job are you after?"

Jim told him promptly, while he exchanged his handshake vigorously; for he liked the look of this young American, and took to him instantly.

"I'm not sure yet exactly what job I'll ask for," he answered. "Guess I'm ready to take anything that's going; but I was wondering whether you'd give me a lesson on the digger."

"Know anything about engines and suchlike?" asked Harry sharply.

Jim nodded. "Guess I do," he said, with that delightful assurance so common to the Americans. "I've handled engines of many sorts, particularly those aboard ship; and for some months past I've been doing diving."

"Git in there, ' said Harry, motioning to the cab, "I'll larn you to work this plant inside an hour or two. Then all that's wanted is jest native gumption, gumption, siree, spelt with a big G, 'cos a man ain't no good on these here chugging machines unless he can keep his head cool. There's times when the digger pulls through the earth quicker than you can think, and when, if you didn't cut off steam, you'd overwind and chaw up all the chain gear. Then the lip of the digger may happen to get hold on a rock that wants powder to shift it, and if there's steam still on, and the engines pulling, you're likely as not to break up some of the fixings, and tip the whole concern over on to its nose. Hop right in; Mr. Barton, I'll see to this here Jim till evening."

CHAPTER V

The Ways of the Steam Digger

To say that Jim could not have been put into better or more capable hands is to tell only the truth. For Harry, the young American operating the steam digger, was one of those eager, hard-working fellows who strive their utmost, who are not satisfied unless they make the very best of a task, and who, given a machine of great power, cause it to produce the biggest results possible, consistent with proper management, and who, unlike some, do not curtail its strength, and limit its output.

"You jest hop up there inside with me," he said, wiping the sweat from his forehead, and tilting his broad sombrero hat backwards a little. "It'll be close quarters, you bet; but when a chap's learning a job he don't kick at trifles."

Jim obeyed his orders with alacrity. He clambered up into the narrow cab, which was merely a metal framework bolted to the huge, sloping steel girder which may be termed the backbone of the leviathan digger, and seated himself upon a hard wooden seat barely wide enough for one person. Just above his head was a toothed wheel, with another, very much larger, engaging with it. Beside him, causing him to start when he touched it, for it was very hot, were a brace of cylinders, with a lever adjacent for operating the throttle. Right overhead was a roof of split and warped boards, which helped to keep away the rays of the sun; for on this isthmus of Panama the heat is fierce at times, and extremely enervating.

"But, bless you, we don't notice it," said Harry, swarming up after him, and seeing that he had noticed the shelter. "Most all of us wear a big hat. In fact you can say as every white man does. Them dagoes don't; they seem to like the sun, same as the Spaniards. Seen anything of 'em, mate?"

Jim nodded. "Not much," he admitted. "There were a few aboard that ship, and they didn't impress me much. They lost their heads and fought like wild beasts."

"Aye, that's them all over; but they're good 'uns to work once they're set to at it, and know you won't put up with any nonsense. I don't suppose there was ever a part where gangs of them Spaniards works better than they do here, and gives so little trouble. Now and agin there's a rumpus, and the police has to intervene; but it ain't often. See 'em over there."

Jim had been so occupied with his inspection of the giant digger that he had hardly had eyes for his surroundings; but as Harry pointed, he swung round in the cab and surveyed the scene. It was remarkable, to say the least of it. Right behind him lay track on track of metal rails, all running direct towards the Atlantic, and the majority of them on different levels. They seemed to hug various gigantic steps, by which the sides of the huge trench in which the digger was situated ascended to level ground. Hundreds of cars were on these rails, with a little, smoking engine at their heads, and a half-closed-in cab behind. Gangs of European and black labourers were disposed here and there, some breaking up rocks obstructing the tracks, others carrying lengths of double rail track bolted together in readiness to be placed in position, while yet again others were engaged in pouring a liquid into trenches at the side of the cutting. Jim looked puzzled, and Harry laughed outright as he caught a glimpse of his face.

"Gee! It do amuse me when strangers come along," he cried. "Guess this here's an eye-opener. Any fellow can tell what we're doing, and why we're doing it, except the reason for those men and the stuff they're pouring into the trench. Say now, what's it for?"

Jim could not even hazard a guess. It was inexplicable, and seemed, indeed, to be an idiotic proceeding. His face must have shown his thoughts, for Harry burst into a loud guffaw, though, unconsciously, pride again crept into his tones as he answered.

"Guess you ain't the first as thought there was madmen about," he said. "But all that stuff being put into the trenches is jest part of this almighty scheme. Without it we wouldn't be able to work; for that's a gang from the sanitary corps, and guess they're nosing round most every day. It's their particular job to see as there isn't a place where a mosquito can breed, or where water can easily lay. Ef there's a spot made in purpose to carry away water, same as that 'ere trench, where some of it's bound to lay, why, they spreads kerosene along it, and no self-respecting mosquito'll go near that stuff. It's a terror to 'em. Guess this Panama zone, stretching five miles either side of the canal line, fairly gives them insects the pip, it's that unhealthy for 'em. As for us, we lives in comfort, and goes on living, which can't be said for others who was here before us. But jest get a grip of that throttle lever, and don't be skeared. Keep cool all the time, and when I cry 'stop', jest jerk it off. She'll come up short jest as ef she was alive, and that's something, seeing as this is a hundred-ton digger. She's able easy to cut her way into well over a thousand cubic yards of dirt in an eight-hours day, and can sling some six hundred double horse loads into them trucks.

But we ain't dealin' with horses here. It's machines all the time, machines, and men, I guess, to drive 'em."

It was grand to hear the fellow talk; unconsciously a glow crept into Jim's face. To think that he, by the movement of his ten fingers, and by the use of his own brain, could control such work, and then to remember that every little task accomplished was setting his country nearer the day of triumph. For triumph it must be: America, in spite of the croakings of a few, cannot and will not fail. She may experience setbacks; but she will prevail in the end. Her native determination and the grit of her workers will compel her.

"You can jest see how we're moving," said Harry, placing a hand on a second lever. "This here digger's set up on a truck heavy enough to take it, with its boiler right away at the tail end of the truck, to counterbalance the stuff we're lifting. We're on rails, as you can see, with a second track beside us that holds a spoil train, as we calls the trucks into which we chucks the dirt. Right clear afore us is the ground we're digging, and you're jest going to take a bite fer yerself. Watch that digger."

Jim cast his eyes upon the huge bucket with its steel cutting lip placed at the end of a secondary beam slanting downwards from the lower part of the main steel girder. Huge chains ran from the upper edge to the tip of the girder, and, as Harry gently pushed his lever, the chains ran out clanking, and the bucket descended till it bumped on to the ground. It was now at the foot of a broken and steep slope some eight feet in height, at the summit of which was the first of that series of big steps ascending to the top of the lock cutting, and accommodating rail tracks. Indeed a spoil train was crunching along it as he looked, while on half a dozen others trains were to be seen. As to the sloping bank itself, it ran on directly till it came to a dead end, where an army of men were engaged in erecting the lake-end wall of the lock. Behind, it dwindled into other banks, and was lost in the distance.

"Where we started, I guess," said Harry, following his gaze. "First the dredgers got to work, then the steam shovels. You see, we cut deep down in the centre first of all, and then take a step out at either side. Then, while diggers get to work to cut other steps we go deeper again in the centre. But let's get at this here bank. That bucket's drawn the chains out by its own weight. This here lever controls a brake, and I can stop the bucket at any point; but it's there, ready for digging. Give her steam, and gently with it. Be ready to cut off if I shout."

Jim moved his lever ever so gently. The proposition was so new to him that he felt somewhat timid of the results; but Harry was as calm as ever. He watched the cutting edge of the bucket dig deep into the bank, while Jim, watching it also, cast an eye upward at the chains where they passed over the tip of the girder. Chug! chug! chug! they went, while the massive beam trembled; but nothing could stop the irresistible course of the digger. The bucket sheared its way upward through the soil, and in a very little while had accomplished the whole height of the bank; then, its work done, it shot upward, causing the machine to shiver and shake.

"Cut her off," cried Harry, and obedient to the word Jim shoved the lever over.

"Now take a grip of this here lever I've been holding, and pull it to you. Give her steam."

Clank! clank! clank! Jim felt the gears engage as he shifted the lever, and once more opened the throttle of the engine. Now he experienced a new and altogether delightful sensation; for the huge mass of machinery to which the cab was bolted, and which was situated on the front of the heavy truck carrying the whole apparatus, swung round easily, the loaded bucket well in front and overhead. Harry grinned: it amused him to watch the delight on his pupil's face. But this was not the moment for allowing his attention to become distracted. He kept a careful eye on the bucket, and, a moment later, just as it began to swing over the dirt truck placed on the side track, he pulled a rope, and with a loud clatter the bottom of the bucket banged open and the dirt fell into the truck.

"Stop her!" he shouted, and Jim at once closed his throttle. "This is the boy that works the shutter for us. See here; pull it and give her steam. Watch those two arms to which the bottom of the bucket are bolted. This here gear just overhead works 'em and closes them over the trigger. Gee! If you ain't working this here like an old hand. Now watch it. That bucket's closed, and you've always to remember to close it afore you swing the machine back again to its work, 'cos the edge of the bottom comes low down and would foul the truck. That'd mean a bust up. Now, round with her. Stop her; get a hold of the brake lever and let her drop."

Confused at first, because of the multiplicity of movements, in an hour Jim was quite at home with the machine. True, he made errors; for instance, he forgot that very important movement to close the bucket, and, as a consequence, though he missed the side of the truck he nearly ripped off the head from a negro. But Harry was there to supervise, and a quick movement on his part arrested the machine.

"Hi! What fo you gwine kill me, yo?" shouted the negro, who had been untouched, as it happened. "Yo take care ob that great big playting ob yours. Not here to dig niggers. Not like hab de head knocked off."

Harry roared. "It's only Joe," he shouted. "He's been as near a blow afore now, and loves to make the most of it. See here, Joe," he bellowed, "I ain't a-goin' to have my machine broken against that 'ere hard head of yours. I'll have to be warning the foreman overseer to shunt yer."

That brought a grin from the negro. He showed his teeth, and shook his fist at Harry; but Jim knew his meaning well enough. The big fellow was just like the rest of his people—just a big, strong, healthy baby, who saw the fun in everything, and, if there were no fun, manufactured it promptly.

"I's gwine to break yo into little pieces," he said, clambering on to the cab and poking his face within an inch of Harry's. "Yo say I hab hard head? Lummy! Me hab hard fist as well."

"Git out!" shouted Harry, striking at him with the slack end of the rope that commanded the bucket trigger.

"Who's he?" demanded Joe, nodding at Jim, and suddenly changing the conversation.

"Him? Why, Jim, of course. Saved Mr. Barton."

"Den I knows him."

To Jim's astonishment the negro stretched out a hand and shook his eagerly. Then he explained the situation. "Know Tom and Sam," he said. "Dey down here now, seein' tings. I show dem round. Tom mighty impressed: he tink yo work de digger better'n Harry."

That brought an exclamation from the latter, while Joe jumped down from the machine just in time to escape the swing of the rope. But his words were true; close beside the digger were Tom and Sam.

"By de poker, but yo run him well!" shouted Tom. "Me's watched yo dis last half-hour. Seems to Tom as ef yo soon have a job in the diggin'."

To the huge fellow everything that Jim did was well done, everything he attempted was sure to be accomplished; and never for one moment did he tire of watching his hero. But Jim had his lesson to learn, and for another hour held to the work. By that time he had filled a whole spoil train, and had watched another shunted into position.

"Ready to fill like the last," said Harry. "That's the proposition that jest beat us at first. There wasn't enough trucks nor locomotives to begin with, and not enough tracks, so these fine diggers wasted half their time; but we've fixed it a while since. Soon as a train's loaded it's pulled back, while an empty spoil train crosses the switches behind. That comes over another switch just behind the digger, and so right on alongside, the last truck just in position for loading, the first 'way ahead. Then, as you've seen for yourself, we move along, a few inches after every dig, filling the trucks as we go."

"And then?" asked Jim. "What happens? Where is the dirt taken? Who unloads the trucks?"

"Gee! You are a chap fer questions. Where does it go? Away up there, at the far end of the river gully, where the Lake of Gatun'll be, there's a sight more dirt than this being taken from the isthmus. Some of that's being dumped at the dam just away over our heads; some of it's being emptied outside Panama, filling up a swamp through which the canal will run. Reckon there won't be swamps when we're done. There'll be good hard ground, and houses'll be built on a spot where there's fever nowadays. We're using dirt at this end in the same way; but you was asking about the dumping?"

Jim nodded, and looked at the spoil train being hauled away. "The gangs of niggers do it, I guess," he said. "But it must take longer than the loading by a long way; at least that's what one would imagine."

"Jest about seven minutes fer the whole train," smiled Harry. "My davy on it! You ask how? Wall, listen here. I've been here a long while, and in them days when we was fixed badly fer more trucks niggers did see to clearing the spoil trains—and precious bad niggers they was, too, about that time. Yer see, they mostly comes from the West Indian Isles, and somehow the place didn't seem to suit 'em. They was too slack to work much; but guess our officials fixed the trouble. They found it was the food, and now every nigger employed on the works gets his meals regular at a Commission barracks, and sech meals as gives him strength. But we was talking of unloading. See that truck 'way in front of the trains, the one just close to the engine? Wall, that's the Lidgerwood apparatus, and guess it beats creation. There's a plough right forward of the train, and a wire rope attached to it. When the spoil train has been brought to the place where the dirt's to be dumped, niggers or Europeans let down the truck ends, so's the whole train's one long platform. The plough then gets pulled from end to end, and shoots the dirt out. Seven minutes for a whole train, siree! Lightning ain't in it!"

Whistles sounded at this minute, and promptly Harry shut down his levers and leaped from the cab.

"Guess you've done right well fer a first time," he said. "In a day you'll be able to get to at it alone. Anyway, you've earned your grub. Come along to the Commission hotel; there's meals there for all whites, and no one can grumble at them."

Wherever he went Jim found something to interest him, so much so that it was a matter of wonder to him that, though he had often been close to the isthmus, he had had no idea of the extraordinary bustle taking place there. It was so extremely surprising to find small towns sprung up where he was assured there was but a single native hut before, to discover buildings so temptingly cool and elegant in appearance, and to learn that America not only employed labour, but provided quarters, food, and recreation for her employees. And here was another example. Harry took him away from the lock cutting, where one of these days a double tier of three locks will elevate ships from the Atlantic, and introduced him to his friends in one of the well-equipped hotels erected for the accommodation of white employees. Hundreds of men were streaming up the steps as they arrived, and passing in behind the copper-gauze screens of the veranda. Jim noticed that all bore much the same appearance—for the most part clean shaven, with here and there some wearing moustaches and beards. Dressed in rough working clothes, with broad-brimmed hats, none showed signs of ill health. There was a buzz of eager conversation as they washed before the meal, and a loud clatter from many tongues as they sat at the tables. As to the food, it was plain, abundant, and well cooked.

"Costs jest fifty cents a day," explained Harry. "If you've finished we'll get to the club. We usually go along fer a smoke at dinner-time. 'Sides, there's a cable of interest now and agin, and sometimes letters."

A few minutes with Harry at the club served, in fact, to banish any doubts which Jim may have had as to remaining on the isthmus. For here was comfort and recreation at the same time, and plenty of men with whom to make friends.

"This here's Jim, him as saved Phineas Barton," Harry told his comrades, and the statement was at once sufficient to rouse interest. Hand-grips were exchanged with our hero. The news of his presence spread round the huge room, in which men were smoking or playing dominoes at little tables, and one by one they strolled up.

"You're stayin' here?" asked one, and when Jim nodded, "I'm main glad: Phineas is one of the best, and a chap who could go in for him as you did must be one of the right kind. What are you going to do?"

"Steam digging, I hope," said Jim. "But of course I'm green yet."

"You'll do. If you've got the grit to face being sucked under by a foundering ship, guess you've the gumption to run one of them diggers. Anyway, I'm glad you're staying. Play yer a game of dominoes one of these mornings."

"Say, siree, ken you sing any?" asked another, when he had shaken hands; "'cos there's concerts here sometimes o' nights, and a new hand aer wanted."

"Guess I can do a little," answered Jim, reddening; for here was a find. No one loved a sing-song more than our hero, and, to give him only his due, he had an excellent voice, badly trained, or not trained at all, to be accurate, but pleasing for all that. "When I've put a little together I'll buy a banjo," he told his interrogator. "I had one aboard the ship, but guess it's deep down below the Caribbean."

"My, that are good news! Say, boys, here's one as can strum on a banjo."

The information was hailed with delight by those present, for a banjo player was an acquisition indeed. These skilled white men engaged in the Panama undertaking were as simple as well could be, and longed for nothing more than mild recreation. After an eight-hours day of strenuous work, and supper at the Commission hotel, it delighted them to gather at one of the clubs and there listen to an impromptu concert. But the midday halt was not the time for dawdling. Already the better part of the interval was gone, and very soon the blowing of steam whistles summoned the workers back to their machines; for nearly every one of the white employees in that hotel managed some sort of machine.

"There's a heap of them engaged with the rock drillers," said Harry, "and ef you go along the line to-morrow, towards Panama, and enter the great Culebra cut, you'll see and hear 'em at work everywhere. Most every night, when the whistles has blown and the men cleared off, you'd think a battle was being fought over there, for there's dynamite and powder exploding on every side, and huge rocks jest bounding down into the trench. Gee! There is a dust up. But I war saying that most everyone who's white has a machine to mind. Of course there are overseers, and lots of officials. Then there's a small army kept going in the repair shops 'way along over Panama direction, at Gorgona. That's a place as would open the eyes of people at New York. I tell you, they turn out a power of work there. See that machine down there running along the rails? Wall, that's home-made, every stick and rod of it put together at Gorgona, and, what's more, it's the invention of one of the employees here."

He was bursting with pride, with a legitimate pride. There was no conceit about Harry, but merely a robust belief in all that his comrades did, and in particular in the brains and muscles at work on this giant undertaking. With a sweep of his hand he pointed to a heavy truck, with a crane-like attachment built on it, running along the rails on one of the higher steps of the huge cutting on which he himself was engaged.

"Jest watch it," he invited Jim. "It's a treat to see it handle rails. You see, our rails wants shifting constantly; for as the diggers clear the dirt they naturally want to get forward or outward, as the case may be, seeing that we cut our steps away to the side. Anyhow, there's need to swap the rails from place to place and lay new tracks, and that 'ere machine is a track layer, which handles the double lengths of bolted rails as if they was sticks."

Jim was fascinated, indeed, as he watched this new wonder; for wonder the machine undoubtedly was. As he looked he could realize that gangs of men and much time might be needed to shift the lines of rails, and time, he remembered, was an item of which his comrades were sparing. Bustle was the order of the day, and of every succeeding day, on the isthmus. As to the machine, it swung its arm over a long length of rail, fastened its clutches upon it, and lifted the double track, ready bolted to its sleepers, into the air. Then it trotted along the rails, and presently deposited its burden somewhere else.

"And by the time it's nipped back for another length, and has brought it, the track gang has got the lengths in line, and has bolted the fishplates to it," explained Harry. "But that digger's waiting for us. Git along, Jim."

Breezy was not the word for this young American. He seemed to enjoy every minute of his life, and would have made an admirable companion for one subject to depression. However, Jim was not that; our hero was naturally inclined to jollity, if at times serious, as became his position of responsibility, but with Harry beside him there was no thought of seriousness. They made a laughing, jolly couple on the digger. The hours flew by, so that Jim was astonished when the five-o'clock whistles blew.

"How's he shaping?" he heard a voice ask, and, turning, found it was Phineas Barton, with another white beside him.

"Shaping! Say, ef there's a digger going free he's fit to take it right off, he's that careful," cried Harry. "See him at it, Major."

"You jest go along as you was before," he whispered in Jim's ear, as the latter hopped back into the cab of the digger. "I ain't going to stay up there alongside of you, 'cos there ain't no need; and you ain't got no cause to feel flustered. The Major's one of the works bosses, and reckon employment lays with him. He'll know in a jiffy that you're able to do the work."

To tell the truth our hero felt somewhat scared at the moment, more even than he had that morning when taking his place for the first time on the machine. But he had perfect confidence now in his powers of control, and, with that assurance to help him, struggled against the unusual feeling of nervousness which had so suddenly attacked him, and let the bucket of the digger rattle down to the bottom of the bank. Time after time he dug his way upwards, and delighted Harry by his management.

"Gee! Ef he ain't got some brass!" the latter exclaimed beneath his breath, as the bucket swung out over the spoil train. "He's copying me with a vengeance. I mind the time when I first started in at the business, and it took me a sight longer to fix the emptying of that bucket. But this here Jim has kind of tumbled to the knack. He swings her out, and ain't stopped swinging afore he opens up and lets his dirt drop. Ef that don't fix the Major, wall he don't deserve to have good men."

As a matter of fact the official was a good deal impressed; but he was a cautious man, and was not inclined to be taken in by a demonstration which might prove to be somewhat freakish. He told himself that under observation there are some men who do better than others, only to break down on ordinary occasions, lacking the stimulus of a gallery to applaud. He yet wanted to prove that this would-be employee had a head on his shoulders, and though he had heard the tale of the rescue, he determined to see if Jim could show coolness on dry land as well as in the water. Therefore he strolled across to the head of the spoil train, to find the driver had not yet quitted his post, in fact he was just in the act of uncoupling from the train, but willingly obeyed an order. Then the official strolled back, to find Jim still busy with the digger, and, waiting a favourable opportunity, waved his arm. What followed made Harry stand up on his toes with anxiety.

"He's sure to boss it!" he growled. "Gee, if I don't talk to that driver! He knows as well as I do that he ought to blow his whistle afore giving his engine steam to draw out. An old hand wouldn't be caught, but most like Jim'll bungle it. He'll get his bucket opened over the train, and the moving cars will catch it."

That, it was evident, was the intention of the Major. He was applying a test which might well strain the cuteness of a raw hand; and, as it happened, it was only watchfulness which saved Jim. Up came his bucket, a mass of dirt tumbling from its edge, and round spun the machine, swinging the bucket over the trucks. In a moment the bottom would fall open. Harry could see him handling the rope which freed the trigger. Then he gave a sigh of satisfaction, for Jim had observed the movement. His hand left the rope, the bucket stopped in its swing, there was the grinding sound of moving gears, and promptly the massive beam returned on its axis.

"That train's moving," he shouted. "I might have had a jam up."

"You might, and no mistake," said Phineas, coming up to the side of the cab. "You jest fixed the business nicely. Reckon if there had been a bust-up the Major deserved to have to pay for the damage. Say, Major, here's a hand wanting a job."

"Bring him to the office to-morrow; I'll take him," was the short reply. "Usual terms; he can get on to a digger way up by Culebra."

Before Jim could thank him the official had departed, leaving our hero still seated in the cab.

"You kin git down off that machine and eat a supper feeling you've earned it," exclaimed Harry, coming up to him and gripping his hand. "I'm main sorry though that you're to work at Culebra, 'cos it would have been nice to meet of an evening."

"And no reason why you shouldn't," cried Phineas. "See here, Harry, Jim's to live with me. He and his sister will have quarters at the house, the two niggers and the Chinaman also. It's an exception, I know, but there it is. Of course he'll get his dinner and supper way up at Culebra; but he'll take breakfast with me, and of an evening he'll come down to the club here. Guess you'll hear more of him."

That the arrangement was likely to prove satisfactory seemed certain, and it may be imagined that Jim was filled with glee. He sat in Phineas's parlour that night, behind the screen of copper gauze, with his mind full of the morrow, wondering what Culebra would be like, and whether the men working there could be half so pleasant as those he had already met.

CHAPTER VI

A Shot in the Dark

Folks in the Panama zone do not keep late hours as a rule, for work begins at an early hour, and he who would be fresh and ready must seek his bed early. However, Jim and his friends were not to find repose on this, almost their first night ashore, as readily as they imagined. Indeed they were to meet with an adventure which was startling, to say the least of it. They were seated in the parlour, Jim and Phineas, discussing their work, while Sadie had retired for the night. Tom and Sam were engaged in an animated conversation in the back regions, and, no doubt, were themselves preparing to turn in. Not one had an idea that a stranger was prowling about outside the house.

"Thought I heard someone about," Jim had remarked, some few minutes earlier, but Phineas had shaken his head emphatically.

"Imagination!" he cried. "There's no one comes around here at nighttimes. You see, this house lies away from the others, and up the hill. Unless a friend's coming up to smoke a pipe with me, there's no one this way of an evening; they don't fancy the climb. Sit down again, Jim. How much do you think you're going to earn on that digger?"

Jim threw himself into his chair again, let his head drop back, and closed his eyes. He already had an inkling of what he would earn. The thought had brought him vast pleasure; for there was enough to pay for his own and Sadie's keep.

"Three dollars, fifty cents, less fifty cents a day for food," he said, after a while.

"Put it at four dollars fifty," said Phineas. "Four dollars fifty cents, less fifteen cents for your dinner. T'other meals you take here. So you'll net four dollars twenty-five a day, and free quarters."

"One moment," exclaimed Jim. "Free quarters! No, Mr. Phineas. You must allow me to pay my way. I couldn't stop with you without making some sort of contribution to the expenses of the house."

"Just as I should have thought," said Phineas, smiling at him. "Any chap with a little pride would want to pay his way: but these quarters are free. The Commission gives you so much a day, and free quarters. If I choose to have a companion, he don't have a call to pay for the rooms he uses; so that's wiped off. Then as to food: if you pay twenty-five cents a day for yourself, thirty for

Sadie, seeing that she's only small, making fifty-five, and another ten for general expenses, there'll be nothing more to be said. How's that?"

Jim thought it was extremely fair, as indeed it was, and at once agreed. The arrangement would allow of his putting by some twenty dollars a week, and at the end of a year he told himself that that would mount to a nice little sum. But again he heard a sound outside, and rose to his feet.

"I'm sure I heard a footstep," he exclaimed. "There!"

Phineas was doubtful, still he went to the door with him, and emerged on to the balcony. There was no one to be seen, and it was so dark that had there been anyone they would have escaped detection. They retired again, therefore, to the parlour, unaware of the figure skulking close down at the foot of the veranda. The man—for a man it undoubtedly was—rose to his feet stealthily, and stood there listening for a while, till he heard voices coming from the parlour. Then he clambered on to the veranda by way of the steps, and crept towards the square patch of light which indicated the gauze-covered window of the parlour. Slowly he raised his head till he was able to look into the room. As he did so, the lamplight flickering through fell upon his head and shoulders so that one could get some impression of his appearance. Decidedly short in stature, the man's face was swarthy, while the eyes seemed to be small and unusually bright, quite a feature of the face, in fact. He wore a long, flowing, black moustache, while his chin was covered with a stubbly growth a week old; but there was something about the face which immediately attracted one's attention more than any other feature. It was the mouth. The lips were parted in something resembling a snarl, showing a set of irregular white teeth, which with the lamplight shining on them looked cruel. A Spaniard one would have said at once. More than that, his features were familiar. Little did Jim guess that the ruffian staring in upon him was one of those who had fought for the boats in the waist of the foundering ship on which he had been voyaging to New York, and that he himself had incurred the man's hatred by a blow which, now that the matter was over, he could not remember having given. But one's actions in the heat of a contest often pass utterly unnoticed and unremembered. Jim had no idea now that this same man had dashed at him with a drawn knife, and that he had floored him with a straight blow from his fist between the eyes. However, if he had no recollection the ruffian had.

"The very one," he told himself, with a hiss of anger, as he peeped in at the two unconscious men. "See the pup. He sits there chatting as if he had no fear, and as if he expected a Spaniard to forget. But I am not one of those; a blow for a blow, I say. I meant to thrust my knife between his ribs aboard the ship; now I will put lead into him. It will be more certain."

His hand went unconsciously to his face, and for a few moments he let his fingers play very gently about his nose, for that was the organ on which Jim's fist had descended with such suddenness and weight. Even now it was decidedly tender, and pained the man as he touched it. That caused his sinister, bright, little eyes to light up fiercely, while the lips curled farther back from his cruel, irregular teeth as the fingers of the other hand fell upon the butt of a revolver tucked into his belt.

"A blow for a blow; if not with the knife, then with the bullet. He who strikes a Spaniard must reckon with the consequences, and afterwards—pouff! there will be no afterwards. The bullet will end everything."

Slowly he drew the weapon, and pulled the hammer back with his thumb till it clicked into position.

"What was that?" asked Jim, hearing the sound distinctly. Even Phineas heard it this time, and stood to his feet.

"Perhaps one of the boys is outside; perhaps your Tom, or Sam," he said swiftly. "Certainly there is someone; we'll go and see."

He went towards the door, while Jim rose from his chair and moved towards him. It was an opportunity of which the Spaniard took the fullest advantage.

"Now or never," he told himself. "If they come out, my chance is gone."

He lifted the weapon till it was on a level with his face. Then he directed it through the gauze window at Jim, and, pressing heavily on the trigger, finally released it. Click!

An oath escaped him, for the weapon had missed fire, while the two men within the room had already reached the door. He pulled again, till the hammer swung upward. Bang! There was a deafening report, a neat little hole was torn in the gauze, while the leaden messenger he had discharged struck the doorpost, an inch above our hero's head, with a thud which caused him to start. As for the Spaniard, he did not wait to see what success he had had. He turned on his heel and fled down the steps of the veranda, and out into the night.

"Gee! A shot! There was someone outside then!"

Phineas swung round swiftly to stare at Jim. The latter nodded curtly.

"Yes," he agreed. "A shot. There's the bullet."

He took the lamp from the table and held it up towards the doorpost.

"Just an inch above my head," he smiled. "I heard the thing bang into the woodwork, and felt the wind of the shot. Close, Mr. Phineas!"

"But—but who fired it? Why? Where from?"

There were a thousand questions he wished to ask, and only the last could Jim answer. He took his friend to the copper gauze stretching across the window, which was otherwise devoid of covering, for no glass was employed, and again with the help of the lamp showed him a neat little round hole punched through the gauze.

"He stood outside there and stared in at us," he said, putting the events as he guessed them. "He cocked his pistol, and we heard the noise. Then he fired as we got to the door. Queer, isn't it, Mr. Phineas?"

"Queer! It's downright, cold-blooded attempt at murder!" shouted Phineas. "Call those boys."

But there was no need to summon them. Tom and Sam were already at the door, while Ching was in the passage, a swaying lantern in his hand.

"What dat?" asked Tom, his eyes beginning to bulge. "Someone fire a shot. Tom not like dat at all; he tink someone try to kill him."

"Boys," said Phineas, keeping perfectly cool, "some scoundrel came to the window of the parlour and fired at Jim here. He missed him by an inch. We must follow and take the fellow, whoever he may be; it may be the work of a lunatic. Bring along that lamp, Ching."

"One moment!" cried Jim. "Best leave someone here in case the fellow returns. Tom, you look after the house. I can trust you to frighten anyone away. Sam and Ching will come with us. Sam, we want you to open those eyes of yours extra wide: that fellow must be followed. Now, are we ready? But first, has anyone seen a stranger about here to-day?"

"Seed a nasty-lookin' Spaniard, I did," admitted Sam, his eyes shining bright and eager in the lamplight. "Him one of de crowd working on de canal I tink; but me recognize him. Same man aboard de steamer, sah; yo knock him down when he come for yo wid a knife. Yo go bang, squelch! Him flop over on to him back, den creep away growling out, and sayin' tings beneath him breath. Him nasty fellow altogether."

"Then there is the motive for the crime," declared Phineas at once. "There is never any telling what some of these Southerners will do. No doubt, in the course of the fight aboard the ship, you knocked him down, though from the look of your face you evidently don't remember the matter. See here, Jim; let Tom go with you. I forgot that I have a broken arm, and am more likely to delay you; but I'll telephone down to the police headquarters in Colon, and put them on the watch. I suppose you'll follow?"

Jim nodded promptly. "At once," he said with decision. "If I passed the matter now, he would make a second attempt, and I don't much fancy that. Sam's a splendid tracker, and if there's a mark he will be able to find it. Then come along, boys. Ching, bring the lamp; perhaps there's another we can have?"

It took but a few minutes to discover another lamp, then the party set out. Meanwhile the diminutive Sam, his eyes sparkling with enthusiasm, had been moving swiftly about the house outside.

"Seen de footmarks, sah," he said, as Jim came out to join him, with Tom and Ching in close attendance. "Look, sah: he come up to de house by here, and hide under de veranda. Den he creep on to it. Dere de muddy boots make a mark. He stand at de window and shoot bang right through. Plenty more mark outside. Soon find de villain."

It had rained that evening, soon after the whistles had sounded for the men to cease work, and, since this side of the isthmus gets more than a fair share of wet weather, the ground is generally somewhat soft. In fact, it was just the place a criminal should not have selected, for it gave opportunities of tracking even to amateurs. But Sam was no amateur.

"When I live down south, often track de nigger," he explained to Ching; whereat the lanky, thin Chinaman wagged his head, shaking his pigtail from side to side.

"Ob course not so easy, not at all, siree," added Sam, an air of importance about him. "Specially when dere so many mens about. But yo see, yo China boy; me soon come up wid dis fellow, and den skin um alive, cook um, see?"

He gritted his sharp teeth together, and in the lamplight looked particularly fierce. Indeed the jolly little fellow seemed to be transformed by the work so unexpectedly placed before him. He was desperately serious now, and eager to proceed with the quest.

"By de poker, but yo talk a heap!" exclaimed Tom, taking the lamp from Ching. "Now yo, Sam, yo get to work quick. Me help, but not jaw; time to chatter when de man found."

"Den yo follow here. See dis! He shoot through de window and den run. He jump from the veranda and come all ob a heap, so he did. Ha! Yo can see dat, eh? Eben a big, fat nigger same as you, Tom, can see dat?"

Tom wisely ignored the remark. He followed Sam's indicating finger, noticed that the dirt marks on the veranda were widely splayed out, as from the feet of a man who was in a hurry, and again saw them, together with a long, curling impression on the soil at the foot of the veranda, showing where the criminal's feet had slipped. Nor was that all. One could detect the spot where his hands had met the earth, together with a deeper mark where the muzzle of the revolver he had used had buried itself in the clay.

"Him sure enough, de blackguard!" growled Tom. "Now den."

Sam led them away from the house at a rattling pace, that caused Jim to marvel. But the little fellow was no fool at the art of tracking, while his eyes, usually so slothful in appearance, were now evidently very sharp and observant. And if our hero thought at times that he was being led on a wild-goose chase, Sam was always able to demonstrate that such was not the case at all.

"Yo tink me not on de track?" he asked, after a while, when they paused to gather their breath. "Well, den, see here. De same marks all de while. Him run like a hare; him wonder if him followed. Soon we come to de house where him hide. Den look out for fireworks. Him shoot like mad. Sam know de sort ob fellow."

The mere suggestion caused our hero to stop and think a little. That a dastardly attempt had been made to kill him he was now sure, and there had crept into his memory, as he followed Sam, the incident aboard the ship which seemed to have been the cause of this attempt on his life. He recollected that a brutal-looking Spaniard, some forty years of age, had rushed at him, and had been sent reeling backward. Then the man had drawn a knife, and had come on again furiously. Jim now brought to his mind his own behaviour. In the heat and turmoil of the contest, when it seemed that the Spaniards would prove too strong for the captain's party, and before the lusty Tom had put in an appearance, the man had rushed furiously forward, and he (Jim) had met him with a terrible blow of his fist. He had seen the ruffian fly backwards and tumble on his back; then the arrival of Tom, and the forward movement of the whole party had occupied all his thoughts, to the neglect of an incident which seemed to be done with.

"And Sam thinks he'll shoot again. Shouldn't wonder," he said to himself. "Still, there's no reason why I should funk following him. He has to be apprehended, for otherwise he might try to shoot someone else who had a hand in that fight. Get along, Sam," he called out cheerily. "If there are fireworks we must deal with them. I'm game to tackle the fellow again."

Tom looked round at him severely. "Yo's got to go extra careful, sah, so yo hab," he said. "Dis fellow not care wheder yo white man; no, not one little piece. He shoot yo down like a dog. Yo leab him to Tom."

"To a big hulking fellow like you! I like that," laughed Jim. "You'd certainly be shot. You couldn't escape a bullet. But we'll see. If he's to be found, we'll take him, however many bullets he may let off."

They pushed on again in wake of Sam, and followed the tracks at a jog-trot. They led in the direction of Colon, and when near the outskirts of the town, turned towards a hut lying to one side of the road.

"Him dere fo shore," declared Sam, pointing. "You find him in de hut. But mind what Sam say. Dis Spaniard not like to be taken. He shoot at eberyone.

Him blaze away widout looking to see who it am. Sah, better yo stay away back here. Tom and Sam and Ching soon finish de hash of dat ruffian."

It was comical and somewhat pathetic to watch their care of Jim, for Tom and the Chinaman both joined with Sam in requesting our hero to remain at a distance. But Jim was not the lad to shelter himself behind the figures of such faithful fellows. Rather was he the one to place himself in the van, to take all risks himself, so that those who obeyed his orders should not be the ones to suffer. Besides, a leader should lead.

"Boys," he said, as if he had not heard them, "we'll surround that hut. Tom at the front, Sam at the back, Ching on the far side, and I will make for the window through which a light is shining. By the way, best douse our lamps. They would show our position. And, another thing, if that fellow rushes at us, or begins to fire, knock him down flat. Don't be too easy with him. I've heard of these wild Spaniards before. Of course they're not all the same as this one. Indeed, Mr. Barton tells me that they are well-behaved as a rule. But this man seems to have a bee in his bonnet, or he wouldn't think so much of that blow I gave him. Anyway, if he rushes, knock him flat. Savvy?"

Ching grinned. The slothful-looking Chinaman enjoyed the thought of a knockout blow, for this Oriental had been now so long resident in the States of America that he had actually acquired some knowledge of the art of boxing. He grinned widely, and began to wrap his swinging pigtail about the top of his head. Sam's eyes bulged widely open; he looked positively ferocious, and stared at the hut as if he wished the contest had already begun. But Tom only laughed inaudibly, and rubbed the palms of his big hands together.

"By de poker, but if him come up agin dat, him not know wheder him man or monkey," he said, doubling an enormous fist. "Massa Jim, yo not tall 'nough to look in at de window. Better leave dat to Tom. Yo go to de front; plenty chance of fightin' dere."

It was only another attempt of the big negro to place our hero out of danger, and Jim promptly scouted the suggestion.

"You'll go to your stations right off," he commanded. "If I whistle, you can come along and join me. The first thing to be done is to see if the fellow is in there."

"Dat sartin; I know him dere. I ready to swear it," declared Sam.

"Then come along."

Without more ado Jim led the way, and presently, when they were within a stone's throw of the hut, they separated, each to seek the position to which he had been appointed. Jim himself stole on tiptoe towards the window of the hut, and, having arrived at it, lifted his head inch by inch, and, pulling off his cap, stared into the room. Then he bobbed down again, and had circumstances permitted of it he would certainly have whistled; for there were five men assembled in the hut, and one of the number was undoubtedly the man for whom he and his friends had set out, the one, in fact, who had that very evening attempted to kill him. In a flash he recognized the ruffian. Then his eye ran swiftly round the circle grouped about a rough plank table, on which bottles and glasses were to be seen, and promptly the faces struck him as likenesses of those he had observed the evening before on a slip presented to all working on the canal. It was a police notification, and had been sent to Phineas so that, in appointing European labourers, he might beware of employing those whose portraits appeared. And Jim brought to memory the words beneath the portraits.

"The police of the canal zone are in search of a number of men, amongst them the above. It has come to their knowledge that a band of European thieves has gathered in the neighbourhood, and several robberies of Commission stores prove their arrival here. Any who recognize the above should at once give notice of their whereabouts. From foreign official sources we are informed that at least one of the men is a dangerous criminal, wanted for acts of violence to the person."

"Phew!" Jim went hot all over. He recollected that Phineas had spoken to him of these men, and had explained to him that it was not until after their arrival on the isthmus that the police received a warning from foreign parts.

"No doubt the fellows had made their last haunt too hot for them," he explained, "so, hearing from their comrades that America had brought a heap of valuable stores here, and that where there are workmen there must also be, often enough, large sums of money with which to pay their wages, these rogues came along to the isthmus, took posts with the gangs of labourers, and then laid their plans to rob. One of our pay offices was broken into and rifled a month ago. That put the police on the *qui vive*. Then came a robbery at the far end of the canal. The culprits were not discovered, but immediately afterwards the police received this information from abroad, together with photographs."

"Which they publish here for the information of canal officials," said Jim.

"Jest so," agreed Phineas. "And I suppose these rascals got to know that their game was ended. Somehow they have means of their own of getting information. Anyway, they disappeared, and weren't missed from amongst the armies we employ. Reckon some of them got aboard that ship that you and I took passage in. If that's so, they're back right here now, waiting for another steamer."

If the whole truth had been known, the gang of desperadoes of whom the Commission police had obtained information had indeed found the zone already too hot for them. They were a band consisting sometimes of five members, sometimes of more or less. And for a long while now their attention had been particularly turned to ports near to the Gulf of Mexico. Appearing to be but Spanish workmen, they escaped often enough the attention of police officers, and had done so at Colon. There they had contrived to burgle two of the pay offices, and, as Phineas had rightly surmised, had sailed on the very steamer on which he and Jim had taken passage. There, having come into contact with our hero, they had met with a misfortune, which had brought them back to the isthmus.

"Just showing that it's here we're meant to do our work," had said the leader of these rascals, a scowling individual boasting the name of Jaime de Oteros, "See here, friends, the police of the zone are looking for us amongst the labour gangs. We've dollars saved in plenty, and no need to work; supposing we find some quiet place near at hand, and take toll of another pay office."

"And first of all pay back the scores we owe," the rascal who had so recently fired at Jim growled. "I've sworn to give back what I was given aboard that ship, and since I believe the young pup who was so free with his fists is staying on here, why, I'll finish him. Eh?"

His suggestion had met with the hearty approval of all. There was not a man in the gang who would not do the same; for to these lawless fellows a blow received demanded repayment. As to the risk, that was nothing. They were accustomed to the feeling that their arrest was aimed at. If theft could pass without actual discovery, then a shot in the night, and the death of a white official, would equally escape detection.

"Five of them." Jim counted them off on his fingers as he again raised his head. He squinted in through the corner of the window, and inspected each one of the gang separately. And now he recognized them not alone from the leaflet which he had seen, but from amongst the faces of the Spaniards who had been aboard the steamer. Of an evening he had often stood at the rail above and looked down into the waist of the vessel, watching the dusky faces of the Spaniards, and scenting the rank odour of the cigarettes they smoked. Features which then had made no great impression on him, but which had, unconsciously as it were, been tucked away within his memory, now struck him as familiar. Little by little he recollected exactly where he had seen each man, and what he had been doing, so that within the space of a few minutes he was sure that every one of them had been aboard the steamer.

"And are now wanted by the police here," he thought, "while the fellow sitting at the far end of the table is wanted more than them all, seeing that he has

67

attempted murder. But how to do it? There are five, and all probably carry arms."

A second glance at the men persuaded him that there was little doubt on the last matter; for the leader of these ruffians had placed his weapon on the plank table before him, while a second was cleaning his revolver with a piece of dirty rag. A third wore a belt, as could be clearly seen, since he had discarded his coat, and carried both a revolver and a huge knife attached to it.

"Ugly fellows to deal with, I guess," thought Jim. "The question is this: ought we to attempt a rush? or ought we to set a watch on the house and send for the police?"

Obviously, with only three to help him, the last suggestion was the one to follow, and having pondered the matter for a little while Jim came to a decision. Peeping in at the window again, he watched the men as they rolled and lit cigarettes, or filled their glasses from the bottles on the table, then he crept away to Sam, and with him went to join Tom. A signal brought Ching to them promptly.

"Come away over here," said Jim softly. "I want to talk."

He led them into a thick belt of bush which had escaped the billhooks of the Commission sanitary corps, for the reason that it stood on high ground, and then came to a halt.

"Wall?" asked Tom, his face indistinguishable in the darkness, but his tones eager. "He's right there, I reckon. He only wants taking?"

"He's there; but for the moment we can't easily take him. Listen here," said Jim. Then he explained that there were five men in the hut, and that if he were right in his surmise, and his eyes had not misinformed him, they were a gang of criminals of whom the police were in search.

"And all armed," he added. "I thought at first that we might rush them; but even supposing they were not armed, one or more might escape. So I guessed the best plan would be to send off for the police, while we watch the place. Say, Sam, you could find the office in Colon?"

The little fellow nodded and gave a grunt of assent.

"Easy as cuttin' chips," he said. "What den?"

"Run there as fast as your legs will carry you, and tell them that we have located the gang of men whose portraits they have been circulating amongst the canal officials. Tell them of the attempt made to shoot me to-night, and warn them to come along cautiously. Get right off. We'll stand round the place till you come along."

Sam set down his lantern at once and disappeared in the darkness, making hardly a sound as he went. Then Jim led the others back towards the hut.

"We'll take the same places," he said. "Of course, if they separate we shall have to follow; but I rather think they live here. If that's so we shall have them."

Waiting till both Tom and Ching had taken up their positions he crept towards the hut, and, having reached the window, raised his head and peeped in. None of the men had moved. The ruffian who had been handling his revolver was still cleaning it with the dirty rag, while the man who had come that evening to the house which Phineas occupied, and had deliberately fired through the gauze window, was staring moodily at the empty glass before him. The others were engaged in an eager conversation, carried on in low tones. Jim put his ear as close as possible, for though he knew only a few words of Spanish it was possible that English was the language employed. Then he heard a sudden, startled cry, and, looking in, saw that the rascal at whose arrest he aimed had risen to his feet. The man was staring hard at the window, and in a flash Jim realized that his own presence had been discovered. He ducked swiftly, and as he did so there came the report of a pistol. An instant later a bullet smashed the glass just overhead, smothering him with debris. Then a babel of cries came from the hut, the door was dragged open, and in a trice five men had thrown themselves upon him.

CHAPTER VII

The Lair of the Robbers

There are times in a man's life when he has no spare moments in which to think, and this occasion may be said to have been one of those urgent periods in that of our hero. For he had no time to do more than move a yard from the window of the little hut located so close to Colon when the door was flung open, and the five ruffians within burst from their cover. Jim had hardly shaken the dust and debris of the shattered pane of glass from his eyes when one of the men was on him. It was Jaime de Oteros, the leader of the gang, a dark, forbidding-looking fellow, as agile as a cat, and a desperado accustomed to scenes of violence.

"A spy! a spy!" he bellowed, catching sight of Jim; for the lamp within the cottage cast its rays through the window and illumined his figure. "Kill him! Down with him to the ground! Stamp on him!"

Quick as thought a blade flashed from his belt, and while Jim was still almost blinded by the dust which was clinging to his eyes, the man struck savagely at him. An instant later a sharp cry escaped from Jim's lips, while he staggered back against the hut; for the dagger had penetrated his left arm, high up near the shoulder.

"Wounded! This is serious. I am in a hole." The thoughts came to him like a flash, while the urgency of the situation seemed to help to clear his eyes. He could now see the villain who had attacked him quite plainly, while, owing to his position close to the wall of the dwelling, his own figure was in the dusk. And it was that fact alone which saved his life; for had the rascal standing so close to him been sure of his bearings that formidable blade would have descended again. Jim caught the glint of the lamplight on it, and, stung by the pain in his shoulder and by the danger of his position, he struck out fiercely with his clenched fist, and as fortune would have it caught the rascal neatly beneath the chin.

Crash! The man staggered backwards, breathing deeply, and a second later cannoned into one of his comrades who was hurrying forward to support him. He gave a low growl of rage, pulled himself together, and flung himself on Jim again furiously.

"Dog of a spy! You struck me. Police or not, I will kill you."

There was a snarl in his tones, while the man's whole person bristled with anger. But Jaime de Oteros was not the ruffian to miss a chance, or spoil his own opportunities, because he was in a passion. Beneath his smouldering rage the rascal kept a level head, and, watching Jim as well as the darkness would allow him, threw himself forward with startling swiftness. Bang! Crash! That terrible knife blade just missed its mark, and passing over our hero's shoulder buried its point deeply in the woodwork of the hut, so deeply, in fact, that Jaime had to pull hard to release it. That effort again helped Jim; indeed it gave him an opportunity he was quick to pounce upon. For out shot his right fist again, and, striking square between the eyes, it sent Jaime hurtling backwards.

"Keep off! I warn you that any further violence will lead to severe punishment." Jim gasped the words, for the suddenness of the attack had taken his breath away. But he was by no means cowed, and, being one of those sharp, shrewd lads of which America is so justly proud, he promptly decided to make use of the few seconds respite allowed by Jaime's downfall. It was a case where force could not greatly avail him, he told himself, as he stood at bay before the desperadoes, his back close to the wall; but bluff might help him.

"I warn you," he said again. "Drop your knives and stand here against the hut with your arms up. If not, I'll whistle to my men to shoot. Yes," he said sternly, "my men, you are surrounded. Jaime de Oteros, the game is up."

As if to support his statement there came a call at that instant, while men could be heard hurrying towards the scene of the conflict. As for the band of rascals, Jaime had, to be sure, been the first to encounter Jim, but his comrades had been quick to support him. They would have thrown themselves on the young fellow before this had there been space; but the hut protected him in rear, while Jaime's swinging limbs kept them at a distance in other directions. The lamp within the hut threw its sickly beams on the figures of the rascals, showing their features plainly, and letting Jim recognize at once the ruffian who had, earlier on in the evening, fired at him so deliberately.

"Come, hands up!" he repeated sharply. "The man who is found with arms on him when my men come on the scene will wish that he had never seen us."

"Massa Jim, Massa Jim! what dat happenin'?" came through the darkness at this moment. "I heard shots; dere was shoutin'. What fo, I want to know?"

"It's that nigger of his," suddenly exclaimed one of the ruffians, hearing Tom. "It's a blind, a big bluff! Down with him! Gee! Stand aside, and see me shoot him!"

Shouts came from all five now, and as if by common impulse they cast themselves in Jim's direction. And if he had remained in his old position there is little doubt but that the gang would quickly have crushed the life out of his body; but Jim was fully alive on this eventful night. There was no drowsiness about him, as may be imagined, seeing the danger in which he stood. The lamplight showed him the staring faces of the villains in front of him, and their changing expressions immediately after Tom had called. He saw their hands dive down for knife or revolver, and quick as thought he darted to one side; but, quick as he was, one of the gang was too swift for him. A hand fell on his shoulder, fingers closed on his coat, while the ruffian made frantic efforts to detain him.

"He is here! Here!" he shouted. "I have the slippery dog! Quick, one of you, slit his throat, and have done with it!"

"Take that! Back with you! Tom, Tom!" Jim shouted for the negro, and a second later struck at the rascal with both fists, sending him staggering backwards; but the blows, sturdy and strong though they were, could not keep off the other desperadoes. They closed round our hero in an instant, and there began at once a conflict the severity of which can hardly be described. The sallow rascal, who had so deliberately attempted to murder him that same night, thrust his comrades aside in his own anxiety to complete the work in which he had so signally failed, and, raising his arm, fired his revolver at point-blank range. However, close shots are not always the ones to kill. The struggling men at the rascal's elbow disturbed his aim, while the bullet buried itself harmlessly in the wall of the tumbledown dwelling close to which the conflict was taking place. Then Jim did a clever thing. He had dodged swiftly to avoid the shot; but an instant later he darted forward, swung his right fist into the villain's ribs with such force that the breath was driven out of his body, and immediately afterwards wrenched the smoking weapon from his hand. It was his turn now, and right well he took advantage of the opportunity.

"Hands up!" he commanded again, levelling the muzzle at Jaime de Oteros's head. "Hands up instantly!"

They fell back from him as if he were infected with the plague, and the same uncertain, flickering lamplight which had helped our hero before now showed hesitation in their scowling faces; but it was only for the moment. Let it be remembered that this gang was composed of men who had been in many a scuffle and come out of them successfully, that one and all were unscrupulous, and would as soon and as easily kill a man as take the life of a fly. Was it wonderful that, seeing one youth alone opposed to them, they regained some measure of courage? Jaime's lips receded from his teeth in an ugly snarl, and, as if shot from a gun, he darted at Jim, ducked beneath the levelled muzzle, and closed with him.

"Now you shall pay with your life, dog of a policeman!" he growled. "This to end our quarrel."

He gripped Jim's right arm as if with a vice, pushing it upward. Then the fingers of his left hand fell upon his chin and forced it backwards.

"Strike with your knife! Strike, fool!" he shouted to one of his comrades. "He is helpless."

And helpless, in fact, Jim was, for a second villain had gripped him from behind. He was just like a sheep held for the slaughter, and though he struggled frantically he could make no impression on those who held him; but Tom could. The lusty negro was not the one to be frightened by a gang of double the strength, and coming upon the scene at this moment he fell upon the men with the ferocity of a tiger. His first charge scattered them, setting Jim free; then a dive to one side allowed him to grip one of the rascals. In a trice he had him swinging at his full arm's length above his head.

"By de poker, but dis fun!" he shouted, waving the man to and fro as if he were merely a package. "Yo's tried to kill Massa Jim, heh? Yo go dere den." He swished round as if he were poised on a pivot, his arms went back, and in an instant he had thrown his burden against the wall of the hut. That done, he dashed forward on the heels of Jim, and helped the latter to secure Jaime de Oteros. As for the others, they melted away into the darkness, and the last that was heard of them was the sound of their quickly moving feet. But Ching reported that he had encountered one of the rascals. Indeed, a minute later he came into the narrow circle of light dragging one of the wretches with him, and giggling with suppressed amusement.

"Him not see Ching," he explained with a guffaw. "Him comee runnin' ever so fast. But Ching knowe him not a good man, and send him silly wid a blow from dis stick. Oh, him hab a velly bad head to-mollow. Him so velly solly him meet Ching."

"And him sorrier still when him come before de police bosses," exclaimed Tom, gripping the arm of the leader of the gang so firmly that the man howled. "What fo you make that to-do?" asked Tom, shaking Jaime as if he were a rat. "Yo no cause to complain. Me hold yo tight, eh? Me hold yo tighter still if yo not stop dat blather. By de poker, but dis fine, Massa Jim! We've caught jest three of de ruffians, and see dem hanged, strung up by de neck, dance tattoo in de air. Eh? Dat good for rascals."

Again he shook the unfortunate Jaime till the ruffian's teeth chattered together, while the man was unable to retain his feet. That he was cowed by the size and strength of his captor there was no doubt, for he made no effort to retaliate or to escape. Instead, he hung listless, his knife fallen at his feet, his left hand clutching at the fingers which compressed his other arm with such painful tenacity.

"Put him there in the hut," said Jim, beginning now to breathe a little more easily. "Ching, take your captive in too. Tom will watch him; if they attempt an escape——"

JIM IN A TIGHT CORNER

"Ha, ha! I like to see dat," cried the lusty negro, lifting Jaime from his feet as if he were a child and beginning to carry him within the hut. "By de poker, but I hope him will try to 'scape. Den yo see; Tom smash um into a jelly. Tom make mincemeat of dis bag ob bones. Yo see; Tom lob to kill um."

He swung the ruffian round till their faces were close together, and, bending closer, bared his teeth and glared at the unfortunate fellow till Jaime recoiled; for, when he liked, Tom could adopt the expression of a demon.

"There; see him safely in the hut, and watch the two of them," cried Jim, smiling even at such a moment, for he could not help but contrast Tom's unusual exhibition of ferocity with his usual self. It was an eye-opener even to him to see this mild-mannered negro so transformed; and Jim, knowing the faithful fellow so well, realized that all his anger and ferocity were assumed.

"Just to scare the ruffian," he thought, "and very thoroughly he has done it, I guess. Now, let's see this other fellow."

He and Ching between them rolled the man whom Tom had cast against the hut on to his back, and then carried him within the dwelling, where the lamp gave them an opportunity of inspecting him.

"Bad luck!" cried Jim at once. "Neither of our prisoners is the one I wished above all to capture. Still, we have accounted for three, and the police will deal with the others. How long will it take them to arrive?"

"Anoder hour, sah," came from Tom immediately. "Me know de road. Dey here about den. But no need to worry; dese blackguard son ob guns not try any little game. Tom make himself happy."

To prove his coolness he dragged a pipe from his coat, filled it with loose chippings which he carried in a pocket, and, stepping to the lamp, held the bowl of the pipe over the flame. Then he puffed big clouds of smoke into the air contained within the hovel, which, to be sure, already reeked with the nauseous fumes of the cigarettes the gang of ruffians had been smoking. Later Tom sat himself comfortably in a chair, crossed one leg over the other, folded his arms, and regarded his prisoners with an air of severity which caused them to cower, though Jim, looking up at him, could distinguish the old twinkle in the negro's eyes.

"By lummy! But s'pose we not wait fo de police," suggested Tom, removing his pipe from his capacious mouth, and baring his fine white teeth in the process. He leered at the two cowering men, and then looked round at our hero. "S'pose save de time and labour ob de police, sah. Hang um now. Plenty room in here, and dat beam jest in nice position. Gee! Fine ting to watch dis scum dance de tatoo in de air. S'pose we get to wid it."

There was an amiable smile on his lips now. He popped the pipe back between his teeth, causing the latter to fasten upon the stem with a click, and stared up at the blackened roof of the cottage. "Him bear de weight ob both together, sah," he laughed. "But not be too fast. One at time plenty much, so as have heap to laugh at. I'm gwine ter commence wid dis blackguard."

He glowered upon Jaime de Oteros, the hardened villain who had led the gang, and who, if the information of the Commission police were correct, had more than once robbed his victims with unusual violence. "Him biggest of de blackguards," said Tom reflectively. "Him gwine ter dance on air fust of de lot."

He rose from his seat, laid his pipe on the table, and approached his prisoner. And Jaime shrunk before him. From being a well-nurtured man, a rascal who, by means of his depredations had been enabled to live on the fat of the land and batten on other people's riches, the wretch, when punishment faced him, shrivelled visibly, till his very stature seemed to be dwarfed, his cheeks shrunken and hollow, and his rounded limbs but half their former size. He grovelled upon the floor, whining for mercy.

"Stop!" cried Jim at once, thinking that Tom's fun had gone far enough. "We will wait for the police, and let them do as they like. But it jest about shows you the cravens these fellows are. Under the same sort of circumstances this Jaime would not hesitate to bully his prisoners, I guess; even to hang them outright. However, it is not our job to give punishment; we'll leave that to the judges. Sit down and watch them."

"Watch dem! By lummy! but dat not necessary; not at all, sah," came the answer from the negro. "Yo dere, yo blackguard. Yo go very careful, or Tom do as him say, massa or no massa. Yo sabbey?"

He scowled at his prisoners till they crouched still lower, and then, turning to Jim, leered again at him, cocking one eye wide open, while the other closed. He was actually grinning, but the next instant, when he reseated himself, and again pulled at his pipe, the eyes which regarded the rascals cowering against the wall were savage.

"Now," said Jim, "lend a hand here, Ching. This fellow is badly knocked about. Bruised all over and stunned I should say: not dead."

The Chinaman wrapped his pigtail round his head, and secured it in position with a pointed piece of stick which he carried about his person for that very purpose. Then he bent over the man whom Tom had dealt so harshly with, and, chuckling all the while, proceeded to examine him minutely.

"Not one little bone ob him brokee, sah," he said. "But plenty fine upset. Got de headachee velly badly. To-mollow, when him wake up, oh him so velly ill. Him groan ever so much. Him giddy and velly sick, and him wish eber so much him neber been a rascal, and neber met dat great big nigger dere. Him tink him one big black debil. Him hate Tom."

"He! he! he! Ho! ho! ho!" came in uproarious tones from the huge negro seated at the table, smoking so comfortably. Then Tom suddenly became very serious.

"Yo Chinee boy," he cried, "yo son ob yellow gun, yo listen here. Tom not like serve a man same as dat always. Him very gentle as a rule. But, by de poker, when a villain try to shoot and cut de throat of Massa Jim, den time to do tings!

Not time to talk. Dat come afterwards. De man dere sorry in course dat he met me; but dat altogether his fault, I guess. He shouldn't hab laid a hand on de young massa. Now yo dere, in de corner, what yo squintin' outer de door for? You tink get away. By de poker, show you dat! Beat you into squash and jelly!" He switched the conversation round to his prisoner, for Jaime was staring out through the door of the hut, as if he had intentions of making a dash for liberty. But Tom's voice brought him to his senses. The man—a Spaniard by his appearance, but one evidently long departed from his own country, and well able to speak and understand English—shrivelled up into his corner, while into his black, beady eyes there came a hopeless expression, the expression to be met with on the face of a condemned criminal who knows he is past relief. It seemed evident, too, that Jaime was in that position, for a little while after, while Jim was bathing the face of the man who lay unconscious on the floor, a force of Colon police arrived, and quickly took affairs into their own hands. A smart officer entered the hut without ceremony.

"Huh!" he exclaimed, when he had taken a swift glance round. "The watchin' ended in a ruction, that's evident. Who's that?"

He stepped to the table, leaned both hands on it, and stared into the corner where the prisoners cowered. Tom coolly removed his pipe from between his lips, nodded to the officer, and then turned on Jaime.

"Dat?" he asked, pointing with the stem of his pipe. "Oh, dat a very brave prisoner dat try to kill Massa Jim, and now very sorry! Stand up dere, yo in de corner. Stand up, or, by lummy, Tom want to know what fo!

"Now den," continued Tom, when the wretch had risen to his feet, shivering with fright. "Who am yo?"

"That don't matter one single brass pin ter me," ejaculated the officer suddenly, his colour heightening, his voice taking on a tone of exultation. "Reckon it's my business to know who every criminal is. Jaime de Oteros, you're badly wanted. Guess there's a score of charges up against you. Boys, jest come in here."

He put his fingers to his lips and sent forth a shrill whistle, which instantly brought a couple of policemen into the hut.

"Handcuffs for 'em both," said the officer shortly. "Search 'em for weapons. Now then, siree?"

He turned on Jim serenely, and extended a hand. "Tell me all about it. Of course the darkie you sent along got to work and poured a whole heap of stuff into my ear as we ran here. Guess I know who you are, where you come from, and the very first day you ever had measles. There ain't many young chaps around same as Massa Jim."

There was a broad smile on his face, and the grip he gave our hero was unusually cordial. "Gee!" he went on; "a real good coloured servant is a thing to be proud of. Reckon you've two. You're jest about lucky. Those boys think all the world of you, and I've been too long amongst them not to have learned that there's always a good reason when things are like that. You've got to be extra good and plucky and all that. But let's get to business. What happened?"

Jim told him abruptly. "It was precious near a case with me," he smiled. "This fellow Jaime did his best to kill me. That's a reminder; he stuck his knife through my shoulder."

Strange to say he had forgotten the matter, and till now had had but little pain. But now he recollected, and, slipping off his jacket, exposed his arm high up near the shoulder. The officer at once inspected the wound, while Tom, and Sam, who had now arrived upon the scene, bent over him anxiously.

"Not enough to stop you enjoying a single meal," declared the officer. "Little more than skin deep, and made by a knife that had cleaned itself as it passed through your clothing. A dressing put there right away will fix the matter for good. Thomas," he sang out. Then, as another man appeared, dressed in Commission uniform: "see here, my lad, we want that first-aid case of yours. Get to work at this gentleman's shoulder. Now, sir," he went on, "you can continue the tale while Thomas is busy. These fellows tried to murder you. You had surrounded the place, I understand, and had sent Sam there back into Colon. Wall, now, what next?"

In a few words Jim described how one of the rascals had detected him as he looked in through the window. How the ruffian, the same who had fired at him earlier in the evening, had again narrowly missed striking him with a bullet, and how the whole five had then thrown themselves on him.

"Here's the result of it all," he ended. "I should have been killed but for Tom. But he arrived just in the nick of time. We took three prisoners between us; two have managed to get away."

"And that man who fired at you?" asked the officer.

"He is one of the two escaped."

"Then there's a chase before us. You'll come right along to the office, sir, where we can talk matters over. Wait while I see these rascals handcuffed to my men. But let me congratulate you and your men, sir. You did as well as any police could have done, and you showed no end of pluck. Boys, get to with those prisoners. Four of you can carry the man who's insensible. Two each to the others will be enough. Bring 'em along, boys. This is a fine evening for the police of Colon."

That the capture of three of these notorious ruffians was indeed a matter for congratulation was brought still more forcibly to Jim's mind some little time later; for, having trudged into Colon, the whole party entered the offices of the Police Commissioner there, and came face to face with that gentleman. He had been hurriedly aroused, and had at once turned out of his bed to learn what had happened. His eyes lit up with a smile as the officer who had gone to the scene of the capture introduced Jim.

"Very glad to meet you, sir," said the Commissioner. "Now tell me all about it. This, of course, will be only a preliminary enquiry; I shall remand the prisoners to the cells, and their case will be taken later. Then, of course, I shall require your evidence, and that of your men. Please state who you are?"

"James Partington, sir; from New York."

"Lately arrived, eh?"

"No, sir. Been cruising in the Caribbean with a salvage plant. Then took a passage to New York. There was a collision, and a number of Spaniards aboard the ship fought for the boats. I—er—I helped the——"

"Pardon, I recollect. Shake hands, sir."

The officer leaned over his desk and gripped Jim's fingers, while a most friendly smile played across his lips. "Of course, I recollect," he said. "The matter was published in the paper. Seen the article?"

Jim shook his head. "I haven't had much time," he said. "There have been so many things to do since I arrived in the zone."

"Then your ears will burn, my lad. The man who wrote that account put the plain truth forward. He had interviewed the captain and his men. Mr. James Partington seems to have been the hero of the occasion."

He laughed outright, seeing Jim flush to the roots of his hair, and then became serious again.

"There, forgive my chaff," he said. "But you behaved handsomely, Mr. Partington. Now tell me how this other matter cropped up."

Jim told him in as few words as possible. "You see," he said lamely, "I couldn't very well help myself. I stayed on in the zone, and Mr. Phineas B. Barton promised to obtain work for me. I had a turn with one of the steam diggers, and it was arranged that I should be appointed to work one. I went back to Mr. Barton's quarters this evening——"

"Last night, you mean," interrupted the officer with a smile. "It is now 2.30 in the morning."

Jim was startled. The hours had simply flown, and he could hardly realize that so much time had elapsed since he set off from his quarters. "I had no idea," he murmured. "But yesterday evening, to be accurate, I was sitting in the parlour with Mr. Barton when a man shot at me through the gauze window."

"At you? How do you know that?" The question came like a pistol shot.

"I guess it. I am not absolutely sure. I may be wrong, but you will hear my reasons. We set out in pursuit. Sam there," and he nodded to the little negro who was following the interrogation with shining eyes and wide-open ears— "Sam tracked the fellow. He took us to a hut in which a light was burning. We surrounded it. I went to the window, and recognized one of the men as a Spaniard who had been aboard the ship, and whom I had knocked down in the fight. He had, apparently, just joined his fellows. There were five in all."

"Points to his being the man who shot at you, and to you being the one at whom he fired. To-morrow we'll settle it. Sam there will follow the tracks if he can."

It was amusing to see the little negro's eyes open wide. There was an expression almost of a feeling of injury about them.

"What dat, sah?" he demanded. "Sam not able to follow track? I like dat, I do. Sam start tracking when him so high." And he placed a hand a couple of feet from the floor, much to the amusement of all. "Sam larn to track way down in de south. Dat rubbish villain leave heap of mark. Plenty soft ground. To-morrow—to-day, sah, I tink, 'cos it's past midnight—to-day Sam pick up de mark and tell you plenty quick who it am and what happened."

"Then that'll fix the matter. What next?" asked the officer.

"I recognized one of the gang as a man whose photograph had been published; in fact, I recognized them all. I remembered the name, Jaime de Oteros. Then I reckoned we had made a find and that you would like to hear. I sent Sam away, and—and there you are."

"Pardon, there we are certainly not yet awhile. I was asleep at the time. Kindly proceed, sir."

Jim answered the officer's encouraging smile by giving him an account of the fight, while the eager Tom burst in with an interruption from time to time.

"Me wanted to hang um quick," he explained. "But Massa Jim angry, scowl at Tom, say tings beneath him breath."

It was pure invention; Jim swung round upon the negro with flashing eyes. But who could be angry with Tom? The fellow's face was wreathed in smiles. His merry features were divided by a wide seven-foot rift, extending from ear to ear, and displayed a double set of teeth which would have been a paying advertisement for a dentist.

"The long and the short of it is this, sir," said the officer. "You and your very eager friends have done the police a great service, for which we are deeply grateful. Now, I will take formal evidence of identity, and send the prisoners to the cells. I advise that you all go back to your quarters by a roundabout route, so as not to spoil tracks. I will send a couple of men to the hut to keep people away. At eight o'clock I will call upon you, when we will go into the question of the tracks and discuss what is to be done. The escape of those two rascals means a chase. We cannot afford to lose them now that we have captured three."

He leaned over and shook hands with Jim. Then, with a pleasant nod, he banished the party to bed. Taking the lamp, Sam lit it and led the way, and very soon they were back at their quarters, there to meet with Phineas's eager questions. At eight o'clock that morning, when Jim imagined that he had hardly enjoyed half an hour's sleep, the Police Commissioner appeared, and very soon it became evident that the canal works would not see our hero yet awhile. In fact, there was another adventure before him.

"We're going to follow those rascals," said the officer. "I'd like you to come along, for you can recognize them. Of course it'll be dangerous. The fellows are armed; I'm not disguising that from you. Are you game to come?"

Was Jim game? He laughed at the officer's caution.

"See here, sir," he said with a smile, "guess I'm not one of the police, and thief catching isn't in my work, but I've a personal stake here. If this man ain't apprehended I stand to be shot at any time. Besides, every American citizen wants to help the police. It's a duty; of course I'm game."

CHAPTER VIII

In Hot Pursuit

"From information received, a small steam launch put out from the Bay of Limon at the first streak of dawn, and steamed towards the east," said Major Pelton, the police officer who had interrogated Jim at night, putting on his most official voice for the occasion. "It was not hired; it was seized by a couple of men. They found the boat lying alongside the staging, ready to take a party out to a hulk we have lying off the coast. They stole her."

"Proof positive that they are the men we are after," ventured Jim, throwing himself back in the well of the little motor launch in which he and his comrades found themselves.

"It's sartin'," came from Sam, his eyes shining brightly, as was usual when he was at all excited.

"Precisely; proof positive, as you say. The useful Sam tracked the man's steps to your quarters from that hut. Then back again, and finally, after a detour in some scrub, where no doubt he remained hidden with his comrade, straight down to Port Limon. We are on the right track; but it will be difficult to adhere to it."

The officer glanced round at the occupants of the launch, and found little to encourage him. True, provided his party could come up with the escaped criminals, it was highly probable that they would be taken; for the handsome launch with which the American Canal Commission had provided its Colon people carried, besides the officer and Jim, three members of the Colon police force, fully armed, as well as Tom, Sam, and Ching.

"You had better bring them all along," the Major had said, when discussing the matter. "Tom is a lusty fellow, and evidently full of pluck, while Sam is a first-class tracker. Some of those negroes one gets from the southern States are extremely quick and skilful, and he is amongst them. Ching, you say, is a good cook."

"Cookee fo ebelybody, sah; make de stew, boil de kettle. Plenty good cookee Ching makee," had been the response of the wily Chinee when he heard of the proposition.

So it turned out that all the friends were together again, armed with rifles on this occasion, and aboard a fine motor launch.

"Thirty horse-power, gasolene motor," explained the Major. "There's not another craft in these waters which can outstrip her. In fact, if only we can trace those ruffians, we shall have them nicely. Now, sir, you've had to do with motors; can you manage for us?"

Fortunately a gasolene motor was one of those things which had always attracted our hero from the first moment he had been able to comprehend its action; and it chanced, seeing that much of his time had been spent in seaports, or closely adjacent thereto, he had had many opportunities of studying the marine variety. Immediately he put foot aboard this launch he had stooped over the half-covered-in engine, and had examined it with a friendly and observant eye.

"Yes," he responded instantly, his eye brightening; "yes, Major, I can run her, I guess. Thirty horse-power! I reckon we shall move along quick. What about gasolene store?"

"Ample aboard. Her tanks are full; I saw to that at the first moment. She has been handed over to us fully equipped, with rations aboard sufficient for a week. I had only to collect men and ammunition. Now, sir."

Jim had already started his engine, and at the word he pushed over his gear lever, retarded the engine a little, and sent the boat gently heading out to sea.

"Due east," said the Major.

"Due east it is, sir," responded Jim promptly.

"And run up alongside any boat you may see in our course. We must make every enquiry."

It was a sensible plan to pursue, for all that the party was sure of was the fact that the miscreants they were in search of had steamed out to sea from the Bay of Limon, and had taken an easterly course. Beyond that fact there was nothing to direct them. Nor were they fortunate in obtaining information till late that afternoon, when they sighted a coaster lazily sailing parallel with the low-lying, muddy shore.

"Have I seed anything of a steam launch hereabouts?" repeated the skipper, a typical Yankee, waddling to the rail of his boat as the launch came alongside. "See here, siree, I observed a launch jest sich as you ask fer steaming easy along the coast twenty mile back of this. She was kinder heading in to find a port. There s lagoons way long there, and, mebbe she's got right into one of 'em. You don't happen to be wantin' the folks aboard?"

He cocked his eye in a knowing wink, and regarded the uniform of the policeman.

"I reckon not," he continued garrulously. "But ef you was—only ef you actually was wantin' 'em—why, I'd get peepin' in at every little hollow with that 'ere queer craft of yourn. Say, what are she? Gasolene?"

The Major nodded. "Thirty horse-power," he said. "Runs well."

"Jest a daisy! Wish I was aboard her instead of this old scow. But I'm too old fer the game. Slow and steady's my motto. Goody to yer."

He helped to push the launch away from the side of his vessel with a long pole, and then stood watching her as she went away through the water, leaving a long, white trail behind her. As for Jim and his friends, they ran in closer to the shore, and, since the light would soon be failing, speeded up their engine and pushed ahead at a pace which was decidedly smart.

"Six or seven knots faster than the steam launch can make," said the Major. "If only we can sight the spot where they have put in before darkness comes, we ought to make short work of them to-morrow. In any case we must discover some sort of haven in which to lie to-night."

But, search as they might, it was already dusk before Tom's sharp eyes hit upon an opening on the flat, dismal coast.

"Fresh water come down dere," he cried, after a while, staring coastward. "Water blue and clean, not same as dis hereabouts. By lummy, but dere a riber in dere, where we can lie fo to-night. Den boil de kettle, cook de meal, hab little sing-song."

"I don't think so," exclaimed Jim at once. "If we make a port there'll be no singing, especially from a noisy fellow such as you are. But I believe he's right, Major; the water does seem clearer here. Probably a stream running into the sea."

"Then we'll explore. We can't venture farther along in any case, and it will be dark even now before we enter unless we hurry. Push her along, my lad; but go easy as we get close in."

Thanks to the fact that the gasolene launch drew but a couple of feet of water, there was no need for extreme caution; and, besides, the coast thereabouts was practically free of rocks. Still, there was mud, mud in abundance, and were the launch to run hard upon it she would stick in that position, so arresting further pursuit.

"Easy now!" commanded the Major, after a while, when the land was close at hand, and a thick fringe of tropical vegetation within close range. "There's the river entrance; narrow enough in all conscience. Take her along to the centre, Jim, and be ready to reverse if I give the order."

He went clambering along past his men till he sat right forward, the diminutive Sam joining him there, as if he thought he needed help. In fact, but for the little fellow's sharp eyes they would certainly have brought the expedition to an abrupt conclusion, for a huge sunken tree blocked a goodly portion of the river channel just at its exit into the sea.

"Hold dere!" shouted Sam, raising both hands. "Back um! Yo see dat snag down dar, sah? Him rip de bottom out ob us quick as noting. Break um up, send de boat to Davy Jones, and all ob us to the sharks or crocodiles. Back um, Massa Jim!"

"He's right! I can see it now—a huge tree," sang out the Major. "That's very awkward. Seems to prove that we are on the wrong track."

"'Spose yo gib Sam de painter, den swim or wade ashore. Easy pull de launch right up to de tree, den see wheder we can get past um. If too much in de way, den put Tom oberboard. Him lift de tree away. If crocodile dere, no matter; Tom very good to eat."

The little man grinned at the big negro, while the latter shook an enormous fist at him, and bared his teeth in just that same manner as had had such effect upon Jaime de Oteros. But Sam recked little of the signal.

"Yo one big, hulkin' nigger, yo," he grinned. "Yo eat wonderful nice and tasty." Meanwhile Jim had been careful to reverse his engine, and lay with his machinery out of gear, awaiting further orders.

"Steady ahead! just a few revolutions!" commanded the Major. "Enough! That has brought us right up to the tree. Now, can one pass by it?"

The dusk was already falling outside, while here, beneath the trees which clung in luxuriant profusion to the banks on either side of the entrance to the river, it was already so dark that a white man was troubled. Neither the Major, nor Jim, nor the policemen, could detect much of their surroundings, but in the case of Sam it might have been brilliant daytime. He peered over the edge of the launch, then flopped full length on to the tiny deck she carried forward, and, pushing himself over the side, finally gripped the tree with one hand, his weight suspended between the latter and the launch. A startled cry came from him, a cry which brought Tom labouring up beside him.

"Yo hurt yoself?" he demanded abruptly. "Hi, yo, Sam, what de matter?"

"Massa Jim, we got um! We bottled dem men up fine and safe. Dey good as hanged. Dey jest as well might be dancin' on thin air at dis very instant."

Sam ignored the huge negro—in fact ignored everyone aboard save Jim—in his anxiety to make a report direct to his master. "Yo see here," he called out, turning slightly so as to be able to look aft, and still clinging half to the launch and half to the fallen tree. "Yo come along and look fo yoself. Tom, yo great big elephant, yo git along to one side. There ain't no sorter room for a person when yo's hereabouts."

There was an air of suppressed excitement about the little fellow which caused Jim to leave his engine and hasten forward.

"Well?" he demanded curiously. "You've found something? What is it?"

"Reckon dem 'ere blackguard run in here full tilt, I do. Dey come whop up agin de tree, and precious nigh upset. Dere's a dent right here big enough to put de hand in. Stop a minute. Sam soon say if dey passed."

Without waiting for his master, he slipped into the water, to discover it deep enough almost to submerge him. But Sam was more like a fish than anything. He struck out for the tree, reached it, and clambered down towards that portion which seemed to have sunk deepest. In the gloom they saw him stretching out a hand to the opposite bank. He gripped a branch hanging conveniently overhead, and then swung in the water.

"Dey come right along plump in here," he sang out "Den dey sheer off, and steam in alongside. Jest room enough. See here, Massa Jim, plenty space to swing de legs. Plenty room to float de launch; but I make extry sure. Yo see in one little bit."

They heard him splash down into the stream, while there came to their ears the swish of the branch suddenly relieved of his weight. Then the fitful rays played upon the splashes as the negro breasted the water and swam upstream. Presently the swish of his strokes ceased, and his voice was heard again, some little distance inland.

"Yo kin jest steer to de right ob dat stump, yo can, Massa Jim. Plenty water. Reckon dem scum come along right in here. We hab um. Dere big lagoon way along a little furder."

Thus it proved when the party had forced the boat past the obstruction guarding the river exit. Jim pushed his lever over a very little, and sent his propeller whirling just for so long as would give the launch way against the sluggish stream. As he did so Tom leaned his ponderous figure over the stem, causing it to dip violently, and, gripping the tree, directed the boat into clear water. A few more revolutions sent the launch through, and in time brought her abreast of Sam. They found the little fellow poised on a branch overhanging the water, for all the world as if he were a monkey, and from that position he dropped like a cat on to the deck of the launch.

"What's this about a lagoon?" asked the Major eagerly. "You couldn't see it, surely?"

Sam made no answer for the moment. He took the officer's hand and led him right forward. Then, while Tom clung to a branch to steady the vessel, his smaller comrade bade the Major lie on the deck.

"Not see um if stand up," he explained. "Dem leaves and branches in de way; but Sam see um when he swim. Easy as talkin'. Dere's a young moon to-night, and now that we's right under de trees it's easy 'nough to look out into de open. Dere: ain't dat a lagoon? Gee! Ef I don't tink so!"

It was laughable to watch his eagerness, while Sam's curious language, often enough sprinkled with long and difficult words, of the meaning of which he had not the remotest idea, was sufficient to make anyone not morose by nature die of laughing. But in any case he had made no mistake. As the Major stooped, so getting beneath the line of overhanging trees and branches, he saw as if from a tunnel a widespreading space filled by water, on the rippling surface of which the moonbeams played. Here and there a patch of rushes reared their heads into the air, while the far distance was hidden behind a cloudy, wet mist which smothered everything.

"And you are sure that those rascals are here?" he asked.

"Sure! Guess so, boss. Dere ain't no room for a mistake. Dem critters comed right in here. I see dere marks on de tree trunk, and den on the bank ob de stream. Dey stepped ashore, I tink, just where we are, den go aboard agin. Dey here; Sam sure as eggs."

"Then, if there is no other exit from the lagoon, we have got them!" came the exultant answer. "We have only to bar the stream, and then set out in search; for, after all, none but a madman would leave the lagoon for the forest. Just hereabouts it is intensely thick, to say nothing of the fever which haunts it. Then, too, savage natives are known to exist, though some of them are friendly. I think, Jim, that we may almost say that we have them. What luck to have pitched upon the very spot they made for!"

"Let us suppose then that they are here, sir," said Jim thoughtfully, as he cut his engine down till it did little more than just turn round. "What is the next movement? To try and find them in that lagoon would be to set oneself the task of discovering a needle in a haystack. There is no chance, even with a bright moon, unless they happened to steam out into the centre. It seems to me that for to-night at least we have come to the end of our efforts."

"Quite so; I agree. We'll haul in somewhere and tie up. We shall all be glad of food and drink. Now, where is a likely place?"

"Right here, I should say," declared Jim briskly. "In the first place, we're in a sort of tunnel, which, therefore, is not easy to discover. Then we lie right in the track those men would take if they were making out to sea. In fact, it's a blockade; we've bottled them so long as we occupy this channel."

It was not a matter which admitted of discussion, seeing that the suggestion was so full of common sense. The Major swiftly realized that fact, and promptly agreed to act upon it.

"Couldn't do better," he said. "Now, see here, boys, we've got to take some precautions. In the first place, we want food cooked, and that means lighting a fire; for no cooking can be done aboard this craft. It wouldn't be safe with our tanks filled with gasolene. Suppose we pitch our camp right away in amongst the trees, where a fire couldn't be easily seen; then we'll tie the launch up right across the stream. She'll reach from bank to bank easily. A man can keep watch aboard her while the rest of the party turn in; how's that, Jim?"

"The very thing, I guess. Say, Major, I'm real hungry; don't mind how soon I sit down to a feed. See here, Ching; jest you and Tom collect those kettles and things, and take off into the trees. Sam, get along with them, and make sure you've chosen a spot where there's plenty of thick stuff about. Supposing we walk along to the edge of the lagoon, Major. By the time we've had a good look round they'll have the boat moored in position and the fire going. There's just a chance that we might have the luck to catch a sight of those two slippery fellows. It's almost as light as day out there, and they might be still moving."

Swinging themselves ashore the two made their way along the edge of the stream slowly and carefully. Indeed, a good deal of care and of agility was required, for the bank was lined by a tangled mass of vegetation which often enough obstructed their path; but as both had encountered the same before, they had brought with them long cutting knives with which to sever the creepers. Underfoot they found the ground firm and even stony in places, while to their right the land seemed to rise abruptly. As to the lagoon, when once they were free of the long, tunnel-like archway of trees leading to the sea, they came into uninterrupted view of the huge expanse of water, for the moon was now well up, and flooded the scene.

"It's so bright that if we were to catch a sight of those rascals we'd be right off after them," said the Major. "But they know their way about. I have had information that this gang, with a few in addition who have left them for one reason or another, have visited many places along this coast. It seems that they came from the States; but they know this coast, and knowing it they will have met with lagoons and forests before. They will be just as careful to keep out of our view when there is light enough to see, as we are careful to hide up our fire at night; but I fancy we shall have them. Quick pursuit is one of the things they have not been accustomed to."

They stared out across the lagoon for some little while, noticing the tufts of reeds which cropped up here and there, and the white mist in the far distance.

Then they turned their faces towards the spot they had left, and felt their way back towards the camp.

"We'll take a couple of grains of quinine apiece to-night," said the Major, halting for a breathing spell by the way. "No white man who comes out to a tropical country can afford to neglect that precaution. Even in the canal zone, where we have reduced the occurrence of malarial fever to an extraordinary figure, we still insist that all employees should take quinine regularly. And out away here it's far more necessary. That mist we've been watching spells malaria, fever that sticks to a man's bones till he's old, even though he gets safe home, and lives in comfort and warmth. Besides, listen to the hum of the mosquitoes; any fool could tell that these parts weren't healthy for a white man."

Jim agreed with him abruptly. He was thinking of his brother, and wishing at that moment that he had been a little more careful to take precautions; but George had been one of those lusty, healthy fellows, never sick or sorry, who had laughed at fever and scoffed at precautions. And see what it had brought him to.

"My brother might have been alive now if only he had taken his quinine," said Jim. "You heard about him, Major?"

"I did. As one of the police at Colon his loss was reported to me as a matter of course. It was bad luck, lad; where did he go ashore?"

"Miles away along this coast. I hunted high and low, as far as a man can hunt a jungle. Reckon he died in the undergrowth."

"Or fell into a swamp, lad. He died, that's sure enough; but come along. There's the fire, and a good meal waiting for us. Gee! we've been getting along; this is better progress than I had dared to hope for."

Skilfully the Major drew Jim's attention from the tragedy which had fallen upon his young life, and very soon had him seated beside a roaring fire, and dipping his spoon into a steaming cauldron of stew which the wily Chinee had provided. In fact, it was a stew which had been prepared ashore in the Major's house, and merely required heating.

"Plenty ob dat fo all, I guess," observed Tom, as he served out helpings all round, smacking his big lips as the savoury odour filled his nostrils. "By gum, but dis night air make a fellow hungry. Yo Sam, yo sit right along down dar, and I help yo. Not trust a little nigger same as yo to help hisself: eat too much. Little man, but plenty big tomach."

He held the huge cauldron in one hand, and with the fingers of the other pressed his small companion to the ground as if he were as weak as a baby.

Then, despite his own words, he gave him a liberal helping, and, having done the same for Ching, sat himself down beside the cauldron.

"So as to see dat dat feller Sam don't play one ob him tricks," he laughed. "By de poker, 'spose him try, den shob him into the pot and cook um."

In the firelight his round, rolling eyes gleamed white. Tom looked a very terrible person for the moment. But he could never preserve an appearance of ferocity for long; his usual smile was soon wreathing his face, particularly when he had taken the first mouthful of stew.

"By lummy, but dat extry good!" he observed. "Hab more, yo fellows?"

In turn he offered it to them all, then helped himself again liberally. In fact, it was not until the last spoonful of gravy had been finished that the party turned to their pipes. Nor was there much difference to be found between the variety of tobacco loved by the British tar or soldier and that favoured in particular by these American policemen. Jim watched them as they cut the cake with their knives and rammed the broken weed into the bowls; then columns of smoke rose amid the branches, while the scent of navy shag made the air redolent.

"And now for the orders," said the Major, when the men had had time for a long smoke. "Sam has been keeping an eye on the water all this time. We must relieve him, though he has hardly been doing duty in the ordinary sense of watchman. Let me see. There are three of my own men, three of yours, making six, and our two selves, eight altogether; suppose we watch in couples. You with one of my men for two hours, then Tom and a second policeman, Sam afterwards with the third, and I last of all with our friend Ching. How's that? Two hours each, four watches altogether, and a good sleep for all of us. It is now eight o'clock, the last spell takes us up to four o'clock in the morning; it'll be light by then. Since Ching will be on duty from two o'clock he can employ himself with our breakfast. By half-past four we shall be able to get the engine going and be under weigh. Now, Jim, get to your duty. One aboard the launch, and the second patrolling as far as the lagoon. Pipes not to be lit unless well amongst the trees. No one to call loudly to another unless there be need. Boys, you've blankets here; turn in."

Ashes were knocked out of pipe stems, and the men at once rolled themselves in their blankets. Then Jim and the comrade who was to watch with him shouldered their rifles, and with pouches filled with ammunition, attached to the belts round their waists, marched towards the stream.

"You get aboard," said Jim. "I'll make along to the lagoon. When an hour has passed I'll come and take your place."

He wended his way through the jungle, and presently was on the bank of the lagoon, admiring its broad expanse of rippling water, which looked so solemn and so beautiful beneath the silvery rays of the moon. Indeed, it was an enchanting scene, and had our hero been of a romantic turn of mind he might well have been excused for giving free rein to his fancy. But Jim was a hard, practical-minded fellow, with the world before him, and his way to make in it. It is not then to be wondered at that his mind strayed from the scene before him to the canal zone, to the gigantic undertaking America had determined on, to the host of workmen labouring there, and to the many problems which confronted them, problems undreamed of by Jim till yesterday, undreamed of now by thousands of Americans, yet problems, for all that, demanding the anxious thought and effort of the Commission staff, in whose able and painstaking hands lay the enormous enterprise. In his mind's eye Jim saw that hundred-ton steam digger again. He fancied himself in the driver's seat, with Harry watching every movement critically, and coaching his young pupil. His hands seemed to fall quite naturally on the levers, and then the hiss of steam came to his ears, just as it had done when he worked the enormous engine.

"Was it all imagination?" To tell the truth he was getting not a little drowsy, but that peculiar hiss was so realistic that——"Gee!" he recovered from his brown study suddenly, and opened his eyes very wide. For there was reality in that hissing steam. He could actually hear it, not over loud, but without doubt steam or gas escaping from some narrow orifice. Moreover the sound came from the lagoon; yes, from the lagoon straight before him. A moment later a long, black shape stole into view from behind a mass of reed some few yards away, then lay still on the water. Silhouetted against the rippling surface he could make out the dusky outlines of a launch, her funnel amidships, the hood of the cab which sheltered passengers when a sea was running, and the little mast on which her flag drooped. And there were figures—two of them. They stood sharply displayed against the light, perched on the deck of the launch, surveying their surroundings.

"Those villains; then they are here without a doubt. Gee, if they try to make out through the opening!"

Jim crouched a trifle lower under the trees beneath which he had taken his station, and watched the launch and her passengers. And steadily, as he watched, the boat drew nearer and nearer.

"Searching for the exit," he thought. "Then they mean to come out. They want to get to sea again, feeling sure that on such a bright night they will be able to find their way. They'll just jump into the trap we've laid for them."

It did indeed look as if fate would play into the hands of those who had set out to take these rascals, and, if Jim had but known what was passing in their minds, he would have learned that a crafty plan was about to be put into execution.

"Of course those police are after us, and quick too," one of the two ruffians had said to the other. "They've steamed along the coast, and no doubt have spoken some skipper who saw us. If they fail to find us to-night they'll get along farther to-morrow, and if we're along there east of this the chances are that we shall be taken. But we know a game better than that; we'll slip clear of this, steam back towards Colon, run inshore just clear of the port, and sink the launch in deep water. There won't be much of a job in getting a passage to New York; how's that?"

It was just one of those plans which, by its very boldness, would mean, provided nothing unforeseen happened, security for those who followed it; for, while all eyes would be searching for them along the coast east of Colon, the rascals themselves would be securely aboard a ship *en route* for New York. But Jim and his friends were to have a say in the matter. Our hero stole back through the trees, gave the warning to his fellow watcher, and then awakened his comrades.

"S-s-s-he!" he whispered, as he touched the Major's shoulder. "The birds are there, on the lagoon. They are searching for the opening. With a little care we shall have them."

It seemed in fact almost a foregone conclusion, this capture of the rascals. For, when all were gathered close to the launch, while two of the men lay with loaded rifles on her deck, the hiss of steam was heard most distinctly. Presently a long, black shape put in an appearance, till all could see it stealing slowly down towards them. Instantly four of the weapons were trained on the men aboard, while the Major, with Jim and Tom to help him, crouched beside the bank, ready to spring on board the stranger. It was a time of intense excitement, because even now there might come a hitch, something might happen to alarm the ruffians.

CHAPTER IX

Jim becomes a Mechanic

"See here, Jim," whispered the Major, as he and our hero, with Tom beside them, huddled close to the bank of the stream which gave exit from the lagoon, "when she comes abreast of us you and I will jump aboard. There are branches in plenty overhead from which we can swing ourselves. We leave Tom to get a grip of the launch itself, and pull her in to the side; got that?"

The big negro wagged his head knowingly from side to side. "Got um safe and sound, sah," he whispered hoarsely. "Tom grip de launch, lift her outer de water if you wants. Lummy! But dis goin' to be a bean feast!"

"S-s-sshe, man! Stay here. Jim, I'll go a little farther up, just a few feet, and pick my branch. You had better do the same; there won't be much time to waste."

"Supposing she doesn't come in; supposing those men discover us, smell a rat, eh?"

Jim asked the question anxiously, and detained the Major on the point of leaving.

"Then we'll be after them quick."

"Will the men fire on them?"

"No; I've given them orders not to do so unless opposition is offered. I never like shooting into men before they open fire. But we're right this time; those fellows are going to jump into the net we have spread for them."

WAITING FOR THE ENEMY

He moved off at once, while Jim stepped a few paces from the spot where the bulky figure of Tom was reclining, and, searching above his head, quickly found a branch strong enough to support his weight. He held to it, and lifted his feet from the ground, making assurance doubly sure. By then the strange launch was heading direct for the opening of the narrow tunnel in which the pursuers were secreted. Jim could hear the splash of her tiny propeller; for the launch was running light, and the blades often rose clear of the water. Then suddenly the noise ceased absolutely, the low, clock-like tick of her engines could no longer be heard, while the moonrays playing upon the ripples at her stern alone showed that she was in motion.

"Coming! In a second I shall have to jump. Reckon we shall have to be pretty slippy with those fellows, for they have arms and are likely to use them."

For some reason or other our hero felt not the slightest trace of excitement on this occasion. No doubt the experiences he had already gone through had helped not a little to steady his nerves, while the overwhelming force of the party he accompanied seemed to argue that there could be now but little prospect of danger; but he was to learn that it is the least-expected thing that happens. For hardly had the words left his lips when the propeller of the launch was heard again thrashing the water frantically, while the ripple ahead suddenly died out altogether, leaving the surface of the lagoon shimmering placidly beneath the soft rays which flooded every portion of it. Then there came a shout, a startled cry from the deck of the launch, a man stood up to his full height forward, his figure silhouetted blackly against the water. A second later he had dived down again, there was another shout, then flames suddenly roared from the funnel, while a glow which illuminated the rear of the vessel showed that the door of the furnace had been thrown open.

Jim rubbed his eyes; the sudden change in the movement of progression of the launch amazed him. He could hardly believe that she was retreating, that those agitated ripples now spreading from her stern right forward beyond the bows meant that she was departing. It was the whirr of her engine and the splashing of her propeller as it churned the water violently which brought the true facts clearly to his mind.

"They're off," he shouted; "we must follow. Quick, on to the launch!"

He dashed along the bank of the stream, calling loudly to the men, and arriving opposite to their own vessel, swiftly cast adrift the rope which had been passed from her stern to a tree growing close down to the water. With a spring he was aboard, and, tumbling at once into the well, he searched in the darkness for the starting handle. But however convenient a gasolene motor may be on ordinary occasions, the fact cannot be denied that there are at times difficulties in connection with them. For instance, it was always a practice of Jim's to shut off his petrol supply when the engine was not running; for otherwise there was risk of leakage through the carburettor, and leakage of such a volatile and inflammable fluid aboard a boat spells danger for those who man her. Then, too, it happened that this engine trusted to drip lubricators for her supply of oil, and though she might reasonably be expected to run satisfactorily for a while without that supply, still, in the exciting time before him, Jim might easily forget to turn up his lubricators, and such neglect spelt failure for his party. After all, this was decidedly one of those cases where it would be better to follow his usual routine, and thereby make sure that the engine had everything in its favour.

"I'll have her running in double-quick time," he shouted. "Get that painter cast off, Major; and, see here, can't you manage to push her along until I have got the engine going?"

"Guess I'se got one mighty big pole here," called Tom, an instant later, whilst the launch heaved and rolled as the ponderous fellow moved about. "You get right along wid dat engine, Massa Jim. I'se gwine astern to pole her."

Once more the launch rolled and heaved as Tom made his way rapidly aft. Then his pole plunged into the water, one of the policemen pushed the bows out from the bank, and, casting his eye upward for one brief instant, Jim saw that they were moving. Meanwhile he had found the gasolene tap and turned it, while the fingers of his other hand as rapidly lifted the six lubricators which fed the engine with that fluid so vital to her.

"Ready?" asked the Major tersely, his voice hard and cold, as if sudden disappointment had changed it. "Get her going quick, my lad, or those fellows will get clear away from us. Already they are steaming right out into the lagoon."

It was true enough; for, casting his eye ahead, Jim could see, through the dark tunnel formed by the overhanging branches of the trees, a wide expanse of shimmering water, across which sped the boat that bore the men in pursuit of whom they had come. There was a white wash at her stern, while sparks and flames shot from her funnel. That and the glow which surrounded her, coming from her opened furnace door, showed clearly that the rascals aboard her were fully prepared for flight, with a hot fire burning and roaring in their furnace, and a head of steam which would drive their boat faster perhaps than she had ever travelled.

"Got it! Now we'll be moving."

With the fingers of one hand Jim had held the float of his carburettor lifted, thereby making sure that the engine would obtain a free supply of fuel; while with the other hand he had discovered the starting handle. It was a simple matter to slip it on to the shaft and turn it till the clutches engaged. Then he bent his back to the work, switched his magneto into circuit and sent the engine twirling round. Poof! poof! poof! Three of the cylinders fired, but the crank ceased turning. Jim lifted his float again, adjusted the handle, and made another effort at starting. Gur-r-rr! bizz! she was off. The rhythmical hum of the machinery told his practised ear at once that the engine was running beautifully.

He dropped the starting handle on to the floorboards and stepped briskly across to his levers.

"Ready?" he asked steadily.

"Let her have it," came from the Major, who, meanwhile, had taken possession of the wheel. "Let her have it all you know, Jim, for we've a long way to make up. Those rascals have obtained a splendid start."

Jim promptly dropped his fingers on the quadrant where throttle and ignition levers lay, and jerked both of them up a few notches. He could feel the thrust of the propeller now, and could hear the wash of the water as the launch pushed her way through it. Then suddenly the vessel cleared the dark tunnel in which she had been lying, and a glorious tropical moon shone down upon her, rendering every figure aboard distinctly visible, while, better than all, the rays flooded the engine well and made Jim's task all the easier.

"Faster!" commanded the Major sharply, and at the word Jim jerked his levers some few notches higher, till the engine buzzed more loudly than before, while the floorboards took on a trembling vibration to which, as a general rule, they were unaccustomed.

"More! We must move faster if we are to catch them," cried the Major, something akin to entreaty in his voice. "Can't you make her do a little more, my lad? We mustn't let those rascals slip through our fingers."

Jim nodded curtly; he disliked racing his engine as a general rule, for common sense told him that such a course if persisted in might well lead to disaster. But these were exceptional circumstances, and, if race her he must, he determined that no precaution on his part should be relaxed so that the motor might come through the ordeal satisfactorily. Once more, therefore, he jerked his levers upwards till the throttle was wide open, while the ignition was advanced to the fullest extent. And how the motor roared! Compactly built and beautifully designed, it could not be expected to revolve at such extraordinary speed and give out its full power without some sign of remonstrance. It answered the persistent goadings of its grim young driver with a tremulous roar, while the planks under foot now shook and rattled ominously. Indeed the whole vessel vibrated, while the bows lifted out of the water, thrusting a huge wave to either side. The surface of the lagoon, hitherto so placid, was now churned to milky foam at the stern of the vessel, while a white wash trailed aft, glimmering in the moonlight.

"Full out, sir," reported Jim to the Major. "How are we doing?"

"Fine, fine, my boy. We'll have 'em yet, if only you can keep her at it; but can she last? Can she keep up this pace much longer?"

"Guess she's got to," laughed Jim, a note of excitement in his voice, in spite of his apparent coolness and unconcern. "Guess she's got to, sir; I'll keep her at it all I know."

He craned his head to one side, and for the space of a minute fixed his eyes upon the black shape ahead which they were following. A column of flame and showers of sparks were being vomited from the funnel, whilst the ruddy hue that had surrounded the escaping launch had now disappeared entirely.

"Closed his furnace; that means that he's got steam up to bursting-point," thought Jim. "But we're gaining on him sure. In half an hour, if all goes well, we'll be alongside."

He let his glance rest for a few seconds on the figures of the policemen huddled in the cab of the launch beside the Major. He even caught the reflection of the moonlight in Sam's big rolling eyes. Then he turned his glance to either side, watching the widespreading bow wave as it swept out over the lagoon. He followed the ripples, and, turning, gazed astern. It came as a shock to him almost to discover two figures there crouching on the little deck aft of the engine well. One was huge and massive, and bore aloft a long, straight pole, while the second sat crouched on his haunches, as motionless as a statue. It was Ching. The Chinaman sat playing with the end of his pigtail, and giggled as Jim looked into his eyes.

"Velly fine! Dis allee lightee, sah; you catch him plenty quick," he gurgled.

"Den hang um," simpered Tom, his eyes rolling. "Dem scum not stand de chance of a dog, I tell yo. Massa Jim, yo make um buzz right along like dis; and den, by lummy, yo see what we do to um. Nobble dem rascals precious quick. Kill um; wring de neck of de villains."

Jim scowled at the negro, for such threats vexed him. Then, seeing the broad smile on Tom's face, he laughed outright.

"Jest like you, Tom, always threatening. I don't believe you'd actually hurt a fly unless you were forced to. But have a care, my lad; this boat's over-loaded, and if I hear too much from you I'll give Ching orders to send you overboard. Get lower, man; your big body meets the wind and keeps us from moving forward."

The mere suggestion that he might be tossed overboard caused the simple-minded Tom to open his big eyes wide in consternation. His huge jaw drooped; then, hearing his young master's merry laugh, the thick lips split asunder, and a loud guffaw came from the negro.

"Wat dat?" he demanded. "Yo ask dis man here to throw Tom overboard? By de poker, but if dis Chinaboy breathe one little word, me smash um. Tom nasty fellow to deal with when him angry."

But Jim had other matters to attend to rather than to listen to the negro's sayings. Indeed he had already turned his back upon the two men crouching astern, and was bending over the engine. Fumbling at the lock of a cupboard, he pulled the door open and extracted a heavy object from within. His finger pressed a button, and instantly a flood of light came from the electric torch he had secured. For five minutes he busied himself with the motor. Carefully adjusting the drips from the lubricator, he set them to give a more liberal supply than was usual. Then he lifted the board which covered the tail shaft bearing, and squeezed down the grease cup secured there. A finger laid on the top of the bearing assured him that it was running cool, while the same precaution in regard to the cylinders disclosed the fact that the water pump was working as it should do. In fact, in spite of the tremendous pace at which the motor was revolving, there was as yet no sign of failure, nothing to point to an immediate breakdown, nothing, in fact, to lead him to suppose that the chase would have to be abandoned.

"Then I can begin to take a little interest in those rascals," he thought, "Ah, we're nearer, we're overhauling them without a shadow of doubt! I give them a quarter of an hour's more freedom."

It did indeed seem as though the pursuit was entering upon its last stage, for the black shape ahead was decidedly nearer—so near, in fact, that one could make out the various features of the launch as well as the two fugitives crouching beside their engine. Tongues of flame and broad showers of sparks still belched from the funnel, while at one moment, when she steamed into the dense shadow cast by some tall trees growing upon the tail end of a group of small islands which studded the lagoon, the funnel itself was seen to be glowing hot. Indeed, while the launch herself was blotted out in the darkness, the glowing funnel remained the one conspicuous object.

"I'm going to give 'em a shot," called out the Major, casting a glance at Jim over his shoulder. "You see, I don't know the ins and outs of this lagoon, and those fellows might yet escape us if they happen to have had time to do a little exploration. See here, Tomkins, send a ball a foot or two ahead of them; and if that does not bring them to a stop, put one right through her funnel. You can do it without fear of hitting one of the men."

"Sure! I'd back myself nine times out of ten to bring off a shot like that. I'll just wait till we're out of the shadow."

Anxious eyes flitted from the dark shape fleeting through the waters of the lagoon to the long, bony fingers of the policeman. He stepped to the front of the cab, leaned forward with his elbows on the deck, and clicked the bolt of his rifle open. Then he dropped the weapon into position, and there was a tense silence aboard as Tomkins squinted along his sights. A second later the report came, for the policeman was too old a hand with his weapon to hesitate. While he shot the empty cartridge out and slipped in a fresh one all eyes went to the boat ahead, and no doubt the bullet which Tomkins had dispatched had passed but a few feet in front of her, conveying a message and a warning; but the effect it had was entirely *nil*. The launch held on her course as though there was no such thing as a pursuing vessel with arms aboard able to reach the miscreants who were escaping.

"Guess they've got to have it then," growled Tomkins. "This time I'll put one through the funnel, and there ain't a doubt that it'll send them bobbing."

As cool as an icicle, the man stretched himself out again, half on the deck and half in the cab of the launch. Once more his eyes went down to the sights, and on this occasion the pause he made was long, so long, in fact, that when the rifle belched forth a stream of fire the suddenness of the report startled his comrades. Then they fixed their eyes upon the launch steaming ahead of them.

"Didn't I tell you! Got it sure, plump through the centre, and a bare foot above their heads," cried Tomkins, dropping his rifle. "See there, the flames tell you what happened."

His finger shot out instantly, and drew the attention of all to the funnel. Flames and sparks were still belching from the opening above, but that was not all, for low down now, but a bare foot above the heads of the two men crouching beside the engine, the sheet-iron tube was punctured, and a thin stream of fire was issuing from the hole. Clank! The sound of the furnace door being dragged violently open came clearly to the ears of the pursuers, in spite of the hum of their own motor, while that same red glow which had once before enveloped the launch again surrounded her. It was the only answer the rascals aboard made to Tomkins's shot, that and a dense column of smoke which now shot up, mingling with the flames and smoke from the funnel.

"Their last kick," cried the Major. "That shot tells them that we mean business. Tomkins, my lad, just give 'em another. Say, Jim, how's the motor running?"

"Fine! fine! Couldn't be doing better. Sing out when you want me to cut her down a little."

To all appearances the end of an exciting chase was already in sight, for there was no doubt that now Jim and his party were running two feet for the one covered by the escaping launch. But they had wily men to deal with, and that fact was impressed upon them within the space of a few seconds, for hardly had the third shot rung out when the launch in front ran into another long shadow by one of the islands, her form being instantly blotted out by the blackness.

There came the clang of the furnace door as it was kicked into place by one of the rascals, and then all that could be seen was the glowing funnel. Even that did not remain long in evidence, for suddenly it swerved to the right, making off at a sharp angle to the course which the launch had been pursuing. Then it disappeared from sight, as if the vessel had gone beneath the water.

"Steady! Stop her!" commanded the Major, swinging his wheel over. "We'll run on a little till we're out of the shadow. Then perhaps we shall be able to see where those fellows have got to. Queer! Seems to me that they know the road. They must have steered direct for the tail end of these islands."

Jim jerked throttle and ignition levers back as the orders came to his ears, and threw his lever into neutral position. But the launch had been ploughing along at a speed of some twenty knots, and the way on her carried her swiftly forward. Dense shadow enveloped her, and for a while there was not one aboard the launch but wondered whether the vessel would dash herself upon a rock, since the course was being followed blindly. The Major had swung his wheel just where he guessed the fugitives had done likewise, and that movement still found the boat in dense shadow. A second or two later she shot out into open water, and once more the moon's rays flooded her from stem to stern.

"Gone! Not a sign of them! This is the queerest thing I have ever——"

"Stop! I can see them!" shouted Jim, interrupting the Major. "They steamed straight between two of the islands, and there they are beyond. Push ahead, Major? Our best way is to run right round this island, and so take up their course again. Ain't that land ahead?"

"Land fo shore! Massa Jim right," sang out Sam, who seemed to have the sharpest eyes of the whole party. "Dem villains know de way; dey been here before. Sam say dey heading for anoder opening."

Whatever was the nature of the evolution practised by the fugitives, the Major, as leader of the party, did not hesitate to follow Jim's advice.

"Forward!' he roared, glancing over his shoulder. "Rocks or no rocks, I'll chance rounding the island. Send her ahead, Jim. Give her full power again."

Bizz! Gurr! How the motor roared as our hero jerked his levers back into their old position. As for that commanding the gears, it was already in position, while the propeller was churning the water into white foam. The launch shot ahead as if propelled from a gun, and in a trice was rounding the island on the far side of which the fugitives had taken their course. A minute later she was again in open water, while right across her path stretched a dark, unbroken line, the edge of which was obscured in deep shadow. It was the margin of the lagoon, without a doubt, while it was equally certain that those whom Jim and his party sought to capture had chosen some point along it on which to land. Either that or their explorations had discovered some exit, for which they were at that very instant racing madly.

"Artful dogs!" cried the Major, wrath in his voice. "They stole a nice march on us by that movement, and gained many yards. Don't fire, Tomkins. You might hit one of them in this uncertain light, and that would defeat my special object. I want to capture the two alive and strong, or not at all."

"See dat? Massa Jim, dere an openin' ober dere. Dose scum race for um!" shouted Sam a moment later, stretching one black arm out in front, and pointing eagerly. "Me see de light shinin' on de water ob a stream, and de launch just about to enter. Steady, sah! Not do to dash right in at dis pace. P'raps smash de launch, run ashore, or pile her up on a mudbank. S'pose we take it easy."

"Steady! Stop her again!" commanded the Major, his eyes fixed on the retreating launch. "Sam is right. Those gentlemen have discovered a channel leading out of the lagoon, and have made for it at their fastest pace. That shows that they have been there before. Look at them; they have sent their boat in without attempting to slow down. Steady, Jim! Let her push ahead slowly; those rascals are a long way from making good their escape. I'll follow them even if it takes me miles into the interior."

Had the Major but known it, there was every prospect of this pursuit carrying him and his party many miles beyond the margin of the lagoon, for the band of ruffians who had so lately attracted his attention, and on the catching of two of which he was now bent, had not confined their thieving attentions to the various settlements along the coast. They had even exploited the peoples of the interior of the unsettled regions lying adjacent to the canal zone. There were wide areas of trackless forest, of jungle, and of swamp, which to this day are unexplored and unknown by the white man. That deadly malarial fever, more than attack by unfriendly natives, has kept the white man at a distance. Only along the immediate line of the coast has trading been done in some of the districts, and even then the results have not been always satisfactory.

"It's a queer place," said Phineas Barton, when describing the isthmus to our hero. "Here along the canal zone you have civilization. Uncle Sam has come in with his dollars and his men, and has worked with an energy which, one of these days, when the facts are known, will surprise the world. As I tell you, you've civilization right here. But jest step out of the canal zone, and what do you find? Savages, sir. Wild men, armed with spears and bows and poisoned arrows. Yes, sir, poisoned arrows that will kill a man inside thirty minutes, even if they only happen to have just broken the skin. And they tell me that 'way along in the jungle, where the fever's that bad that a white man don't dare to go, there are gangs of tall natives that won't allow a stranger to put so much as his nose into their territory."

It is all true enough, and is, indeed, one of the curious features of the Isthmus of Panama. There, where one of these days, when America has completed her gigantic task, a mighty canal will stretch from coast to coast, bearing the commerce of the nations to and fro between Pacific and Atlantic Oceans, there lie side by side the modern dwellings and the civilization which an enormous undertaking of this description must inevitably produce, and a condition of savagery unchanged since the Middle Ages. Even Spain, with her huge capacity for conquest, failed to penetrate into many of the wide areas of jungle adjacent to Panama and Colon. Doubtless her gallant sons made the attempt; but history records the fact that the fierce tribes within drove them back, murdering those upon whom they could lay their hands, and showing such courage and ferocity that further attempts were not embarked upon. Moreover, the malarial fever, which haunts these jungles in its most virulent form, was deterrent enough, without thought of the natives.

Still, there were some who had contrived to open up negotiations with the tribes. There are men who will risk anything for a handsome profit, and the gang of rascals we are dealing with had seen in these tribes an opportunity of enriching themselves. They tempted the natives with the offer of guns and powder, and already the bartering of those weapons had given them access to a part which would have brought inevitable destruction, had they entered on any other pretext. Cheap guns and powder were to be obtained, and in return the natives willingly parted with huge quantities of precious stones and gold. Sam was perfectly right when he suggested that the man aboard the steam launch had visited the lagoon and its surroundings before.

"I's sure of that," he cried, bending forward and peering into the gloom. "Dem scum know ebery foot of de way, for dey steam hard ahead for a place dat no one else can see."

"Know it or not, we're going on after them," growled the Major. "Where they can run we can follow. But steady with her, Jim. This chase is not going to be finished yet awhile, and we shall do better now that there is no longer a chance of catching them on the lagoon. Take it easy. After all, they can't go on for ever; some time or other the stream they are making for will fail them, and then they must take to the jungle or fall into our hands. Steady with her! Slow but sure must be our motto."

"Steady it is, sir!" cried Jim. "But say, I can see a line of water running out of the lagoon. Those fellows are steering straight ahead into it."

All eyes aboard followed the movements of the fleeing launch, and watched as she crossed in the gleam of the moonlight the last few yards of open lagoon. They saw her shoot across the dark line which till a moment before had seemed unbroken; she sped on up the stream to which Jim had called their attention, then once again she was lost to sight. The blackness swallowed her; there was not even a glowing funnel to show her whereabouts.

"Forward!" cried the Major hoarsely. "But see here, Jim, send one of your men right up into the bows, for there's no knowing what may happen. We may run into a mudbank, and if we have a man forward with a pole we can get pushed off in a twinkling."

The launch heaved and shook as the huge Tom rose to his feet. As agile as a cat, in spite of his size, the ponderous fellow went crawling along, past Jim and his motor, past the Major and his man, and finally established himself right forward in the bows.

"Come a mudbank and Tom push de launch off quick," he called. "But hab no fear. Me able to see much better right away here; dere no mudbanks in dis stream, sah. All open water; plenty room for eberyone."

By now Jim and his friends had reached the very edge of the lagoon, and were able to make out their surroundings more distinctly. The bright moon above helped them wonderfully; thanks to the light it shed, and to the fact that the stream ahead was wide, and branches could not reach across it, they could discern the path which they were to follow. Not a stump, not a single object, broke the shimmering surface of the water. A bright lane stretched before them, with a deep black shadow on either hand.

"Give her steam," commanded the Major, forgetting that the launch which he and the others manned was of the gasolene variety. "Send her ahead, Jim. We've a clear road, way up there ahead, and we'll take it. Boys, be on the lookout for trouble; those rascals are not the only ones we are likely to come across in such an out-of-the-way part."

Jim jerked his levers forward promptly; the motor buzzed and roared, while the propeller bit into the water, and, taking a grip of the fluid, shot the launch forward. She swept on gallantly into the unknown, her commander and crew careless of the consequences and determined to do their duty whatever happened.

CHAPTER X

Running the Gauntlet

There was tense silence aboard the launch from the moment when she had plunged from the placid waters of the lagoon on to the brightly lit surface of the stream which the two fugitives had followed. For half an hour scarcely a word was spoken, while all eyes searched the path ahead, and peered vainly into the deep, impenetrable shadows on either hand. But at length Tom broke the trying silence, a sharp exclamation coming from the bows, where he was stationed.

"By lummy," he called, "but dat precious queer. Minute ago dere a bright lane ob water ahead; now noding, jest noding, all dark and black. Massa Major, yo ain't gwine ter steam ahead like dis all de while! S'pose dere a big rock ahead. S'pose de water come to an end. Dat be very awkward."

"Steady," called out the Major. "Guess it is queer, as Tom says; for a minute ago I could have sworn that this stream ran on clear and unbroken a good mile ahead. Now, it's suddenly blocked out. Perhaps there's a bend 'way there in front."

"I'm sure," answered Jim promptly. "If we run on gently we shall find that the stream opens up again before we get to that patch of darkness. Gee! Guess I'm right; it was a bend."

Meanwhile he had slowed down his motor; and it was fortunate he had done so, for as the launch covered the intervening space lying between herself and the dense shadow, to which Tom had drawn attention, it was noticed by all that the fairway had narrowed considerably. At the bend, when she was gliding slowly forward, the banks came together very abruptly, leaving a stream of water between them which was but a few feet wide. And while the rays from the moon fell upon the surface for some dozen boat-lengths ahead, beyond that point the distance was shrouded in darkness, the jungle cut off the rays as if with a shutter, casting a dense shadow on every side. Instantly the Major issued his orders.

"Stop her," he cried in low tones. "This is a teaser. I don't much care about going on through that narrow lane; for if there were folks round here to attack us, we might have a job to get out again. Chances are we couldn't turn the boat, and that would mean reversing all the way. What do you say, Jim? It's a teaser, ain't it?"

But for the moment our hero was engaged with his engine. He threw out his lever at the Major's orders, and then pushed it right forward, till the propeller was reversing. Having brought the boat to a standstill, he left the motor running gently, and clambered forward till he was beside the officer.

"Guess it'd be better to stay right here," he said shortly. "I quite agree that if we went along that narrow lane we might be placing ourselves in a difficulty. We might find curselves in a regular bottle, with only a narrow neck from which to make our escape. Best lie here till morning, when we shall see where we are, and what sort of a place that stream leads to."

"Den boil de kettle an' hot up de food," sang out Ching, who was still huddled at the stern of the vessel. "Plenty hungry and thirsty, Mass Jim, an if havvy food to eat, den de time slippy along velly quickly."

The Major nodded his head vigorously. "You are a man in a hundred, Jim," he said, giving vent to a laugh. "'Pon my word, when I am next sent off on an expedition I shall make it a point that you come along with your servants. A more useful lot I never hit upon. Gee! Of course we're hungry. Jest get to with it, Ching."

"Drop de anchor, eh!" demanded Tom, standing to his full height forward, and holding the pole erect in the air. Indeed, for the moment he looked, with the moon playing upon him, for all the world like a dusky sentry, keeping guard over all on the launch and her surroundings. Then he set the pole down with a clatter, there came to the ear the clank and chink of a chain being dragged across the boarding. Tom lifted the launch's anchor from its rests, and held it out at arm's length, as if it were a feather.

"Drop um in?" he asked, poising it above the water. "Wat you say, sir?"

"Let her go," cried the Major. "When she's fast, haul in the slack, and let me know what depth we've got. Reckon this is as good a place to lie in as we could have, for we're well in midstream, and those rascals could not easily reach us from the banks. But of course they could send their bullets whizzing amongst us, and that's a risk we shall have to laugh at. What's the time, Jim?"

"Want's half an hour of midnight, sir. Guess we might have a feed, and then turn in."

The arrangement was one to be recommended, and the Major fell in with it instantly. Jim stopped his motor, shut off the gasolene and oil, and made a careful inspection of the machinery with the help of his electric torch. Ten minutes later Ching announced that hot coffee was ready, and, rising from the petroleum stove situated as far forward from the motor as was possible, and over which he had been bending, proceeded to deal out the beverage to each member of the expedition. Sam followed him with a tin of biscuits, while the ponderous and good-natured Tom thrust his arm over the shoulder of his diminutive comrade, offering squares of cheese which he had cut ready, and had placed upon the lid of the box to serve as a tray.

"Guess better eat as much as you can," he laughed, opening his cavernous mouth. "S'pose dose scum come along fine and early; den hab noting to eat, but p'raps plenty bullet. Den very sorry yo not fill up to-night."

In any case he availed himself of his own advice, and sat on the edge of the well devouring enormous mouthfuls. As to the others, each ate according to his appetite, and we record but the truth when we say that in no case did that fail them. Their rush across the lagoon in the wake of the fugitives, the excitement of the chase generally, and the freshness of the night had given them all a feeling of briskness, and with that feeling came undoubted hunger. Besides, it might be necessary to push on without a pause, once there was light enough with which to see, then he who had not partaken of a full supper might regret the fact, and might have many hours to wait before an opportunity occurred of taking food.

"Jest you turn in and take a sleep, Jim," said the Major, when the meal was finished. "It's just midnight now, and between two and three in the morning we shall have light. I'll take the watch till then, and Tom may as well be along with me. That big chap somehow seems to make one feel quite secure and safe."

Within five minutes silence once more reigned over the launch, while the moon peeped down upon a number of figures huddled in the well. The Chinaman lay bunched in a little ball right aft, which he seemed to have appointed as his own particular quarters, while Sam lay curled up like a faithful dog at his master's feet. The Major sat beside the engine, a rifle barrel resting against his shoulder, and Tom was perched on the rail, his big eyes searching every shadow, a smile of serene happiness on his face. And at length the morning came. While the moon still hung low in the sky, prepared to disappear altogether, a rosy hue lit up the dense banks of green on either hand, and, falling upon the tree trunks, brought them into prominence. Swiftly the light increased in strength till the banks beneath the trees were visible. The surface of the water gleamed white and cold, and every feature of the launch stood out distinctly. It was time to move. The Major rose from his seat and peered into the narrow channel through which he had not dared to take his men during the darkness. He was on the point of issuing an order when at a spot a little to the right, still hidden somewhat by the lack of light, a puff of white smoke was seen to burst. Flame ringed it in the centre, while the smoke itself rose and spread in wide billows. Something thudded heavily against the side of the launch, while an instant later a deafening report broke the morning silence, and reverberated along the forest.

"Eugh!" cried Tom in alarm, his eyes prominent. "Yo hear dat, massa? Dem scum do as I say and start in right early. Tom not like de bullets singing and humming about his head."

As if the Major could have failed to hear! He started violently as the report swept across the water, and then clambered across into the cab. Jim and the others were already on their feet, while the crafty Ching had uncurled himself, and now lay full length upon his face, a rifle at his shoulder.

"Do dat again and me fire fo sure," he cried. "Mass Jim, you call out if dis Chinaboy to send dem a bullet."

But Jim had other matters to attend to, for he realized that any instant it might be necessary to set the launch in motion. He crawled along into the engine well, and with the light now to help him, had his motor running within the space of a few seconds.

"One of you boys get that anchor lifted," commanded the Major, his eyes fixed upon the spot from which the shot had come. "Tomkins, just fix your sights 'way over at that corner, and if there's another shot, send 'em a bullet. You needn't be careless either; this time they're asking for a lesson."

The words had hardly left his lips when another shot rang out from the bank, the smoke blowing up again into the cool morning air. It was followed by another and another, till from some twenty places smoke obscured the bank and the forest. As to the missiles, they flew, hummed, and screamed overhead, some dropping into the water beyond, others thudding against the far bank, while a few, just a few only, struck the launch, making her wooden sides rumble. Not a man aboard was hit, though many escaped narrowly.

"Precious near every time," cried Jim, reddening under the excitement, and finding it extremely difficult to refrain from bobbing. "Gee! I declare that one of those bullets went within an inch of my arm while another struck the top of the cylinder here, and—hi! look at this!" he shouted.

That last bullet had, in fact, done real damage; for it happened to be a big one, discharged from a huge muzzle-loader, sold to the man who had fired the weapon by men who palmed it off as of the latest construction. Almost as big as a pigeon's egg, the mass of lead had struck the cylinder heavily, and with disastrous results. A column of water was spurting upward from the rent made in the copper cooling jacket.

"Done any damage? Not harmed the engine, I hope?" said the Major, looking across at Jim, and then at Tom, who meanwhile was tugging at the anchor chain. "I hear her running; that sounds hopeful."

Jim did not answer for the moment. At the first hasty inspection he imagined that the missile must have made a rent in the copper jacket and also cracked the cylinder casting itself. But a close survey of the damage showed him that the worst had not happened. The motor was heavily built, and no doubt the casting had been strong enough and thick enough to stand up to the blow. As to the water jacket, the damage was serious, but could be remedied. He could make a temporary repair inside half an hour, if given the opportunity, some sheet copper, and a soldering lamp. But for the present the rent must remain; the water must continue to pump up into the air.

"We'll get along in spite of the damage, Major," he sang out cheerily. "But I shall want a man along here to bail. Ching, jest you hop in here with me and bring some sort of a pannikin."

"Got um! By de poker, but I tink dat anchor fixed down below beneath a rock," shouted Tom at this instant, lurching back on the for'ard deck and just saving a fall into the well. "Dat ting stick like wax, and Tom not move um at fust. Hi, by lummy, you ober dere, yo do dat again and Tom say someting to yo. He skin yo alibe. He roast de flesh on yo bones and eat you."

Jim grinned; even in the midst of such excitement the huge negro amused him, so that he was forced to laugh. Indeed the antics Tom indulged in were enough to cause a shout of merriment. It seemed that a bullet, fired at him a second earlier, just as he was hauling up the anchor, had struck him on the back of the hand; and though it had done nothing more than break the skin, it had caused a great deal of pain. It was that, and the suddenness of it all, which had roused the ire of the negro.

"You black son ob gun yo!" he bellowed, shaking a huge fist towards the bank from which the shot had come. "Me break yo into little pieces, smash yo into fine jelly."

"Hop right down off that deck, and see that you've placed the anchor out of harm's way," commanded the Major sharply. "Bullets are bad enough, but when they ricochet from an anchor they give very nasty wounds. Ah!"

He had hardly finished speaking when there came another rolling discharge from the bank, followed by the rush of the bullets, and then by a dull thud. The officer commanding the expedition fell forward in the cab, struck his forehead against the edge, and subsided in a heap on the floor. Instantly one of his men bent over him.

"Knocked silly, sir," he said, addressing Jim. "What's to be done?"

He looked at his two companions and awaited their answer. But one of them was busily engaged. Tomkins crouched in the well, his rifle to his shoulder and a perfect stream of fire issuing from the muzzle. Indeed, no one could have handled a magazine rifle better. But he came to the end of his supply of cartridges within a minute, and faced round quickly.

"What's that?" he demanded anxiously. "The Major hit? Say, this is bad!"

"Knocked silly; not killed," explained his comrade, shooting a cartridge into his own barrel. "What's to be done?"

Tomkins cast a sympathetic glance at the Major, and then across at the river bank. A second later his eyes strayed to Jim's figure, and for a few moments he watched the young fellow as he tended to his engine, and with Ching's help placed a board padded with oiled cotton waste over the rent in the cooling jacket.

"See here," he cried abruptly. "The Major's down. Guess that young fellow had best take his place. He knows how to work this concern, and he ain't no fool by a long way. Get to at it."

He took it for granted that Jim would accept the post of commander, and promptly turned towards the bank again, his magazine already replenished.

Meanwhile it may be wondered who had caused the whole commotion, who were the miscreants who had so suddenly and treacherously fired into the launch.

Five minutes almost had passed since the first shot came, when the banks were hardly visible. But the dawn comes quickly in the tropics. The day was full upon them now, and, looking up, Jim could perceive the mass of tangled undergrowth beneath the forest trees, while right by the edge of the water were a number of dusky figures. If he could have had any reasonable doubt that they were natives Tomkins speedily helped him to a decision. For the man was a first-class marksman, and now that the light was strong enough he began to make good use of his rifle. As Jim stared at the bank, one of the dusky figures turned and scrambled towards the jungle. But it seemed that the man had already been hit; for suddenly he swerved and almost tumbled. Then he faced round again, and stood unsteadily leaning on his weapon. The next instant a terrible shout escaped him; the native, for a dusky individual it was without question, dropped his weapon and thrust both arms high into the air. Then he seemed to crumple up entirely, and, falling forward, rolled with a loud splash into the river. Within a second a comrade had followed him to the same destination, dispatched thither by the policeman's unerring rifle.

Bang! Bang! From a long length of the bank splashes of smoke came, and once more bullets sped towards the launch. Jim heard their thudding, and even noted the various queer sounds they made, the dull blow of one striking her broadside, the cheep of another which merely grazed her rail, and then the nasty screaming of a missile which hit the anchor chain, and, being deflected in its course, rose almost vertically, and later on brought a shower of leaves from the trees beyond. But that was not all. Two bullets at least passed with a peculiar whizz, and went on into the jungle on the other bank, as if they had been driven with greater force than all the rest.

"Revolvers!" exclaimed our hero at once. "Tomkins, I think there were two revolver shots then. Eh?"

The man nodded; he had hardly time to speak.

"Guess so," he said abruptly. "Revolvers—those villains we're after. They've set a whole crowd on to us."

"Then the sooner we are out of their reach the better. See here," cried Jim; "try to find out where those particular ruffians have got to and pepper them. Sam, get to the wheel; we'll make over to the far bank; that'll bother them."

The motor buzzed and roared as he switched his levers forward, while the water pump gathered such power from the momentum that the pressure within the jackets increased wonderfully. Ching, despite all his efforts and all his cunning, could no longer seal that rent made by the bullet. True, he reduced the leakage wonderfully; but from all round the margin a spray of hot water swept broadcast, quickly drenching our hero to the skin. It was a trifle, however: Jim congratulated himself that he was not likely to be scalded.

"With a motor on a car ashore it would be different," he told himself, as he put the launch in motion. "Here the temperature cannot very well rise too high. She takes in her supply direct from the river, and pumps it right through the jackets and out again. Swing her over, Sam. See here, Tomkins, I'm going straight for the far bank, and will swing round in a circle when I get near. We'll bring up end on, beneath a tree if possible; then we shall present less of a mark. Ah! Good shooting! That'll make 'em careful."

As yet he had had no time in which to reckon the odds opposed to them, nor the imminence of the danger in which the expedition stood. Minor matters occupied his attention, those and vague queries as to how he should proceed. He noted with satisfaction that Tomkins and his two comrades were making excellent practice. At least half a dozen of the enemy had already fallen.

"Round with her, right round, Sam," he commanded, when the launch was near the bank. "Steady! Back her! How's that for a tree?"

With Sam aiding him at the wheel, and he himself controlling the pace of the launch, Jim soon manœuvred her beneath a tree which swept its branches right into the water. Then he threw his lever out, slowed the motor, and crawled into the cab. With Tom's help he laid the Major on his back and carefully searched for a wound. And very soon they came upon the result of the bullet. There was a huge, discoloured bump on the top of his head, while an ugly graze crossed the forehead. For the rest, he was breathing deeply and regularly, while the pupils were equal.

"Bullet knock de sense clean out ob him head," explained Tom, as if he were completely conversant with the matter. "Knock de Massa Major silly. Tomorrow, when he wake up and come to himself, he hold de hands to him head. Oh, how him ache! Him feel more silly den dan he look now. But, Massa Jim, dis a bit ob hot stuff. Dis quite all right. Once de fun begin Tom like it hot and plenty. Yo bide little bit; soon dem debil fire away all dere powder and ball. Den time to make a move; den Tom hab someting more to say about de wound. Yo see dat!" and he held out a bruised and swollen hand for Jim's inspection; "scum of a black nigger do dat. Yo see. Tom not forget when de time come."

Really the big fellow was too much for Jim. Grave though the situation was, he was forced to laugh again. For Tom did not stop at threats; his words lost all their impressiveness without the gestures. And the latter, terribly fierce though they were—for when he bared his teeth in a snarl no one could look more like a demon than Tom—were instantly banished and forgotten by the fellow's well-known merry smile. Tom's six-foot smile was too catching. His comical face never failed to draw laughter from his audience.

"If you stand up and expose your ugly head like that you won't be left when the powder has been done with!" exclaimed Jim severely, suppressing his mirth. "Now, listen to this: Tom will watch up stream, Ching will keep a lookout in the downward direction, while Sam will hop ashore. Don't go more than a few feet away, lad," he warned the little negro. "Just enough to keep us from being surprised, and to allow you to rejoin instantly. Say, Tomkins, supposing we give over firing?"

A flushed face turned towards him, while the policeman regarded our hero as if he thought him demented.

"Let 'em go on shootin' and not answer!" he gasped. "Why, of all——"

"It's like this," explained Jim curtly. "All the time you fire they know where we're lying. I don't say we're likely to get bad wounds at this distance, for most of the weapons yonder are gas barrels, I reckon, but a revolver bullet might hit by accident, and then it'd be a case with one of us."

There was indecision on Tomkins's face for the space of a few seconds. To tell the truth, though an excellent fellow, he was one who boasted unusual independence, both in word and act, and while it was a fact that he had suggested that Jim should take the Major's place, he had taken it for granted that orders from our hero would not be very frequent, and that he would mainly direct by managing his motor, and seeing that a course was steered. And here he was fighting the vessel. There was something approaching a scowl on Tomkins's face as the thought flashed across his brain. He swung round to look at the enemy. But a second later he was glancing up at Jim once more, his weapon idle beside him.

"You're a conjuror, I guess," he said abruptly. "I'd forgotten those revolvers. I thought your suggestion was a bad one; then, blessed if one of them rascals didn't drop in a shot. Look there! He winged me!"

He grinned as he held out a finger of his left hand for inspection.

"That's what I got for being foolish. You're right, sir," he said with decision. "What next?"

"See that you don't touch the branches overhead. They'd see them moving from the far side. Sam there? Come aboard. Now," he went on, when the negro had dropped into the well of the launch, "not a sound from anyone. They won't hear the motor while she is running light. We'll run down stream under the trees, and then make a break into the open. A hundred-yards start will allow us to laugh at all their weapons."

There was agreement on all the faces about him. Tomkins nodded very decidedly, showing that the plan met with his approval.

"Then lie out there right forward, Tom," said Jim, lowering his tones. "Those long arms of yours will do as fenders. Push us off if we get too near to a tree. But don't touch 'em if you can help it. Get on to that wheel, Sam; I'm moving off at once."

He threw in his lever and set the propeller turning very slowly, but the launch felt the effect instantly. She was already heading in the right direction, and at once began to glide away beneath the leafy covering. It happened, too, that she was able to pursue this course for more than a hundred yards before a break in the bank, where there had been a species of landslide, and where the trees receded sharply, caused her to come into the open.

"Take her clear into the centre, and then head her for the lagoon," said Jim, calling gently to Sam. "Tom, slip back into the cab. All hands keep their heads as low as possible. Don't fire a shot unless there's actual need, and if there's trouble, let every man who has no other special duty pepper those rascals for all they're worth. Over with her."

Bizz! gurr! gurr! The motor roared at his bidding, while the propeller lashed the shallow water into foam. Ching grabbed at the covering placed over the rent in the water jacket, and then turned his face from the engine. For, though there was nothing there to harm one, still the spray forced in all directions by the pump was disagreeable, to say the least of it, and made seeing almost impossible! Bizz! Gurr! the launch shot down the last few yards of the dark lane beneath the trees. Sam, his eye fixed on the opening, swung his wheel right over, while Jim nudged his levers a trifle higher. The planks at his feet had started to dither again, and practice told him that the vessel must be moving. But they were not shaking and vibrating to such an extent as to make standing upon them uncomfortable. There was no need for such an exhibition of haste yet awhile.

"Might bust the jacket altogether," Jim told himself. "Might have a bad breakdown. Better get along as we are. I can squeeze a little more out of her if there's occasion. Ah, here she goes round into the open!"

Turning abruptly, as Sam swung the wheel over, the launch canted on her heel till a stream of water swamped far up the rail-less deck astern. The bows lifted from the surface in spite of Tom's enormous weight, while a big bow wave collected beneath her cutwater, and, gathering in size as the propeller shot the boat forward, was presently spreading across the surface of the river, and washing heavily against the nearest bank. Straight as a dart the vessel was directed to the point that Jim had mentioned. She cut obliquely across the stream, and, almost before those aboard could have believed it possible, was heeling again to the swerve of her rudder.

"Done them brown. Cut out below them, and left 'em well behind. Boys!" cried Tomkins, beside himself with delight, "I 'low as we've something to thank the chief for. He's done a cute thing; he's stolen a real march on them blackguards."

"Not know so much, siree," answered Tom from his post in the cab, where he had retired at Jim's orders. "Massa Jim all right, don't you fear. He know right well what him up to; but what yo say to dat, and to dat? Dem bullets buzz too close fo Tom's likin'."

That the passage of the launch had been observed there could not now be a shadow of doubt, for the far side of the river had already displayed several patches of smoke, billowing from the rifles of the enemy. But Tomkins laughed at the idea that they could prove harmful.

"Jest you squat right down here at my feet, darkie," he laughed. "Then you won't have no cause to get wonderin' whether a bullet's coming along. Fer me, I guess as we're well out of a ruction that looked at one time likely to get too hot fer anything. You ain't got sich a thing as a light along of you?"

Tom grunted. It annoyed the big fellow to have a recommendation to place himself in safety. His eyes gleamed white in the morning light; his sharp teeth gritted together.

"Yo policeman," he said, as he extracted his pipe from his pocket, and still leaned on the edge of the cab, within full view of those on the bank of the river, "yo Tomkins, yo ain't the only one as wants a smoke. By gum, but Tom like a draw too, 'specially early in de mornin', when dere a chance of gettin' a bullet. Yo sit right there and wait. Matches ain't so plentiful in this locality."

He stuffed his pipe methodically and slowly. Then he put the stem between his teeth and, slowly again, struck one of his matches. He was on the point of offering the light to the policeman when a sudden exclamation came from Sam. "Look dar!" he shouted. "Not tink dat good for dis here party. Tings is all changed round. Dey's chasin' us instead of we bein' after dem. Massa Jim, dis am a bit of a conundrum."

Conundrum or not, the situation was sufficiently serious. Even Tomkins went red and hot as he realized to the full the gravity of this new movement. For the motor launch was not the only one on the river. The launch on which the two ruffians had escaped from Colon, and which they themselves had chased in the late hours of the previous night, was now chasing them, but under altered circumstances. There were fifty dark figures swarming over her decks.

"Right straight down the centre!" cried Jim, waving to Sam. "You hold on dead straight unless I give you an order. I think we shall just clear her."

But would they? That was the question. The steam launch which had disappeared so mysteriously on the previous night had suddenly darted out from the opposite bank of the river, her decks crowded with men. Moreover, she was fully prepared for a speedy journey, for steam was hissing and whistling from her escape. There was a white wave under her foot, a spreading surf behind her, while the course she followed promised to bring her alongside Jim's vessel before the latter could make her way down the long stretch of water that led to the lagoon. Indeed it looked very much as if the stranger would intercept their passage, and then—what was the prospect?

"Boys," called out Jim after a minute, during which time he had pushed his throttle and ignition levers as far forward as was possible, "see here, boys, there may be a tussle before us. Get to work right now with your rifles. Give it to 'em hot. We may be able to scare 'em."

Pip! Pop! The sharp reports of the Government rifles punctuated the semi-silence which followed, while screams of rage came from the crowded decks of the enemy. Pip! Pop! Tomkins and his friends splashed their bullets in the centre of the throng, and sent more than one of the dusky warriors rolling. Meanwhile, under Jim's guiding hand, the motor launch sped faster towards the lagoon, till her whole frame shivered and vibrated. In such acute cases a second's space of time will change the complexion of matters entirely, will advance the fortunes of one party against those of the other. And here there was an illustration of the fact. Jim's engine raced madly, while the propeller took a firm grip of the water. The vessel bounded forward at a pace which easily outdistanced that of the steam launch. Very soon it became apparent that Jim and his friends would slip past the launch that was steaming from the opposite bank to intercept them.

"Keep at it with those rifles, boys!" he shouted, delighted at the turn matters had taken, and, heedless of the spray of water which gushed in all directions from the rent in the cooling jacket of the motor. "Keep down their fire, and if you catch a sight of those rascals, pepper them properly. Hooray! We'll best 'em yet."

"Run past dem as if they was lame and walking," sang out Tom, bubbling over with excitement. "Den turn and gib dem what fo. Yo tink dat good advice, massa. Yo do as I say; den we knock dem into little pieces. Tom able to find de blackguard dat fired dat shot; den smash um to a jelly."

But seconds bring great changes in the fortunes of parties, as we have already observed, and now, having smiled upon Jim and his comrades, Dame Fortune—a fickle dame at any time—turned her face from them. That rent in the water jacket, the spray which the pump forced past the plug which Ching held in position, proved the undoing of the party. The rhythmical buzz of the engine suddenly ceased. The explosions came haltingly, while the revolutions lessened sensibly, so much so as to reduce the speed of the boat. Then Jim's practised ear told him that the ignition had given out, that the vital spark, without which the motor was useless and now deficient, had been cut off, and thus the motor had been sent adrift. Let us express the matter in proper terms— the flow of water had smothered the magneto, and the current was shorted; no longer did it flow uninterrupted and insulated to the cylinders. It expended its force elsewhere, sent sparks flashing about the magneto, and in the short space of a minute entirely stopped the motor. But the steam launch made no pause in her progress. She pushed on towards the stranded boat swiftly, while a shriek of delight and triumph burst from the horde of natives crowding her decks.

CHAPTER XI

Barely Escaped

Tall and lean, the natives aboard the steam launch were plainly visible for a moment, so much so that Jim, having regarded his useless motor desperately for some few seconds, was compelled to give his attention to the enemy. Tall and thin, each one of the natives was almost naked. Their bodies were painted with broad stripes of white, which at a distance made one think of skeletons; while vermilion was daubed on the cheeks, giving each individual the same air of ferocity. For the rest, these men wore their long hair plaited into queues, and bore about their persons a simple belt in which a long knife was suspended.

But when events are moving fast, and disaster stares one in the face, details and trifles escape attention. Jim and his comrades had their safety to think of, so that it is not wonderful that they failed to observe too closely the appearance of their dusky enemies. But however urgent the position, none could fail to see the short spears, with long narrow blades attached to them, which each dusky warrior carried. Half a dozen at least were gripped in each left hand, while the right held a single one in readiness to discharge it. As for the gun, the cheap gas barrels with which these wretched natives had been supplied, they were without exception muzzle loaders; and now that events were moving so fast and so furiously there was hardly time to load. A few of the men handled their ramrods, but the rest had discarded their weapons and stood prancing upon the deck of the launch, causing her to heave and roll dangerously, and prepared to throw their spears the instant they came within range of Jim and his party. It was not until that moment that our hero realized that if their fortunes were desperate they were at least lucky in one particular.

"Gee, ain't I glad!" he exclaimed. "From what Phineas told me I quite expected them to be armed with bows and arrows—the latter poisonous. Tomkins, you and your men had best concentrate your force aft of the launch, where the engine is. I caught a glimpse of those rascals there; and though I don't suppose that the death of one or both would cause the gang to sheer off, yet it might do so, and in any case if we could put them out of action there would be no white man to lead the natives."

"Right, sir, right," came from Tomkins instantly, while he and his two comrades promptly moved to the back of the cab, from which point they could best command that portion of the launch upon which they were instructed to concentrate their fire.

"You, Tom and Sam, fire on the natives," shouted Jim. "I'm going to help you. Ching, get hold of some of that clean cotton waste and wipe up all round this magneto. Dry every part you can, and don't forget those plugs on top of the cylinders."

He had already pointed out the ignition plugs to the Chinaman, for they, like the rest of the engine, had been heavily sprayed with water. Then he seized a rifle, jerked the magazine open as the Major had instructed him when they first set out on the expedition, and levelled his sights upon the advancing natives.

By now the latter were dangerously near, and already clouds of spears were flying. It looked as if within a few seconds the steam launch would be right alongside, and the black demons aboard her hurling themselves upon the decks of the motor. But suddenly there came a high-pitched shriek amidst the howls of the enemy, and to the relief of all in Jim's party the course of the other vessel was abruptly altered. She shot away obliquely to the left, while one of the white men who had been manning the wheel was seen to tumble backwards.

"A grand shot," shouted Jim. "Now is our time to get this motor running. Out of the way, Ching, and let me get to her. We'll see how she'll run without water in her jackets."

The idea had suddenly flashed into his brain, and he proceeded promptly to put it into execution. But, first of all, now that he had a short breathing space, it was necessary to supervise the work that Ching had been doing.

"It'll take 'em a good five minutes to round up and get back here within range," he told himself, glancing across at the enemy. "That splendid shot and the fall of their steersman have caused no end of confusion, and now is the time to best them."

Laying his rifle down hurriedly, he bent over the magneto and seized a handful of dry cotton waste.

"Me mop up all de water," grinned Ching, looking the coolest person aboard the launch. Indeed, there seemed to be little doubt that he was actually the least concerned of all the party, for his inexpressive features had not changed in the slightest. There was not so much as a tinge of red in his sallow cheeks, sure indication of some excitement. His almond eyes—all aslant, as is common to this Eastern race—regarded Jim, the useless motor, and the howling band of natives steaming across the water with the same tranquillity. "Wipey all de water up, Mass Jim," he repeated. "Now, s'pose you start him. He go velly nicely p'laps. Den run away from dem rascals, and Ching put de kettle on, hab someting to eat, 'cos Ching hungry, velly."

"Get out of this!" cried Jim irritably. "Breakfast, man! Why, if we don't get out of this in the next few minutes there won't be one of us left to take a bite!"

He pushed the Chinaman to one side, and rapidly ran over his ignition system. Ching had done his work with that painstaking thoroughness for which the Chinaman is noted, and though hollows and crevices in and about the motor still held pools of water, the vital parts were dry.

"Then I'll try it," he said. "Those beggars have managed to turn rather quicker than I had imagined; but if I can only get her going within a minute we ought to be able to escape them. Ah! here come their bullets again, boys; get in at them with your rifles."

All the while he had been troubled with the want of one small article. To keep the water out of his motor he must plug the opening which led from the vessel's side direct to the pump. For the rest, it was an easy matter, there being a tap which would drain all the jackets within the space of but a few seconds. But that alone was insufficient; with the water port still open, the pump would drive a column of fluid through the jackets, and the ignition would be again drenched.

"A cork! a cork!" he cried. "Something with which to fill this port."

He leant over the side of the vessel and pointed out the opening to Ching. And the wily, cunning Chinee immediately came to his assistance.

"A cork, sah; I's got the velly thing. You wantee someting to push in dere. Ching hab plenty fine cork."

He moved with exasperating slowness across the engine well, and rummaged in a locker in which his cooking utensils were stored. There came the characteristic sound of a bung being extracted from a bottle, and then Ching came back again, still slowly, still unconcernedly, still with that unruffled countenance.

"He, he, he! him come out of the vinegar bottle," he giggled. "Him one velly fine cork, Mass Jim. But yo gib him back when yo finished? Eh? Velly fine cork dat."

Jim snatched it from his hand without ceremony, in fact with a brusqueness altogether foreign to him. Then he leaned over the side of the launch and gave a shout of triumph when he discovered that Ching had supplied him with an article which fitted nicely. He rammed it home forcibly, driving his fist through the water against the cork. Then he bounded to the engine, jerked the starting handle into position, and sent the motor whirling. Bizz! She was off. The engine went away with an encouraging roar, while but a few ounces of water escaped from the rent in her jacket.

"Wipe it up," he commanded Ching. "And guess you'd better keep clear of the magneto and plugs and suchlike. If you touched them you'd get a shock that would knock you endways. Gee! Ain't she buzzing! Hooray! we'll best them."

Sam was already at the steering wheel of the launch, watching his master out of the corner of his big eyes, and paying some attention to the enemy. Indeed he would not have been human had he failed to cast more than one anxious look in their direction. Sam was not the same stolid, supernaturally unemotional individual as the Chinaman. He had nerves; excitement told on the little fellow.

"Dey almighty near, sah," he sang out. "Dat motor goin'? den, fo' goodness sake, put de gear in, push on, get away from dem demon."

"Dodge 'em; swing her about. Put out their aim," Jim called to him, and at once pushed his gear lever home. Then, like the practical young man he was, he reached over to his lubricators and sent them dripping at a pace which, while they would not flood the engine and overlubricate her, would still supply a more abundant amount than usual, and so in a measure serve to counteract the want of water cooling.

"She's bound to run hotter," Jim told himself, "and as a permanent arrangement the thing wouldn't do; but for the time being it's got to. Round with her, Sam."

The launch meanwhile had floated quietly on the surface of the river, and, owing to the fact that her propeller was stationary, being thrown out of gear by the failure of the engine, she had lost steerage way, and had drifted completely round. She was heading upstream when Jim set her propeller thrashing the water again, and for a while she raced away from the other vessel, the manœuvre drawing shrill yells of rage from the natives. But Sam had her in hand. The fine little fellow had not been with Jim and his father all this time without learning how to steer a launch, and at once, with a glance over his shoulder, he sent his wheel round, causing the boat to flop over and heel till her rail was almost under the surface. Round she spun on her keel, and within the half-minute was heading direct for the enemy. A growl broke from Tomkins as he laid his cheek once more down on the butt of his rifle.

"This time guess we'll make hay with 'em," he shouted. "Don't you be in too much of a hurry, sir. You can make rings all round 'em and still keep out of range. Dare say their bullets'll reach right enough, but they won't strike hard enough to hurt more'n a fly. It's the spears I'm frightened of."

And everyone else, too; for the natives aboard the oncoming launch had again discarded their firearms, and were now standing, spear in hand ready poised, waiting for the moment when they might cast them. Sam gave every dusky warrior a start when he headed the launch direct for them. It looked as if he were bent on a collision; but a minute later, when effective range for the spear throwers had almost been reached, he put his wheel over again, and shot the launch away at a right angle. Then a figure aboard the enemy was seen to rise erect beside her steering gear, and within the space of a few seconds she paid off in the same direction as Jim's craft had taken—on a course, in fact, which would bring the two boats alongside very shortly. Either that or they must run hard into the bank.

"Right round with her again; dodge them!" shouted Jim, his heart in his mouth. "Then take her up stream a little. We have the legs of them, and if only we can shake them clear for a while we shall get past them."

That was the difficulty. The enemy remained all the while between them and the lagoon, and in that direction safety lay. Even a swift boat such as the motor launch had proved herself to be could not slip by easily, unless she risked running so close into the other as to place her crew in danger of those terrible spears; but Sam seemed fully to have realized the difficulty, and at Jim's command he brought the boat heeling round again. Hardly three lengths separated the combatants when he swung the wheel again, and, driven by her fast-rotating propeller, the launch shot obliquely up the stream, leaving the other heading helplessly for the bank. Tom roared with delight, brandishing his rifle overhead, while Ching giggled and simpered as if he looked upon the thing as a glorious joke. But Jim's face was set and stern. He had been so close when the vessel turned that he had been able to look into the eyes of the natives; and the ferocity of their appearance, their terrible shrieks and howls, and the cloud of spears which they had discharged brought realistically to him the depth of their danger. Within a foot of his hand a spear stood quivering, the blade sunk deeply in the woodwork. It needed but a glance to tell him that the weapon was capable of dealing death to anyone. However, they were out of range now, and the time had come to practise a further manœuvre. Jim waved his hand in Sam's direction.

"Over," he shouted. "Let her rip for the lagoon."

Meanwhile the course of the other launch had been hurriedly arrested; for the ruffian aboard her was a clever skipper, and handled the craft with decision. The waters churned into white foam beneath her rudder, and before Jim and his friend had completed their slanting run upstream the rascal had his boat running rapidly astern in an effort to intercept them.

"Gee, he'll do it, too!" shouted Tomkins. "Say, sir, we'll have to charge them. But that would mean the end of everything for them and for us."

Jim shook his head emphatically. "You're asking for a funeral," he said bluntly. "We've got to dodge 'em, even if we play at the game for the rest of the morning. Steady there, Sam; do anything rather than let them get within close range of us. Boys, if only you could pick off that rascal who commands them we would soon make an end of the others."

But the man aboard the other boat proved to be as crafty as he was capable. True, they had obtained a clear view of him on one occasion, at least, when he had dashed for the steering gear of his vessel. But now a gaudily painted native occupied that responsible position, while the Spaniard himself lay out of sight in the engine well, but near enough to prompt him. The rim of his hat could be seen on occasion as he glanced across at Jim and his party. As for our hero, seeing that the course was blocked, and that for the moment their escape was cut off, he coolly threw his lever out of gear and slowed down his engine. Then he reversed his propellor for a while until the launch had come to a standstill.

"Two can play at this sort of game," he told himself. "We'll wait and see what that fellow proposes to do; but listen here, Tomkins, and you other fellows. Next time we attempt a rush we have to make a big impression on these natives. We'll get them end on, if we can, and then try them with volleys. We want to make every shot tell, and that hasn't been the case up to the present. A moving target isn't too easy to hit from a launch when she's heaving and rolling."

"Lummy! Look dere! By de poker, dere more of de scum. Yo see dem black sons ob guns coming right away dere? Dey likely to be very troublesome."

It taxed the perception of all to decide where this new arrival could have come from; for up till that moment the banks on either hand had seemed to be untenanted. Not a shot had come from them for quite a while, and all imagined that every native taking part in this sudden and unprovoked attack upon Jim and his comrades was embarked aboard the other launch. And here, as Tom had brought to their notice, was another boat, steering out from a bank to join her consort. It was a long, dark-coloured craft, with sides protruding some little distance out of the water, a stem erected high into the air, and bearing upon it a hideous carving, while astern there was a platform perched up on the post, and squatted upon it a painted and feathered savage, whose steering oar controlled the course of the vessel. As for her crew, a swarm of natives filled her from end to end; those in advance standing ready, spear in hand, to join in the engagement, while the remainder, situated aft, squatted on the floor and churned the water with their paddles. In a little while she had come alongside the steamer, which now rested across the centre of the stream.

"They'll talk for a bit now, I guess," growled Tomkins. "Then, like as not, they'll make a dash for it. This here business ain't going to be ended without a rare lot of bloodletting. It's that launch that's the bother. She ain't as quick as we are, but she's swift enough to turn and stop us now that she's got a position downstream. If only we had half a dozen more men aboard here! I wouldn't funk, then, running aboard her. We'd show 'em who was going ter be master."

The man's eyes were set and shining. There was a good deal of the bull dog about Tomkins, and one had only to glance at him to feel satisfied that when the crisis came the American could be trusted.

"As ef we was goin' down before a lot of black chaps same as they are!" he growled. "But you can't get away from numbers. It's the crowd that tells, and ef we lets 'em get close enough ter get their teeth fixed—gee, it'll be a case! Funerals ain't in it. I for one ain't goin' ter drop into the hands of sich rascals. I'll clear out all I can, and then——"

His eyes were bent on his rifle, while his fingers—strong, brown fingers—played with the lock.

Gurr! Jim switched the conversation in another direction by throwing his gear in. "They're moving," he said. "Best get steerage way on the boat. See here, boys, we've a heap of room upstream, and if they don't separate directly I shall run up gently. We've always enough water to turn in, and if only we can once fool the launch, and get by her, I don't care a row of chips for the other craft. I'll run her down in a winking. Ah, they're coming along! Swing her over, Sam. There's no hurry: we'll see if the movement won't make them part company."

But the steamer and the huge war canoe held together. In fact, ropes had been passed from one to the other, and the launch provided the power. But men were stationed ready to cast off the bonds between them, so that each craft could go separately. Jim's sudden movement produced nothing more than a howl, while the steamer swung gently over towards him.

"That'll suit me as well as anything," he cried. "Let 'em hold together. I'll tempt them across towards this bank, then double and be away before they can cut the canoe adrift. How's that?"

The enemy answered the question. For, of a sudden, the ropes were cast off, the canoe lay to in the centre of the stream, while the launch steamed to intercept the other. It was a crafty move on the part of the rascal who commanded the natives; for now he could rush at Jim. If he failed to come to grips with him, and the latter attempted to slip downstream, there was a formidable obstacle which was by no means to be sneered at because she had no motor aboard. There were lusty arms to ply the paddles, and when the backs of the natives were bent to the work they could make their craft slip through the water at a pace which had to be witnessed to be believed.

"Round we go, upstream for the moment," called Jim to the negro at the wheel. "Easy does it: I'm only letting my motor out a little. We'll make things hum before we have finished. She's coming along too. Well, we'll make a race of it to the far side of the river."

All the time he was attempting to get the enemy so near one bank that, in the race across to the other, the launch propelled by an internal-combustion motor, which had already proved herself far the speedier, would outstrip the other by so much that it would be safe to head downstream and sweep past her without risking those formidable spears. But always there was the crafty ruffian aboard the steamer to be reckoned with. He turned as Jim's craft ran direct across to the far bank, and followed swiftly. Then, as the motor launch approached close to the far bank, the rascal coolly stopped his engine. When Sam swung his boat round again the enemy had actually gained. A direct run upstream would almost allow him to meet the motor launch.

"Gee, he's got us there!" cried Jim, disappointment in his voice. "I thought we were going to do the trick nicely. But wait a little: we'll be more successful on the second occasion. Run her slick across, Sam," he called. "I'm going to try and trick him."

There is little doubt that had the enemy desired it he could almost have arrested their progress on this occasion, or forced Jim and his party to change their course. But the commander of the steamer had his own ideas as to how to accomplish his purpose. Ching simpered when he discovered the truth of the matter, but had the good sense to mention his fears to our hero.

"Oh, him one velly clever person!" he giggled. "Yo see what him up to, Mass Jim. All de time him run across alongside ob us him slippey nearer and nearer. Presently him so close dat de black man able to dig dere spears in."

Jim shivered in spite of the heat, for the sun was now streaming down upon the contestants. Then he looked closely at the enemy, and realized that Ching had given him valuable information. For though the steamer was cutting across the river on an apparently parallel course to his own, yet all the while her steersman was jerking his helm over, bringing her by degrees closer to Jim and his party. It was a difficulty which needed to be faced promptly, and Jim's lips were hard set together as he made his plans to meet it. Very gradually he slowed down his motor, keeping a keen eye all the while upon the stern of the steamer, where white foam showed how her propeller was working.

"I don't know that his game won't suit me very well after all," he said to himself. "So long as he actually doesn't come within spear range of us we are all right, and my aim all the while is to get him dead on a line with us. Once there he can't catch us by suddenly swerving off from his course, as was nearly the case this last time. Sam, boy," he called out, "when I shout, bring her clear round and face her back on her tracks right away for the other side. Tomkins, you can get your men ready for a little bit of quick business."

For the past five minutes not a shot had left the rifles of his comrades, though an occasional ball came from the deck of the steamer. It was remarkable that the rascal there made no attempt to use his revolver; but perhaps he had run out of ammunition, and in any case the management of the craft occupied all his attention. As to the men under Jim's command, all wore a grim determined expression. Even Ching seemed to take some definite interest in the adventure, and, though one could not be quite sure of the matter, those slanting, almond eyes bore just the merest trace of anxiety. Otherwise, there was tense excitement on board, for by now each man had realized the nature of the manœuvre about to be attempted, and the narrow margin which must necessarily lie between themselves and safety. It was Tomkins who put in an encouraging word.

"Jest you get in at it, pard," he said, moistening the palms of his hands preparatory to gripping his rifle. "You ain't got no cause to fear that we won't fight. When the ruction comes you can count on us, every blessed mother's son of us; and, see here, siree, ef you don't happen to bring off this trick, and there's a chance of them chaps driving us up into a corner, jest round her and go baldheaded for 'em. I'm getting sick of this here runnin'."

His two comrades nodded curtly to show that this statement met with their full approval, while Tom, the noble fellow, who always seemed to carry his young master's interests uppermost in his mind, stepped across to the rear edge of the cab and leaned over towards the motor.

"We ain't gwine to knuckle down to dem black niggers," he said in a voice which was meant to be a confidential whisper, but which as an actual fact was a deep-chested roar that wellnigh drowned the noise of the engine. "Yo ain't got no cause to fear, 'cos this here boy and all de odders wants to get back right along home again. We ain't a-goin' to let scum like this stan' in de way. Nebber. We's gwine to do as we wants. Sam, jest see that you're nippy."

Tom gave his master one of his most expansive smiles; then, as if to relieve his overwrought feelings, he swung round and glowered upon the harmless but extremely energetic Sam. Indeed, if the fortunes of the day were due to some extent to those who had wielded rifles, they were none the less the work of Jim and Sam and Ching between them, while at this very critical moment they may rightly be said to have rested in the hands of our hero and the little negro only.

Jim glanced swiftly across at the steamer. By now she was almost abreast of them, and if only he had but known it her commander was on the point of bringing his scheme to a termination by a rapid movement. He imagined that the slowing down of the launch was due again to further trouble of her motor. It was distinctly an opportunity to be snatched at, and, with a promptness which did him credit, he caused his steersman to swing his helm over. In an instant the steamer had changed her course and was heading for the broadside of the other vessel.

"Now," shouted Jim excitedly. "Right round with her. Let her rip. We've got 'em nicely."

It is one of the advantages of a gasolene motor, that the engine is capable of instant acceleration. A second before it had been purring gently, whilst the propeller was barely turning; but now the machinery gave out a sudden roar, while every plank and strut aboard shivered and vibrated. Under her keel the blades of her propeller churned the stream into milky foam, while the craft itself gathered way promptly. Once more she rolled heavily as Sam swung his wheel. Then she came round on her former course as if she were a living thing that understood, and was in full sympathy with the work expected of her. She bounded forward, raising her bows clear of the water, and by the time she had reached midstream had gained five lengths on the steamer.

"Edge her down, Sam; edge her down," urged Jim, giving hasty directions to his steersman. "Be ready to bring her over. That will be the time for you, Tomkins, and the others with the rifles."

It hardly needs the telling that the din from those aboard the steamer was now bewildering and deafening. But a few short seconds before the game had seemed entirely in their hands; it looked as though they would be aboard the other craft in a twinkling. Now they were hopelessly left behind; every instant made their failure more certain. Puffs of smoke burst from the crowded decks, while the huge bullets discharged from the gas barrels owned by the natives splashed all round Jim and his friends. Then there was a roar of anger as the launch turned once more on her heel, exposing her bottom boards right down to the keel as she rolled to the movement. A cloud of useless spears filled the air, while right aft of the steamer a figure sprang on to the stern deck waving both arms and shouting furiously. Tomkins's eye fell upon the man, and he gripped hard to the rail of the vessel to steady himself whilst she was rolling. Then down came his rifle, the weapon cracked forth a bullet, and the figure beyond collapsed across the engine and was hidden from view in the depth of the well which housed it. There were others amongst the natives who met with their deserts about the same moment; while, as if to put the question of the steamer's further utility entirely beyond discussion, there came suddenly from the neighbourhood of her funnel a thick column of hissing steam which rose in clouds over the river.

127

"I guess I'd had to shoot him," declared Tomkins grimly; "and well he deserved it. Say, sir, you needn't think no more of that steamer, for she's put clean out of the running. Reckon a bullet found her boiler and plugged a hole clean through it."

Whatever the cause of that cloud of escaping steam the effect was to bring the launch to a standstill. Indeed the position of affairs seemed to have become suddenly reversed. A little while before it had been Jim's motor which was *hors de combat*. He and his friends were stranded and helpless on the water. Now the situation was pleasantly reversed. As Tomkins had said, the steamer was out of the running.

"Dead straight ahead for them," called Jim, his eye fixed upon the huge war canoe hovering farther down the stream. "If they swerve, swing over towards them, and, when within a couple or more lengths, cut off in the other direction. Don't forget to keep them a spear throw from us."

"And meanwhile pepper 'em with the rifles, eh?" asked Tomkins, grinning over his shoulder, and wearing now a very different expression to the grim, determined look he had shown but a short while before. "Pepper 'em nicely, eh, so as to give 'em a taste of what's coming?"

But Jim shook his head decidedly. "There's been enough bloodlettin' already," he said, using the very words which the policeman had employed already. "We've done well with these other fellows, and have shot the two rascals for whom we came in this direction. These ignorant natives don't know any better. Guess we'll give 'em a chance."

A flush of vexation rose to Tomkins's face as he heard his suggestion scouted. He turned with shining eyes upon our hero, and doubtless, had the incident happened some few hours before, would have blurted out a protest. But Jim's manly form, his stern, set face, and his coolness disarmed the policeman and smoothed down his ruffled temper. He recollected that it was to our hero's guidance that the party, so far, owed in great measure its security. The young fellow had done right well, as his worst enemy must needs admit. Then why should he, Tomkins, step in to disturb him? True, Jim was not his lawful commander; but then he himself had placed the lad in that position of responsibility, while a sense of discipline urged him to support one who filled the post of officer.

"Dash it all, man," he growled, "play the game! Don't he deserve it?"

"Right, sir," he said pleasantly, turning to Jim. "You've shown us a cool head so far, and, gee! if I don't think you'll pull us through this business. Not a trigger will we draw on those darkies till you give the word, or till there's actual reason to teach them a lesson. Now, sonny, you ain't got no need to glare at me as if I'd stolen yer last dollar. I ain't done nothing to hurt your master."

It was Tom to whom he addressed himself on this last occasion, for the watchful negro had overheard the words which had passed between Jim and the policeman. Incensed at Tomkins's seeming disloyalty, and always eager to protect our hero, Tom was on the verge of indignation. His big, broad face, which had lost its happy smile since the beginning of the action, now wore an expression akin to anger. His sharp, white teeth were gritted together, while he leaned toward the policeman as if he would do him an injury. But in an instant his manner changed. Tom could not be resentful for more than a moment; besides, there were other pressing matters to engage his attention.

"Yo hab a care, yo policeman," he cried; "me smash dem niggers easy. If me commence on yo, knock de stuffing out ob yo altogether, make yo terrible ill and shaky. Savvy dat? Den put dem in yo pipe and smoke dem."

But Tomkins had already turned away from him with a grin and a shrug of his shoulders, while Jim silenced the negro peremptorily.

"Get a grip of that pole," he cried, nodding to the one that Tom had used on the previous evening, "just in case they happen to come within close distance of us. I hope they won't. We ought to run slick past them."

And that, in fact, seemed to be the most likely termination of the matter, though it was a little disconcerting to notice that the huge war canoe still lay stationary in the very centre of the river. So far it had not been necessary for Sam to swerve the launch in the slightest, and now, as before, she was running head on towards the enemy. In a minute it would be necessary to cut away to one side or the other, the choice resting entirely with Sam, the negro. Deliberately he swung his wheel to the right, and shot the launch obliquely across the river. At the very same instant the man squatting upon the high platform right aft of the canoe shouted, and some fifty paddles plunged into the water. With incredible speed the native craft made off, and shot forward at an angle which would bring her alongside the launch. In spite of the latter's speed it became evident, with startling suddenness, that she could not escape contact with the enemy. It was Sam who decided the course of Jim's party. He bent over his steering wheel till he seemed to hug it. Then he twisted it to the left abruptly.

"Down under with you all!" shouted Jim. "We shall strike her. Tom, get your pole ready." But the negro's services were not required, for the collision and all that followed was ended with startling swiftness. The bows of the launch swung round till they pointed but a few feet ahead of the canoe. Then they came round a little more, while a terrible shout burst from the enemy. There was a gentle shock as the launch struck the stem post of the huge native craft, spears rattled upon her deck, and then they were passed. As for the canoe, the collision had driven her to one side just as she had seemed on the point of running along in close company with the launch. She was now some twenty yards in rear, her crew paddling hopelessly. That she had very nearly run aboard Jim's boat there could be no doubt, for one of the warriors had actually managed to leap forward and reach her. Tom discovered him clinging to the rail amidships, his mouth wide open to hold his spears.

"Oh, dat yo, my frien'!" he laughed, peering over at him. "You hab a free ride all fo' noding. But goodbye now. Sorry to lose yo: we a bit in a hurry."

The burly fellow pushed his pole beneath the man, and by sheer strength lifted him clear out of the water. He held him there for a little while, casting choice expressions at him, then he cast him back into the water, as if the native were some species of fish for which Tom had no use whatever.

"Lucky him swim so well," he laughed. "Tom almost sorry he not kill um. Not so sure dat blackguard not de one who shoot and hit him hand."

"Nonsense!" cried Jim. "Nothing of the sort. That man was aboard the steamer. Stand out of the way, Tom! I think we may take it easily."

There was, in fact, no longer any reason for haste; therefore Jim slowed down his motor. They cruised slowly across the lagoon, and lay close to its exit. There, with the help of the kit of tools carried aboard, and a strip of tinned iron cut from a biscuit box, our hero effected a temporary repair to the water jacket, soldering the patch into position. It was a triumphant crew which returned to Colon, for the Major was himself again, and their duty was accomplished.

CHAPTER XII

An American Undertaking

"I never did meet such a fellow as you, Jim Partington," cried Phineas Barton, when our hero and his comrades turned up at the house situated above the huge dam of Gatun, in progress of building. "No, never before. You get introduced to me after a likely enough adventure. Perhaps I ought to say that I was introduced to you; reckon anyway our meeting was as strange as one might imagine, and there was no end of excitement in it. You behaved like a plucky young beggar." Jim went very red at once. "I thought we weren't to hear anything more about that," he said bluntly. "That was our agreement."

But Phineas only grinned at him. "Agreement or no agreement," he said seriously, "there are times when a chap has just got to sit down and listen. Reckon that time is here now, and you're the chap. I was saying, when you interrupted me—ahem!—that you were a beggar for adventures. You come to my house, do one day's solid work, and then get gallivanting off with an exploration party. Of course, being fired at in the meanwhile and the ruction you had with those rascals down at the hut above Colon is nothing—just a kind of act between supper and breakfast, as it were. Now there's this launch expedition, and there's Tomkins—a surly sort of fellow, who don't often open his mouth, and then not always to be pleasant; there's this policeman, with the Major, his commanding officer, singing your praises down at the club, till the boys are jest jumping to get a grip at you. Time supper's ended to-night you've got to come right along there with me; and, jest remember this, they ain't got an agreement with you."

Jim was horrified at the suggestion. Though he was American born, and was blessed with an American's average allowance of assurance, the lad was undoubtedly modest when his own actions were in question. He would have given anything to escape from what promised to be an ordeal, and made numerous excuses. But Phineas bore him off in spite of all of them, and Tom and Sam and Ching fell in as a bodyguard in rear, in case his protégé should attempt to escape.

"It's not what you owe to yourself," he said, with a laugh, "but what you owe to the boys. Remember that they're working here all day, with little chance of getting news but what comes to them at the club. We're steadygoing stagers here on the canal, and it isn't often that a chap like you turns up. When he does he's got to stand the ruction, and guess that's what you've got to do. Don't I jest wish you and I could change places."

Jim agreed with him heartily, though, as a matter of fact, when he came to face what in his imagination would be an ordeal, he discovered it to be but the pleasantest ceremony. Quiet, earnest men crowded round him to shake his hand; then he was bidden to sit at a table in the centre of his new comrades.

"Yer see," said Harry, who regarded our hero with an envious expression, "that 'ere Tomkins ain't the man to talk, while the Major's much too busy; besides, guess his head's much too sore for chatting. You jest get right in at it, and give us the yarn from start to finish."

ATTACKED BY NATIVES

Jim did as he was bidden, describing every incident, and drawing a growl from many of his audience when he came to that part of his narrative which dealt with the injury to the engine; for it can well be imagined that amongst those white employees on the huge canal a goodly number were, if not actually engineers by profession, certainly most strongly imbued with a leaning towards it. All may have been said to have had mechanical knowledge, since there were few who did not run a steam navvy, a rock drill, a rail-laying plant, or a lifting derrick of some description.

"Gee whiz! That's hot!" exclaimed one of them, interrupting for a moment. "One of those muzzle-loading gas barrels chucked a shot right at your motor, did it? And knocked a hole clean through the water jacket? My, that must have been awkward! Reckon the water pumped up most everywhere, and swamped the ignition. Tell us jest how yer fixed it."

Jim described exactly what had happened, how he had plugged the water entrance to the pump of his motor, and drained the jackets dry. "It was a near thing," he admitted, with a grin. "I thought I should never get going again; but we mopped the water from the magneto, and reckon we fixed it just in time. Of course I gave her plenty of oil, and all the time I was scared that the motor would become overheated."

"Excuse me, sir," said one of the audience, suddenly pressing forward and disclosing himself as one of the officials. "All the time you were fixing this motor, shots were flying, and I understand that there was a boatload of dark-skinned gentlemen thirsting for the lives of yourself and your comrades, and not forgetting to let you know it either. Reckon many a man would have been too upset to think of extra lubrication, though everyone here who knows a gasolene motor realizes well enough that it was extra lubrication, and that alone, which saved your engine from overheating."

He looked round at the assembled audience enquiringly, and was rewarded with many a sharp nod of approval.

"You've got it, siree," cried one of them. "You've jest put your finger on the very point I was about to ask."

"It's as clear as daylight," went on the official, "our young friend here saved the whole party by keeping his head well screwed down and his wits about him. If that motor had overheated, as any self-respecting engine might well have been expected to do under the circumstances, you were all goners. All dead, sir. Wiped out clean by those natives."

There came a grunt of acquiescence from the audience, while Jim went red to the roots of his hair.

"You don't happen to have got fixed on a special job yet awhile?" asked the official pointedly.

"I'm to take a steam digger away up by Culebra."

"And you wouldn't change, supposing I was to come forward with an offer? See here," said the official eagerly, "I'm from the machine shops 'way over at Gorgona. You've heard of them?"

Everyone in the canal zone had heard of these immense shops to which the official alluded, for there a great amount of engineering work was undertaken. In such a colossal task as this building of a canal between Panama and Colon, between the Pacific and Atlantic Oceans, the reader will readily comprehend that an enormous number of locomotives, steam diggers, and machinery of every sort and description was in constant operation, and that, like machinery all the world over, such implements break down on occasion and require repair. The works at Gorgona coped with all such matters, and was staffed by such keen engineers that they even did not stop at repairs of whatever description. There, in those sheds, engines were constructed, from the smallest bolt down to the heaviest crank shaft, according to the designs produced at the drawing offices at Gorgona. The workers on the canal had long since discovered that special machines were often required to deal with the special jobs they had in progress. And clever heads at Gorgona invented means to satisfy them. Witness the ingenious rail layer, without which the task of delving would have been much delayed; witness that other clever arrangement which did in seven minutes the work of a hundred men, and swept the dirt clear from a whole line of earth wagons.

"You've heard of those shops 'way over at Gorgona?" asked the official again.

"I have," Jim admitted. "I'm longing to see them."

"Then you shall, I promise. But, see here, about this job. A good man deserves a proper place for his knowledge and his energies; down there, at Gorgona, we've just turned out a gasolene rock driller that'll knock the other steam-driven concerns into the shade. I'm looking for a man to run it, one used to gasolene motors. Say, if I apply for you, sir, will you take the work?"

Jim looked round the circle before he replied, and almost smiled at the expression he caught on Harry's face. The genial fellow who had given him a day's instruction in the working of a hundred-ton steam digger did not look best pleased; but that was to be put down to his own keenness, to the keenness which he inherited in common with every white man labouring on the canal. For in Harry's eyes it was the machine which he himself ran which was helping the progress of the canal; it was the enormous mouthfuls of dirt which his digger tore from the soil that placed the undertaking nearer completion. And every man he coached in the task was something approaching a traitor if he abandoned that particular machine for another. Then, of a sudden, his face took on another expression.

"You ain't got no cause to think of me, young 'un," he said pleasantly. "I don't deny as I'd have liked to see you running a digger, 'cos it's me as taught you; but, then, I don't forget that you've shown that you know one of these gasolene motors right away from the piston to the crank shaft. You close with the offer if you like it; there'll be more dollars in it, I reckon."

He addressed the last remark to the official, who nodded acquiescence.

"Special work, special pay," he replied curtly. "We want a man, and we must be prepared to spend dollars on him. I offer a dollar more than digger rates. What's the answer?"

"Of course he takes it!" burst in Phineas eagerly. "It ain't in human nature to refuse advancement, and of course Jim'll take that motor. Do you want him yet awhile?"

"In a couple of weeks perhaps. We're not quite ready."

"Then I accept, with many thanks," said Jim, his heart beating fast with pleasure at such rapid progress; for here was advancement, here was pay which made his own future and that of Sadie all the brighter. "In two weeks' time; and in the meanwhile perhaps you'll allow me to see the machine and get an idea of its construction."

"You can come along whenever you like and handle the concern. It'll knock spots out of those steam drills," declared the official.

"And now, as this here business interview seems to have come to an end, supposing we get to with a song," cried one of the audience. "Didn't I hear tell as you could play a banjo, Jim, and sing a tune when you was axed?"

"I've done so before; I can try," answered our hero, breathing more freely now that his ordeal was over. "I'll buy a banjo as soon as I can; then I'll let you see what I can do."

"You'll get right away in at it, siree," said the man severely, grinning at his comrades. "See here, there's a banjo I brought along with me from the States. Not that I can tune on it; I allow as I've tried, but, gee! the performance was enough to make a cat laugh. The boys passed a resolution axing me to give over at once, and fer that reason the instrument's been lying idle in my quarters this three months past. Get in at it, siree."

He produced a stained and somewhat battered instrument from behind his chair and passed it to Jim. Now Jim was by no means a poor instrumentalist, and in addition was one of those fortunate individuals gifted with a fair voice. Thousands of men have found before this that the power to sing and entertain their fellows is the key to popularity, and Jim was no exception. It had been his fortune to live as a rule amongst small communities, where any form of entertainment was appreciated, and none more than a song. It followed, therefore, that here again, as in the case of the gasolene motor, he had had experience, and seeing that his audience were determined to hear him, he settled down to the work without more ado. A fine young fellow he looked, too, seated in their midst, the banjo in correct position as he leant over it, touching the strings and tightening them till his keen ear was satisfied. Burnt a deep brown by the hot sun of those parts, his hair somewhat dishevelled, and his clothing by no means improved by the adventures through which he had passed, Jim had a rugged, healthy, out-of-doors appearance which was most attractive. That he was by no means a weakling was at once apparent, for he filled his clothing well, and presented a fine pair of broad shoulders. When he lifted his face and glanced round at his audience, smiling in his own serene, inimitable manner, there was not one who did not know in his heart that our hero was a stanch and jolly individual, free from side and that stupid conceit which spoils some young men of his age, but full of go and energy as became an American; ready when his work was done, and only then, to enjoy himself as much as possible and help to give enjoyment to others.

"See here," laughed Jim, looking round the circle of men, all of whom had their eyes on him, for there was no little curiosity to see how he would accomplish the task; "if I break down, you must forgive me, for, gee! it's like being in a cage with a whole crowd watching."

Down went the head over the banjo again, while his fingers played on the strings; and at once, by the notes which issued, it became apparent that here was no novice. Jim struck up a gay tune, and in a little while had given his audience the first verse of a jaunty song, to which there was an equally jaunty chorus; so that before the evening had passed the rafters above were ringing to the sound made by a hundred or more lusty voices.

"Fine, jest fine!" cried one of the men.

"Gee! If he don't take it!" shouted Harry.

"I'm shaking hands with myself," declared the official who had offered him a post at Gorgona. "You men down here needn't think that you're going to have young Partington all to yourselves. A fortnight to-day he'll be a Gorgona man, when we'll send you invitations to our concerts."

There was a shout at that, a shout denoting some displeasure. Phineas Barton rose from his chair, his fractured arm swathed and bandaged and slung before him, and regarded the official triumphantly. "Not a bit of it, siree," he said. "Jim's my lodger. Don't matter whether he works along here at Gatun or way over there at Culebra or Gorgona, he jest comes home every night of the week. The Commission's jest got to pass him a free ticket, and ef he's in a concert, why, guess it'll be here, and the folks at Gorgona will be the ones to be invited." There was a roar of laughter at the sally, and Jim was called upon for a second song. Modestly enough he gave it too; for such open praise as had been bestowed upon him is not always good for a lad of his age, and might well be expected to turn the heads of many. Our hero had his failings without doubt, and we should not be recording truly if we did not allow the fact, but a swelled head was not one of the ailments he was wont to suffer from. So far his friends and acquaintances had never known Jim Partington to be too big for the boots he stood up in.

"Which is jest one of the things that made me take to him right away from the first," said Phineas, when discussing the matter that same evening with the police officer who had been in command of the launch expedition. "He ain't bumptious, Major. He's jest a lively young fellow, full of sense and grit, and I tell you, if there's one lad here in the zone who's made up his mind to make a job of the canal, it's Jim. He's fixed it that he's going to rise in the world, and if nothing unforeseen happens we shall find him well up the ladder one of these days, and making a fine living."

They called Jim over to them, where they were seated at a small table in one corner, and at once the Major gripped our hero's hand, while he acknowledged that he felt wonderfully better. His head was heavily bandaged, for the bullet which had struck him had caused a nasty gash in the scalp.

"Not that it did any great harm," laughed the Major. "They tell me that there was tremendous swelling at first, but the blood which escaped from the wound brought that down wonderfully; but I admit that at first I felt that my head was as big as a pumpkin. How's your own wound?"

Jim had forgotten all about it, though on his arrival that morning he had taken the precaution to have it dressed. But it was already partially healed, and caused him not the slightest inconvenience.

"I think I had the best of the matter altogether," he answered, "for though up there on the river I was unable to distinguish the man who began all this business by firing at me, yet both were hit, and I fancy pretty badly."

"You can count them as almost wiped out completely," agreed the Major. "But I have serious news to give you regarding the other three. During our absence Jaime de Oteros and his comrades broke out of prison and made good their escape. The scoundrels are once more free to carry on any form of rascality. Of course I have sent trackers after them; but the latest news is that they have disappeared into the bush, and pursuit there is almost hopeless. I own I'm vexed, for there is never any knowing what such men may be up to. A Spaniard with a grudge to work off is always a dangerous individual."

The information of the escape of the prisoners was indeed of the most serious moment, and Jim and his friends were yet to learn the truth of the words that the Major had spoken. For Jaime de Oteros had indeed a grudge, and with all the unreasonableness of men of his violent disposition he had already determined in his own mind that our hero Jim was the cause of all his troubles. He brushed aside the fact that one of his ruffianly comrades had most deliberately attempted murder, and that the effort made to capture the offender was but a natural reprisal. That effort had led to the discovery of the gang and its break-up, and in Jaime's eyes our hero was the culprit. He swore as he lay in prison to take vengeance upon him, while he did not forget his animosity towards the police officials.

"I tell you," he cried fiercely, once he had contrived to break out of the prison, "I don't move away from these parts till I've killed that young pup, while as to these others, these Americans, I'll do them an injury, see if I don't. I'll wreck some of the work they're doing; break up the job they're so precious proud of."

Meanwhile Jim had many other things to think of, and very promptly forgot all about the miscreants. He sauntered back to the house with Phineas, and on the following morning boarded a motor-driven inspector's car running on the isthmian railway.

"We'll just kop along first to Gorgona," said Phineas. "And on the way we'll take a look at the valley of the Chagres River. You've got to understand that right here at Gatun, where we're building the dam, and where the river escapes between the hills which block this end of the valley, we shall have the end of the lake we're going to form. For the most part the valley is nice and broad, running pretty nigh north and south. This track we're on will be covered with water, so that gangs of men are already at work fixing the track elsewhere on higher ground. But I want to speak of this valley. It runs clear south to Obispo, where there is hilly ground dividing it from the valley of the Rio Grande, and there, at Culebra, which is on the hill, we're up against one of the biggest jobs of this undertaking. You see, it's like this: from Gatun to Obispo we follow a route running almost due south, with the Chagres River alongside us all the way; but at Obispo, which I ought to have said is just twenty-six miles from the head of Limon Bay, the Chagres River changes its course very abruptly, and if followed towards its source is found to be confined within a narrow valley through which it runs with greater speed, and in a north-easterly direction. Now, see here, to figure this matter out correctly let's stand up in this car. There's the track running way ahead of us through the Chagres valley in a direction I described as southerly, though to be correct it is south-westerly. Dead behind us is Limon Bay; right ahead is Panama. I've given you an idea of the works we're carrying out at this end—first dredging Limon Bay for 4-1/2 miles, then canal cutting for say another 4 miles. There you get three tiers of double locks, and the Gatun dam that's going to fill in the end of this valley, and give us a lake which will spread over an area of no fewer than 164 square miles, and which will fill the valley right away up to Obispo, where the Chagres River, coming from a higher elevation, will pour into it."

"And then," demanded Jim, beginning, now that he was actually in the valley, to obtain a better conception of the plan of this huge American undertaking. "I can see how you will bring your ships to the Gatun locks, and how you will float them into the lake. I take it that there will be water enough for them to steam up to Obispo. After that, you still have to reach Panama."

"Gee! I should say we had. But listen here. Taking this line, with Panama dead south-west of us, we come at Obispo to a point where the designers of the canal had two alternatives. The first was to cut up north-west, still following the Chagres valley where it has become very narrow, and so round by a devious route to Panama. That meant sharp bends in the canal, which ain't good when you've got big ships to deal with, and besides a probable increase in the cost and in the time required to complete the undertaking."

"And the second?" demanded Jim.

"The second alternative was to cut clear through the dividing ridge which runs up at Obispo some 300 feet above sea level. Following that route for 9 miles in the direction of Panama you come to the alluvial plain of the Rio Grande, and from thence to the sea in another 6 miles. Forty-one miles from shore to shore you can call it, and, with the dredging we have to do at either end, a grand total of 50 miles. But we'll leave this Culebra cutting till we reach it. Sonny, you can get right along with the car."

Jim would have been a very extraordinary mortal if he had not been vastly interested in all that he saw from his seat in the rail motor car. To begin with, it was a delightfully bright day, with a clear sky overhead and a warm sun suspended in it. Hills lay on either hand, their steep sides clothed with luxuriant verdure, while farther away was a dark background of jungle, that forbidding tropical growth with which he had now become familiar. On his right flowed the Chagres River, winding hither and thither, and receiving presently a tributary, the Rio Trinidad. Along the line there were gangs of men at work here and there laying the new tracks for the railway, while, when they had progressed on their journey, and were nearer Obispo, his keen eyes discovered other subjects for observation. There were a number of broken-down trucks beside the railway, which were almost covered by vegetation, while near at hand on the banks of the river a huge, unwieldy boat seemed to have taken root, and, like the trucks, was surrounded by tropical growth.

"Queer, ain't they?" remarked Phineas. "Guess you're wondering what they are."

"Reckon it's plant brought out here at the very beginning of this work, and scrapped because it was found to be unsatisfactory."

"Wrong," declared Phineas promptly. "Young man, those trucks were made by the Frenchmen. That boat is a dredger which was laid up before you were born, and was built by the same people."

The information caused our hero to open his eyes very wide, for he, like many another individual, had never heard of the French nation in connection with the isthmus of Panama; or if he had, had entirely forgotten the matter. But to a man like Phineas, with all his keenness in the work in which he was taking no unimportant part, it was not remarkable that French efforts on the isthmus were a matter of historical interest to him.

"A man likes to know the ins and outs of the whole affair," he observed slowly, as they trundled along on the car. "There's thousands, I should say, who don't even know why we have decided to build this canal, and thousands more who don't rightly guess what we're going to do with it when it's finished. But Columbus, when he discovered the Bay of Limon round about the year 1497, thought that he had found a short cut across to the East Indies. He didn't cotton to the fact that the isthmus stretches unbroken between the two Americas, and only came to believe that fact when his boats came to a dead end in the bay he had discovered. Cortés sought for a waterway at Mexico, while others hunted round for a channel along the River St. Lawrence, and all with the one idea of making a short passage to the East Indies.

"Then the Straits of Magellan were discovered, while some of those bold Spaniards clambered across the isthmus and set eyes upon the Pacific Ocean. You know what happened? Guess they built and launched ships at Panama, and the conquest of Peru was undertaken, and following it gold and jewels in plenty were brought by mule train from the Pacific to the Atlantic, across from Panama to Colon. So great was the traffic that even in the days of Charles V of Spain the question of an isthmian canal was mooted; for, recollect, Spain drew riches from the Indies as well as from Peru. And now we come to the nineteenth century. America badly wanted an isthmian crossing which would bring her western ports closer to those on the east, and vice versa. A railway seemed to be the only feasible method, and we tackled the job splendidly. That railway was completed in 1855, in spite of an awful climate, and guess it filled the purpose nicely. Just hereabouts came our war, North against South, and, as you can readily understand, there wasn't much chance of canal building.

"Now we come to the Frenchmen, to Ferdinand de Lesseps," said Phineas, pointing out another group of derelict trucks to our hero. "You want to bear in mind that the question of an isthmian canal was always in the air, always attracting the attention of engineering people. Well, de Lesseps had just completed the Suez Canal, connecting the east with the west, and guess he cast his eye round for new fields to conquer. He floated a company in France, and raised a large sum of money. Then he bought out the Isthmian Railway for twenty-five and a half million dollars. You see, he knew that a railway was wanted to carry his plant, and I guess that the fact of having that railway made him decide to build his canal across where we are working. But there was mismanagement. De Lesseps, like many another man, had been spoiled by success, and had lost his usual good judgment. His expenses were awful, and finally, when the money ran out, his company abandoned the undertaking. In eight years he had spent more than three times the amount for the Suez Canal, and had got through some three hundred million dollars. He and his staff left behind them the trucks you see, besides a large amount of other machinery. At this day there's many a French locomotive pulling our dirt trains right here in the Culebra cutting, while his folks set their mark on the soil. They, too, started to cut through at Culebra, and in those eight years did real honest work. But shortage of money ended their labours, and, as I've said, they've left behind these marks of their presence, with rows and rows of graves over at Ancon; for fever played fearful havoc with the workmen. Yes, it was that which gave America her warning, and set our medical folk at work to tidy up this zone and sweep it clear of mosquitoes and fever."

It was all very interesting, and Jim listened most attentively, though, to be sure, every now and then his mind was distracted for a brief instant by some new object to right or left of the line; while from the very beginning the desire to ask one question and to receive information in reply had been present.

"That tale of the French is new to me," he said, "and I hadn't the faintest idea that a canal had been previously attempted. You've said that Spain desired one by means of which to reach the East Indies and so save the long trip round by the Straits of Magellan; how does America stand when all's finished?"

The fingers of Phineas's only usable hand were clenched instantly. Was it likely that a man such as he, who had counted the cost of the undertaking, and knew something of its vastness, would not also have counted the gain?

"What do we get when all's ended?" he cried eagerly. "Guess for that you require a map by rights, though I can tell you something from memory. To begin with, take New York as our important eastern port, and San Francisco as that on the west coast. Of course I know that we have an inter-oceanic railway. But if goods in bulk were shipped, the boat would have to steam right away south, round by Cape Horn and the Straits of Magellan. The Oregon, one of our best battleships, was lying away up in the Pacific when our war with Spain began. She had to steam more than 13,000 miles to reach Key West, and guess a ship wants overhauling after such a long journey, putting aside the risks she ran of capture *en route*, owing to her isolation. Well now, this isthmian canal will knock the better part of 9000 miles off the route from New York to San Francisco. The English doing business with our firms in that port will have a journey less by 6000 miles, while New York will be closer to the ports of South America by a good 5000 miles. It'll be a shorter journey from Japan or Australia to New York than it is to-day to Liverpool, while there's scarcely a trip from east to west that won't be helped by this canal we're building. Just think of it, Jim! Where this trolley's running there'll be, one of these days, deep water, with bigger ships floating in it than you can dream of now. You and I will have helped to bring about that matter. When we're old we'll be able to tell the youngsters all about it; for America will know then that she owns something valuable. Her people will have had time to grasp its full significance, and guess then the question will not be, as now, 'Where is the Panama Canal? What are our folks doing?' but 'How was America's great triumph accomplished?' My! Ain't I been gassing? Why, there's Gorgona. Hollo, sonny! Pull her up."

They descended from the car promptly, and made for the huge sheds where one portion of the engineering staff undertook the upkeep of the machinery engaged along the whole line of the canal. The friendly official was waiting for them, and very soon Jim's eyes were bulging wide with delight at the sight of the motor drill he was to manage.

CHAPTER XIII

Hustle the Order of the Day

Never in the whole course of his short existence had Jim come upon such a busy scene as he encountered, when Phineas Barton at length contrived to drag the eager young fellow away from the engineering shops at Gorgona.

"My!" cried Phineas, simulating a snort of indignation; "I never did come across such a curious chap in all my born days. I began to think that you'd stick in the place, grow to it as the saying is. But there, I don't blame any youngster for liking a big works same as this. There's so much to see, huge lathes and planing machines running and doing their work as if they were alive and thinking things out. Steam-hammers thudding down on masses of red-hot metal, giving a blow that would crack a house and smash it to pieces, or one that would as easily fracture a nut. Then there are the furnaces and the foundry: guess all that's interesting. But you've got more to see; it's time we made way up for Culebra. Look here, boy, set her going, and mind you watch the spoil trains."

The precaution and the warning were necessary, for the double track of the Panama railway at this point was much occupied by the long trains of cars filled with earth coming from the trench that was being cut through the high ground just ahead. It was not until they actually reached the neighbourhood of Culebra, which may be said to occupy a place in the centre of the gigantic cut, that Jim gathered a full impression of the work, or the reason for so many freight cars. But it was true enough that the driver of the motor truck had to keep his wits about him to escape collision; for every three minutes a spoil train came along, dragged perhaps by a locomotive made at Gorgona, or by one imported by the French, and of Belgian manufacture. Every three minutes, on the average, a train came puffing down the incline from Culebra, and nothing was allowed to delay it. In consequence, the motor inspection car on which Phineas and his young friend were journeying was compelled at times to beat a hasty retreat, or to go ahead at full power before an advancing empty train—returning from the great dam at Gatun, where it had deposited its load—till it arrived at a point where a switch was located. There was nearly always a man there, and promptly the car was sidetracked.

"It's the only way to do the business," explained Phineas. "The getting away of those spoil trains means the success of our working. If they don't get clear, so as to be back at the earliest moment, there's going to be any number of steam diggers thrown out of work; for it's no use shovelling dirt if there aren't cars to load the stuff in. If there's a breakdown with one of the cars, guess the whole labour force is pushed on to it, so as to get the lines clear. Telephone wires run up and down the line, and a breakdown is at once reported. But we're just entering the cut, and in a little while you'll be able to see and understand everything."

To be accurate, it took our hero quite a little while to grasp the significance of all that he saw, for the Culebra cut extends through nine miles of rocky soil, and at the period of his inspection it had already bitten deep into the hilly ground which barred the onward progress of the canal at Obispo. One ought to say, in an endeavour to give facts accurately, that this mass of material forms the southern boundary of the huge Chagres valley which, when the works are completed, will be flooded with water. It bars all exit there, though by turning sharply to the left one may follow the course of the river through a narrow, ascending valley. However, the scheme of the undertaking required that there should be no sharp bends, and in consequence the host of workers were toiling to cut a gigantic trench, of great width and enormous depth, right through this hilly ground. What Jim saw was somewhat similar to the works below Gatun, at the Color end of the canal, but vastly magnified. There were the same terraces, with tracks of rails laid, bearing an endless procession of spoil trains and numbers of steam diggers. There was the same pilot cut in the very centre, from which the terraces ascended step by step, as if they were portions of another Egyptian pyramid. But there comparisons ceased. This huge ditch extended for nine miles, and throughout its length presented an army of toilers, any number of dirt trains, and a constant succession of white steam billows, at various elevations, pointing to the places where the hundred-ton diggers were at work.

"You have to get right on the spot to see what's happening," said Phineas, looking proudly about him. "You can see for yourself now that it means everything to us to get rid of the dirt as quickly as possible, and everything to have spare trains ready to fill the place of those taking the spoil away. This concern is simply a question of dirt, and of how rapidly we can shift it. If I was the President of the Republic of the United States himself I should have to look lively all the same, and dodge about so as not to get in the way of the dirt trains. But we'll get out here and climb; I'll show you a thing or two."

He chuckled at the prospect before him, for to expatiate on the canal works to a keen young fellow, such as Jim undoubtedly was, was the height of enjoyment to the energetic official. Their car was switched on to a side track at once, and, descending from it, the two clambered up the scarped side of the trench till they were on the summit of the rocky ground. Then it was possible to obtain a bird's-eye view of the whole cut, and to appreciate its vastness. Jim noticed that the path he had clambered by shelved rather gently, while elsewhere the bank of the trench was steeply scarped, and at once drew Phineas's attention to the matter.

"You don't miss much, siree," came the answer. "We've come face up against more than one tough job 'way up here at Culebra, and the question of the slope of our banks is one. You see, this trench will be mighty deep, and if we were to cut the sides perpendicular they would soon fall in. Most of the stuff's rock, of course, but it's queer rock at that. It's soft, weathers quickly, and becomes easily friable when water has got to it. So we've had to spread the banks wide, and make the slope easy, except where the rock's harder and allows a steeper slope. Now, guess we're near about the centre of the cut. You've seen what's happening to the north. Dirt trains run down the incline, enter the tracks of the Panama Railway, and run 26 miles to the dam at Gatun. South of us the tracks fall to the plain of the Rio Grande, and the spoil trains run down and dump their stuff on either side of the line the canal will take. You've got to remember that this trench is 'way up above tide level; so at the end of the cut, at Pedro Miguel, there is to be a lock, or, rather, a double lock—one for a vessel going north and one for a ship coming south. A matter of a mile farther along there is another lock—the Milaflores lock—double, like the last, but with two tiers. It will let our ships down into the Pacific. But you've got to remember that there is a tide in that ocean, so the lift of the Milaflores lower lock will be variable. Now, lad, come and see the rock drills."

They descended into the bottom of the trench again, Phineas explaining that when it was completed there would be a bottom width of 200 feet, ample to allow the passing of two enormous ships.

"Guess it's the narrowest part of the canal," he said, "though nó one would call it narrow; but it's through hard rock, which is some excuse, and then this narrowest part happens to be dead straight. North of us the cut widens at the bottom to 300 feet, while elsewhere, outside the cut, the minimum width is 500 feet. You've got to bear in mind that I'm talking of bottom widths. Recollect that the banks slope outwards fairly gently, and you can appreciate the fact that the surface width of the canal stream will make a stranger open his eyes. Ah, here's a drill! This is the sort of thing you'll be doing."

To the novice the machine to which Phineas had drawn attention was indeed somewhat curious. It looked for all the world like an overgrown motor car, constructed by an amateur engineer in his own workshop, and out of any parts he happened to have by him; for it ran on four iron wheels with flat tyres, and bore at the back the conventional boiler and smokestack. In front it carried a post, erected to some height, and stayed with two stout metal rods from the rear. The remainder of the machine consisted of the engine and driving gear which operated the drills.

"It'll get through solid rock at a pace that will make you stare," declared Phineas, "though our friend at Gorgona believes that this new model that you're to run will do even better. But you can see what happens; these drills get to work where the diggers will follow. They drill right down, 30 feet perhaps, and then get along to another site. The powder men then come along, put their shot in position, place their fuse, wire it so that a current can be sent along to the fuse, and then get along to another drill hole. At sunset, when all the men have cleared, the shots are fired, and next morning there's loose dirt enough to keep the diggers busy. Guess you'll be put to work with one of these drillers, so as to learn a bit. You can't expect to handle a machine unless you know what's required of you."

The following morning, in fact, found our hero dressed in his working clothes, assisting a man in the management of one of the rock drills. He had risen at the first streak of dawn, and after breakfasting, had clambered aboard an empty dirt train making for Culebra.

"Yer know how to fire a furnace?" asked the man who was to instruct him. "Ay, that's good; I heard tell as I wasn't to have no greenhorn. Ain't you a pal o' Harry's?"

There might have been only one Harry amidst the huge army of white employees; but Jim knew who was meant, and nodded promptly.

"And you're the chap as went off into the swamps, across a lagoon, along with the Police Major, ain't you?"

"Yes," responded our hero shortly.

"Huh! You and I is going to be pals. Harry's been blabbing. You don't happen to have brought that 'ere banjo along with you?"

Jim had not, but promised to do so if this new friend liked.

"Why, in course we like," cried Hundley, for that was the man's name. "Seems that you're to live 'way down there at Gatun, so the boys along over there will get you of an evening; but you'll feed with us midday. I tell you, Jim, there's times when a man feels dull out here, particularly if he's had a go of fever, same as I have. It takes the life out of a fellow, and ef he ain't brightened he gets to moping. That's why I'm precious keen on music; a song soothes a man. There's heaps like me up at the club; jest steady, quiet workers, sticking like wax to the job, 'cos the most of us can't settle to pack and leave till we've seen the canal completed."

There it was again! Right along the fifty miles of works Jim had come across the same expressions. It mattered not whether a man drove a steam digger or a dirt train, whether he were official or labouring employee, if he were American, as all were, the canal seemed to have driven itself into his brain; the undertaking had become a pet child, a work to be accomplished whatever happened, an exacting friend not to be cast aside or deserted till all was ended and a triumph accomplished. But Jim had heard the request, and promptly acceded.

"I'll bring the banjo along one of these days right enough," he smiled. "Perhaps you'll make a trip down to Gatun and hear one of our concerts. They tell me there's to be one within a few days."

Hundley eagerly accepted the invitation, and then proceeded to instruct our hero. As to the latter, he found no great difficulty in understanding the work, and, indeed, in taking charge of the machine. For here it was not quite as it was with a hundred-ton digger, when the lip of the huge shovel might in some unexpected moment cut its way beneath a mass of rock, and be brought up short with a jerk capable of doing great damage. The rock drill, on the other hand, pounded away, the engine revolving the drill, while the crew of the machine saw that the gears were thrown out when necessary, and an extra length added to the drill. If the hardened-steel point of the instrument happened to catch—as was sometimes the case—and held up the engine, then steam had to be cut off quickly, the drill reversed and lifted, so as to allow it to begin afresh.

"You never know what's goin' to happen," explained Hundley; "but most times things is clear and straightforward. You lengthen the drill till you've run down about 30 feet: that means eight hours' solid work—a day's full work, Jim. You don't see the real result till the next morning; but my, how those dynamite shots do rip the place about! For instance, jest here where we're sinkin' the drill we're yards from the edge of the step we're working on. Well now, that shot'll be rammed home, and the hole plugged over it. Something's got to go when dynamite is exploded, and sense there's all this weight of stuff to the outside of the terrace, and the shot is 30 feet deep, the outer lip gives way, and jest this boring results in tons of rock and dirt being broken adrift. It's when you see the huge mass of loose stuff next morning that you realize that you ain't been doin' nothin'."

At the end of a week Jim was placed in entire charge of a rock drill, while a negro was allocated to the machine to help him. Then, somewhat later than the official had intimated, the motor driller was completed, and our hero was drafted to the Gorgona works for some days, to practise with the implement and get thoroughly accustomed to it. It was a proud day when he occupied the driving seat, threw out his clutch, and set the gears in mesh. Then, the engine buzzing swiftly, and a light cloud of steam coming from the nozzle of the radiator—for, like all rapidly moving motor engines designed for stationary work, the water quickly heated—he set the whole affair in motion, and trundled along the highroad towards the cut.

"If you don't make a tale of this machine I shall be surprised," said the official, as he bade him farewell. "This motor should get through the rock very quickly, quicker a great deal than the steam-driven ones. But go steady along the road; steering ain't so easy."

Easy or not, Jim managed his steed with skill, and soon had the affair on one of the terraces. He had already had a certain part allotted to him, and within an hour of his departure from the works had set his first drill in position. Nor was it long before he realized that the desire of the staff at Gorgona was to be more than realized; for the drill bit its path into the rock swiftly, more so than in the case of the slower revolving steam drills, while there were fewer sudden stops. That first day he accomplished two bore holes, giving four hours to each operation. His cheeks were flushed with pleasure when he reported progress to the official.

"And the engine?" asked the latter. "She ran well?"

"Couldn't have gone better," declared Jim. "She gives off ample power, and there is plenty of water for cooling. That machine easily saves the extra dollar wages you offered."

"And will pay us handsomely to repeat it, for then there will be more dirt for the diggers to deal with, and the more there is the sooner the cut will be finished. We can always manage to get extra diggers."

That the innovation was a success was soon apparent to all, and many a time did officials come from the far end of the canal works to watch Jim at work, and to marvel at the swiftness with which his machine opened a way through the rock. It was three months later before anything happened to disturb our hero, and during all that time he continued at his work, coming from Gatun in the early hours, usually aboard an empty spoil train, but sometimes by means of one of the many motor trolley cars which were placed at the disposal of inspectors. At the dinner hour he went off to one of the Commission hotels, and there had a meal, and often enough sang for the men to the banjo which he had since purchased. When the whistles blew at sundown he pulled on his jacket, placed a mackintosh over his shoulders if it happened to be raining, which was frequently the case, and sought for a conveyance back to Gatun. And often enough these return journeys were made on the engine hauling a loaded spoil trail.

As for Tom and Sam, the two negroes had received posts at the very beginning, the little negro working with the sanitary corps and the huge Tom being made into a black policeman.

"He's got a way with the darkies," explained Phineas, when announcing the appointment, "and I've noticed that they're mighty civil to him. You see, the majority of our coloured gentry come from the West Indies, and, though they are likely enough boys, they are not quite so bright, I think, as are the negroes from the States. Anyway, Tom has a way with them, and don't stand any sauce; while, when things are all right, he's ready to pass the time of day with all, and throw 'em a smile. Gee, how he does laugh! I never saw a negro with a bigger smile, nor a merrier."

It may be wondered what had happened to the worthy and patient Ching. The Chinaman was far too good a cook to have his talents wasted in the canal zone, and from the very beginning was installed in that capacity at Phineas Barton's quarters, thus relieving the lady who had formerly done the work. The change, indeed, was all for the best, for now Sadie received more attention.

Three months almost to a day from the date when Jim had begun to run the motor drill the machinery got out of order.

"One of the big ends of a piston flew off," he reported to the official, when the latter arrived. "Before I could stop her running the piston rod had banged a hole through the crank case, and I rather expect it has damaged the crank shaft."

It was an unavoidable accident, and meant that the machine must undergo repair.

"You'll have to be posted to another job meanwhile, Jim," said the official. "Of course I know that this is none of your doing. We shall be able to see exactly what was the cause of the accident to that piston rod when we've taken the engine down. Perhaps one of the big end bolts sheered. Or there may have been a little carelessness when erecting, and a cotter pin omitted. But I don't think that: my staff is too careful to make errors of that sort. How'd you like to run one of the inspection motor trolleys? They were asking me for a man this morning; for one of the drivers is down with fever. You'd be able to take on the work at once, since you understand motors. Of course there isn't any timetable to follow. You just run up and down as you're wanted, and all you've got to learn really is where the switches and points are; so as to be able to sidetrack the car out of the way of the dirt trains."

So long as it was work in connection with machinery Jim was bound to be pleased, and accepted the work willingly. The next day he boarded the inspection car at Gatun, and within half an hour had made himself familiar with the levers and other parts. Then he was telephoned for to a spot near Gorgona, and ran the car along the rails at a smart pace. Twice on the way there he had to stop, reverse his car, and run back to a siding, there to wait on an idle track till a dirt train had passed.

"You'll get to know most every switch in a couple of days," said the negro who was in charge of this particular point, "and sometimes yo'll be mighty glad that you did come to know 'em. Them spoil trains don't always give too much time, particularly when there's a big load and they're coming down the incline from way up by Culebra."

The truth of the statement was brought to our hero's mind very swiftly; for on the following morning, having run out on the tracks ahead of an empty spoil train, and passed a passenger train at one of the stations, he was slowly running up the incline into the Culebra cut when he heard a commotion in front of him. At once he brought his car to a standstill beside one of the points.

"Specks there's been a breakdown, or something of that sort," said the man in charge, coming to the side of the car. "The track's clear enough, but I guess there'll be a dirt train along most any minute. Are you for runnin' in over the points out of the way?"

At that moment Jim caught sight of something coming towards him. Suddenly there appeared over the brow of the incline the rear end of a dirt train, and a glance told him that it was loaded. A man was racing along beside one of the cars, somewhere about the centre of the train, and was endeavouring to brake the wheels with a stout piece of timber. Jim saw the timber suddenly flicked to one side, the man was thrown heavily, then, to his horror, there appeared a whole length of loaded cars racing down towards him, with nothing to stop the mad rush, not even an engine.

"Gee, she's broken away from the loco!" shouted the man at the points. "She's runnin' fast now, but in a while she'll be fair racing. Time she gets here, which'll be within the minute, she'll be doing sixty miles an hour. She'll run clear way down to Gatun. Come right in over the points."

He ran to open the switch, so that Jim could reach safety, while our hero accelerated his engine in preparation for the movement. Then a sudden thought came to his mind. He recollected the passenger train which was coming on behind him.

"Man," he shouted, "there's a passenger coming 'way behind us! The cars were filled with people when I passed. She's ahead of the dirt trains, and of course does not expect to have a full spoil train running down on this line. She'll be smashed into a jelly."

"So'll you if you don't come right in," cried the man, waving to Jim frantically.

But he had a lad of pluck to deal with. Jim realized that between himself and the oncoming passenger train, now some six miles away perhaps, there lay a margin of safety for himself, if only he could run fast enough before the derelict spoil train racing towards him. But that margin might allow him to warn the driver of the passenger train. He took the risk instantly, shouted to the pointsman, and began to back his car. Fortunately it was one of those in which the reverse gear applied to all speeds, and, since there was no steering to be done, he was able to proceed at a furious pace.

"Get to the telephone," he bellowed to the man as he went away. "Warn them down the line."

Then began an exciting race between his car and the spoil train; for the latter was composed of many long, heavy trucks, all laden to the brim with rock debris, consequently the smallest incline was sufficient to set them in motion if not properly braked. Now, when the whole line had broken adrift from its engine, and had run on to the Culebra incline, the weight told every instant. The pace soon became appalling, the trucks bounding and scrunching along the tracks, shaking violently, throwing their contents on either side, threatening to upset at every curve, gained upon Jim's car at every second.

"I'll have to jump if I can't get clear ahead," he told himself. "But if I can only keep my distance for a while the incline soon lessens, when the pace of the runaway will get slower. But that man was right; she's coasting so fast, and has so much weight aboard, that the impetus will take her best part of the way to Gatun."

Once more it was necessary for Jim to do as he had done aboard the motor launch. His ignition and throttle levers were pushed to the farthest notch. He was getting every ounce of power out of his car, desperately striving to keep ahead. But still the train gained. They came to a curve, our hero leading the runaway by some fifty yards, and both running on the tracks at terrific speed. Suddenly the inside wheels of the inspection car lifted. Jim felt she was about to turn turtle and promptly threw himself on to the edge of the car, endeavouring to weigh her down. Over canted the car till it seemed that she must capsize. Jim gave a jerk with all his strength, and slowly she settled down on to her inside wheels again, clattering and jangling on the iron track as she did so. Then he glanced back at the dirt train racing so madly after him.

"She'll be over," he thought. "She'll never manage to get round that bend at such a pace."

But weight steadies a freight car, and on this occasion the leading trucks at least managed to negotiate the curve without sustaining damage. The long train, looking like a black, vindictive snake, swung round the bend, with terrific velocity, and came on after him relentlessly. Then, as the last truck but one reached the bend, there was a sudden commotion. The dirt it contained heaved spasmodically and splashed up over the side; it seemed to rise up at the after end in a huge heap, and was followed by the tail of the truck. The whole thing canted up on its head, then swayed outwards, and, turning on its side, crashed on to the track running along beside it. There was a roar, a medley of sounds, while the actual site of the upset was obscured by a huge cloud of dust.

"That'll do it," thought our hero. "If we have any luck, that upsetting truck will pull the rest of the cars off the road, and bring the whole train to a standstill."

But he was counting his chickens before they were hatched. The cloud of dust blew aside swiftly, and, when he was able to see again, there was the line of cars, nearer by now, leaping madly along, trailing behind them the broken end of the one which had overturned. Right behind, the other portion, together with the greater portion of the last truck of all, was heaped in a confused mass on the second track of rails, disclosing its underframe and its two sets of bogie wheels to the sky.

"That passenger train must be only a couple of miles from us now," said Jim, as he desperately jerked at his levers, in the endeavour to force his car more swiftly along the track. "If I can keep ahead for half that distance I shall manage something, for then the incline lessens. Just here she's going faster if anything. If only I could send this car along quicker!"

He gazed anxiously over his shoulder, in the direction in which he was flying, and was relieved to discover that the rails were clear. Then he took a careful look at the line of cars bounding after him. There was no doubt that the train was nearer. The leading car was within two hundred yards of him, and a minute's inspection told him clearly that the distance between them was lessening very rapidly; for the runaway now seemed to have taken the bit between her teeth with a vengeance. Despite the weight of earth and rock in the cars they were swaying and leaping horribly, causing their springs to oscillate as they had, perhaps, never done before. The wheels on the leading bogie seemed to be as much off the iron tracks as on them, and at every little curve the expanse of daylight on the inner side beneath the trucks increased in proportions, showing how centrifugal force was pulling the heavy mass and endeavouring to upset it. It was an uncanny sight, but yet, for all that, a fascinating one. Jim watched it helplessly, almost spellbound, conscious that the few moments now before him were critical ones. He unconsciously set to work to calculate how long it would take, at the present rate of comparative progression of his own car and the runaway train, for the inevitable collision to occur. Then, seeing the heaving bogies of the trucks, he leaned over the side of his own car and watched the metal wheels. They clattered and thundered on the rails, the spokes were indistinguishable, having the appearance of disks. But at the bends this was altered. The car tipped bodily, the inner wheels left the tracks, and at once their momentum lessened. Then, though he could not see the individual spokes, the disk-like appearance was broken, telling him plainly, even if his eyes had not been sufficiently keen to actually see the fact, that the wheels and the track had parted company.

"Ah!" It was almost a groan that escaped him. In the few minutes in which he had been engaged in examining his own wheels the runaway train had gained on him by leaps and bounds. He could now hear the roar of its wheels above the rumble and clatter of his own, that and the buzz of the motor so busy beneath the bonnet. He cast his eye on either side, as if to seek safety there, and watched the fleeting banks of the Chagres River, bushes and trees, and abandoned French trucks speeding past. A gang of workmen came into view, and he caught just a glimpse of them waving their shovels. Their shouts came to his ears as the merest echoes. Then something else forced itself upon his attention. It was the figure of a white man, standing prominent upon a little knoll beside the rails, and armed with a megaphone. He had the instrument to his mouth, and thundered his warning in Jim's ears.

"Jump!" he shouted. "Jump! She'll be up within a jiffy!"

Within a jiffy! In almost less time than that; there were but two yards now between the small inspection car and the line of loaded trucks. Jim could see the individual pieces of broken rock amongst the dirt, could watch the fantastic manner in which they were dancing. He looked about him, standing up and gripping the side of the car. Then away in front, along the clear tracks. He thought of the passenger train, and remembered that he alone stood between it and destruction.

"I'll stick to this ship whatever happens," he told himself stubbornly. "If the train strikes me and breaks up the car, the wreck may throw it off the rails. Better that than allow it to run clear on into the passenger train. Ah! Here it is."

Crash! The buffers of the leading truck struck the motor inspection car on her leading spring dumb irons, and the buffet sent her hurtling along the track, while the shock of the blow caused Jim to double up over the splashboard. But the wheels did not leave the tracks. Nothing seemed to have been broken. The dumb irons were bent out of shape, that was all.

"Jump, yer fool!" came floating across the air to Jim's ear, while the figure of the man with the megaphone danced fantastically, arms waving violently in all directions.

But Jim would not jump; he had long since made up his mind to stick to his gun, to remain in this car whatever happened; for the safety of the passenger train depended on him. True, a telephone message might have reached the driver; but then it might not have done so. He recollected that at the switch where this mad chase had first begun there was no telephone station closely adjacent. It would be necessary for the man there to run to the nearest one. That would take time, while his own flight down the tracks had endured for only a few minutes, though, to speak the truth, those minutes felt like hours to our hero.

Bang! The cars struck him again, causing the one on which he rode to wobble and swerve horribly; the wheels roared and flashed sparks as the flanges bit at the rails. The bonnet that covered the engine, crinkled up like a concertina; but the car held the track. Jim was still secure, while the second buffet had sent him well ahead. Better than all, he realized that he was now beyond the steeper part of the incline, while his engine was still pulling, urging the car backward. If only he could increase the pace, if only he could add to the distance which separated him from that long line of trucks bounding after him so ruthlessly. Then a groan escaped him; for along the Chagres valley, where, perhaps, in the year 1915 a huge lake will have blotted out the site of the railway along which he flew, and where fleets of huge ships may well be lying, there came the distinct, shrill screech of a whistle. Jim swung round in an agony of terror. He looked along the winding track and his eyes lit upon an object. It was the passenger train, loaded with human freight, standing in the way of destruction.

CHAPTER XIV

The Runaway Spoil Train

Barely a mile of the double track of the Panama railway stretched between the inspection car, on which Jim was racing for his life, and the oncoming passenger train. Glancing over his shoulder he could see the smoke billowing from the locomotive and the escape steam blowing out between her leading wheels. Behind him there was the scrunch, the grinding roar, of the long line of steel wheels carrying the runaway spoil train. He kneeled on his driving seat and looked first one way and then the other, hesitating what to do. The rush of air, as he tore along, sent his broad-brimmed hat flying, and set his hair streaking out behind him. His eyes were prominent, there was desperation written on his face; but never once did he think of taking the advice which the megaphone man flung at him.

"Jump for it! No! I won't!" he declared stubbornly to himself. "I'll stick here till there's no chance left; then I'll bring this machine up sharp, and leave her as a buffer between the spoil train and the one bearing passengers. Not that she'll be of much use. That heavy line of cars will punch her out of the way as if she were as light as a bag; but something might happen. The frame of this car might lift the leading wheels of the spoil train from the tracks and wreck her."

There was an exhaust whistle attached to his car, and he set it sounding at once, though all the time his eyes drifted from passenger train to spoil train, from one side of the track to the other. Suddenly there came into view round a gentle bend a mass of discarded machinery. He remembered calling Phineas's attention to it some weeks before. Broken trucks, which had once conveyed dirt from the cut at Culebra for the French workers, had been run from the main track on to a siding and abandoned there to the weather, and to the advance of tropical vegetation, that, in a sinister, creeping manner all its own, stole upon all neglected things and places in this canal zone, and wrapped them in its clinging embrace, covering and hiding them from sight, as if ashamed of the work which man had once accomplished. Jim remembered the spot, and that it was one of the unattended switching stations rarely used—for here the tracks of the railway were less encumbered with spoil trains—yet a post for all that where the driver of an inspection car might halt, might descend and pull over the lever, and so direct his car into the siding.

"I'll do it," he told himself. "If only I can get there soon enough to allow me to reach the lever."

He measured the distance between himself and the pursuing spoil train, and noted that it had increased. His lusty little engine, rattling away beneath its crumpled bonnet, was pulling the car along at a fine pace. True, the velocity was not so great as it had been when descending the first part of the incline, that leading out of the Culebra cut; but then the swift rush of the spoil train was also lessened. The want of fall in the rails was telling on her progress, though, to be sure, she was hurtling along at a speed approximating to fifty miles an hour; but the bump she had given to Jim's car had had a wonderful effect. It had shot the light framework forward, and, with luck, Jim determined to increase the start thus obtained.

"But it'll be touch and go," he told himself, his eye now directed to the switching station, just beyond which the mass of derelict French cars lay. "There's one thing in my favour: the points open from this direction. If it had been otherwise I could have done nothing, for, even if I had attempted to throw the point against the spoil train, the pace she is making would carry her across the gap. Why don't that fellow on the passenger engine shut off steam and reverse? Ain't he seen what's happening?"

He scowled in the direction of the approaching passenger train, and knelt still higher, shaking his fists in that direction. It seemed that the man must be blind, that his attention must be in another direction; for already the line of coaches was within five hundred yards of the points which had attracted Jim's attention, and he realized that she would reach the spot almost as soon as the spoil train would.

"'Cos she's closer," he growled. "If he don't shut off steam, anything I may be able to do will be useless. He'll cross the switch and come head on to the collision."

A minute later he saw a man's figure swing out from the cab of the locomotive on which his eyes were glued, while a hand was waved in his direction. Then a jet of steam and smoke burst from the funnel, while white clouds billowed from the neighbourhood of the cylinders. Even though it was broad daylight, Jim saw sparks and flashes as the wheels of the locomotive were locked and skated along the rails.

"He's seen it; he knows!" he shouted. "But he ain't got time to stop her and reverse away from this spoil train. If that switch don't work there's bound to be a bad collision."

There was no doubt as to that point. The driver and fireman aboard the locomotive recognized their danger promptly, and, like the bold fellows they were, stuck to their posts.

"Brakes hard!" shouted the former, jerking his steam lever over, and bringing the other hand down on that which commanded the reverse. "Hard, man! As hard as you can fix 'em! Be ready to put 'em off the moment she's come to a standstill. This is going to be a case with us, I reckon. That spoil train's doing fifty miles an hour if she's doing one. We can't get clear away from her, onless——"

He blew his whistle frantically, and once more leaned out far from his cab, waving to the solitary figure aboard the flying inspection car.

"Onless what?" demanded the fireman brusquely, his eyes showing prominently in his blackened face, his breath coming fast after his efforts; for both hand and vacuum brakes had been applied.

"Onless that 'ere fellow aboard the inspection car manages to reach the points in time and switch 'em over. Guess he's tryin' for it; but there ain't much space between him and the spoil train. There's goin' ter be an almighty smash."

Thus it appeared to all; for by now men, invisible before, had appeared at different points, and were surveying the scene, holding their breath at the thought of what was about to happen.

"Best get along to the telephone and send 'way up to Gorgona for the ambulance staff," said one of these onlookers. "That 'ere passenger train ain't got a chance of gettin' clear away. She ain't got the room nor the time. Fust the spoil train'll run clear over the inspection car, and grind it and the chap aboard to powder. Then she'll barge into the passenger, and, shucks! there'll be an unholy upset. Get to the telephone, do yer hear!"

He shouted angrily at his comrade, overwrought by excitement, and then set off to run towards the points for which Jim was making. As for the latter, by strenuous efforts, by jagging at his levers, he had contrived to get his engine to run a little faster, and had undoubtedly increased his lead over the spoil train. He was now, perhaps, a long hundred yards in advance.

"Not enough," he told himself. "Going at this pace it'll take time to stop, though the brakes aboard this car are splendid. I know what I'll do. Keep her running till I'm within fifty yards, then throw her out of gear, jam on the brakes, and jump for it just opposite the switch. I'll perhaps be able to roll up to it in time to pull that train over."

It was the only method to employ, without doubt, though the risk would not be light. For, while a motor car on good hard ground can be brought to a standstill within fifty yards when going at a great pace, when shod with steel wheels and running on a metal track the results are different. Jim's steed lacked weight for the work. Though he might lock his wheels, they would skate along the tracks, and reduce his pace slowly. The leap he contemplated must be made from a rapidly moving car. That might result in disaster.

"Better a smash like that than have people aboard the train killed by the dozen," he told himself. "Those points are two hundred yards off; in a hundred I set to at it."

He cast a swift glance towards the passenger train, which was now retreating, and then one at the spoil train. He measured the distance between himself and the latter nicely. Then he dropped his toe on the clutch pedal, and his hand on the speed lever. Click! Out shot the gears, while the engine raced and roared away as if it were possessed. But Jim paid no attention to it. He let it continue racing, and at once jammed on his brakes. It made his heart rise into his mouth when he noticed with what suddenness the spoil train had recovered the interval between them. She was advancing upon him with leaps and bounds. It seemed as if he were not moving. With an effort he took his eyes from the rushing trucks, and fixed them upon the points he hoped to be able to operate. They were close at hand. His glance was caught by the operating lever. The moment for action had arrived, while still his car progressed at a pace which would have made the boldest hesitate to leap from it. But Jim made no pause, more honour to him. He left his seat, placed one hand on the side of the car, and vaulted into space. The ground at the side of the track struck the soles of his feet as if with a hammer, doubling his knees up and jerking his frame forward. The impetus which the moving car had imparted to his body sent him rolling forward. He curled up like a rabbit struck by the sportsman at full pace, and rolled over and over. Then with a violent effort he arrested his forward movement. With hands torn, and every portion of his body jarred and shaken, he brought his mad onward rush to a standstill, and, recovering from the giddiness which had assailed him, found that he was close to the all-important lever governing the points. With a shout Jim threw himself upon it, tugged with all his might, and jerked the points over.

"JIM TUGGED WITH ALL HIS MIGHT"

Meanwhile the thunder of the spoil train had grown louder. The scrunch of steel tyres on the rails, and the grinding of the flanges of the wheels against the edges of the track drowned every other sound, even the singing which Jim's tumble had brought to his ears. The runaway, with all its impetus and weight rushing forward to destroy all that happened to be in its path, was within a yard of the points when our hero threw his weight on the lever. The leading wheels struck the points with violence, and Jim, watching eagerly, saw the rims mount up over the crossway. Then the bogie frame jerked and swung to the right, while the four wheels obeyed the direction of the points and ran towards the side track. But it was when the first half of the leading car had passed the points that the commotion came. The dead weight of the contents—projected a moment earlier directly forward—were of a sudden wrenched to one side. The strain was tremendous. Something was bound to give way under it, or the car would capsize.

As it happened, the wreck was brought about by a combination of movements. The front bogie of the truck collapsed, the wheels being torn from their axles. At the same moment the huge mass capsized, flinging its load of rock and dirt broadcast across the track. The noise was simply deafening, while a huge dust cloud obscured the actual scene of the upset from those who were looking on. But Jim could see. As he clung to the lever he watched the first truck come to grief in an instant. After that he himself was overwhelmed in the catastrophe; for the remaining trucks piled themselves up on the stricken leader. The second broke its coupling and mounted on the first; while the third, deflected to one side, shot past Jim as if it were some gigantic dart, and swept him and the lever away into space. The remainder smashed themselves into matchwood, all save five in rear, which, with retarded impetus, found only a bank of fallen dirt and rock that broke the collision and left them shaking on the track. When the onlookers raced to the spot, and the people aboard the passenger train joined them, there was not a sight of the young fellow who had controlled the inspection car and had saved a disastrous collision.

"Guess he's buried ten feet deep beneath all that dirt and stuff," said one of the men, gazing at the ruin. "I seed him run to the lever. Run, did I say? He jest rolled, that's what he did. He war just in time, though, and then, gee! there war a ruction. I've seen a bust-up on a railway afore, but bless me if this wasn't the wildest I ever seed. Did yer get to the telephone?"

His comrade reassured him promptly.

"I rung 'em up at Gorgona," he answered. "There's a dirt train coming along with the ambulance and Commission doctor aboard, besides a wrecking derrick. That young chap saved a heap of lives you'd reckon?"

It was in the nature of a question, and the answer came from the first speaker speedily.

"Lives! a full trainload, man. I seed his game from the beginning, and guess it war the only manœuvre that was worth trying. It was a race for the points, and the man aboard the inspection car won by a short head. He hadn't more'n a second or two to spare once he got a grip of the lever; but I reckon he's paid his own life for the work. He war a plucked 'un—a right down real plucked 'un!"

He stared fiercely into the eyes of the other man, as if he challenged him to deny the statement; but there were none who had seen this fine display of courage who had aught but enthusiasm for it. There was no dissentient voice; the thing was too plain and palpable.

"Some of you men get searching round to see if you can find a trace of that young fellow," cried one of the Commission officials who happened to come running up at this moment. "If he's under this dirt he'll be smothered while we're talking."

Every second brought more helpers for the task, and very soon there were a hundred men round the wreck of the spoil train; for the driver of the passenger train had stopped his reverse movement as soon as he saw that all danger for his own charge had gone. Then he had steamed forward till within a foot of the inspection car which Jim had driven. The latter, thanks to the fact that the brake was jammed hard on, came to a halt some thirty yards beyond the points, and stood there with its engine roaring. But the fireman quickly shut off the ignition. Passengers poured from the coaches—for it happened that a number of officials were making a trip to the far end of the Culebra cut to inspect progress—and at once hastened to the side of the wreck. But search as they might there was no trace of the lad who had saved so many lives by his gallantry and resourcefulness.

"Come here and tell me what you think of this," suddenly said one of the officials, drawing his comrades after him to the tail end of the train, to the shattered remains of the two trucks which had overturned at a bend, and which had been trailing and clattering along the track in wake of the spoil train. He invited their inspection of the couplings which had bound the last of the cars to the locomotive. There came a whistle of surprise from one of his friends, while something like a shout of indignation escaped another.

"Well?" demanded the first of the officials. "What's your opinion?"

"That this was no accident. This train broke away from her loco. when she was on the incline because some rascal had cut through the couplings. That, sir, 's my opinion," answered the one he addressed, with severity.

There was agreement from all, so that, at the first examination, and before having had an opportunity of questioning those who had been in charge of the spoil train, it became evident that there had been foul play, that some piece of rascality had been practised.

"But who could think of such a thing? There's never been any sort of mean game played on us before this. Whose work is it?" demanded one of the officials hotly.

"That's a question neither you nor I can answer," instantly responded another. "But my advice is that we say not a word. There are but six of us who know about the matter. Let us report to the chief, and leave him to deal with it. For if there is some rascal about, the fact that his work is discovered will warn him. If he thinks he has hoodwinked everyone there will be a better opportunity of discovering him."

The advice was sound, without question, so that, beyond arranging to get possession of the coupling, which showed that it had fractured opposite a fine saw cut, the party of officials preserved silence for the moment. Meanwhile American hustle had brought crowds of helpers to the spot. A locomotive had steamed down from Gorgona, pushing a wrecking derrick before it, and within thirty minutes this was at work, with a crew of willing helpers. A gang of Italian spademen was brought up from the other direction, and these began to remove the rock and dirt. As to Jim, not a trace of him was found till three of the overturned and wrecked trucks had been dragged clear by the wrecking derrick. It was then that the actual site of the lever which operated the points was come upon, the most likely spot at which to discover his body.

"We'll go specially easy here," said the official who was directing operations. "Though one expects that the man is killed, and smothered by all this dirt, yet you never can say in an accident of this sort. I've known a life saved most miraculously."

The hook at the end of the huge chain run over the top of the derrick was attached to the forward bogie of the overturned car, then the whole thing was lifted. Underneath was found a mass of dirt and rock which the impetus of the car had tossed forward. At the back, just beneath the edge of the truck, where it had thrust its way a foot into the ground, one of the workers caught sight of an arm with the fingers of the hand protruding from the debris. "Hold hard!" he shouted. "He's here. Best wait till we've tried to pull him out. The car might swing on that chain and crush him."

They kept the end of the wrecked truck suspended while willing hands sought for our hero. A man crept in under the truck, swept the earth away, and passed the listless figure of the young car driver out into the open. Jim was at once placed on a stretcher, while the Commission surgeon bent over him, dropping a finger on his pulse. He found it beating, very slowly to be sure, but beating without doubt, while a deep bruise across the forehead suggested what had happened. A rapid inspection of his patient, in fact, convinced the surgeon that there was no serious damage.

"Badly stunned, I guess," he said. "I can't find that any bones are broken, and though I thought at first that his skull must be injured, everything points to my fears being groundless. Put him in the ambulance, boys, and let's get him back to hospital."

An hour later our hero was safely between the sheets, with a nurse superintending his comfort. By the time that Phineas arrived on the scene he was conscious, though hardly fit for an interview; but on the following morning he was almost himself, and chafed under the nurse's restraint till the surgeon gave him permission to get up.

"As if I was a baby," he growled. "I suppose I fell on my head, and that knocked me silly. But it's nothing; I haven't more than the smallest headache now."

"Just because you're lucky, young fellow," quizzed the surgeon. "Let me say this: the tumble you had was enough to knock you silly, and I dare say that if you hadn't had something particular to do you would have gone off at once. But your grit made you hold on to your senses. That car, when it overturned, as near as possible smashed your head into the earth beneath it. You'll never be nearer a call while you're working here on the canal. Low diet, sister, and see that he keeps quiet."

Jim glowered on the surgeon and made a grimace. "Low diet indeed! Why, he felt awful hungry."

But no amount of entreaty could influence the nurse, and, indeed, it became apparent to even our hero himself that the course of procedure was correct. For that evening he was not so well, though a long, refreshing sleep put him to rights.

"And now you can hear something about the commotion the whole thing's caused," said Phineas, as he put Jim into a chair in his parlour, and ordered him with severity to retain his seat. "Orders are that you keep quiet, else back you go right off to the hospital. Young man, there were forty-two souls aboard that passenger train, and I reckon you saved 'em. Of course, there are plenty of wise heads that tell us that the driver, when he'd stopped his train, should have turned all the passengers out. Quite so, sir; but then it takes time to do that. You might not have opened the points, and the spoil train would have been into them before the people could climb down out of the cars. So the general feeling is that everyone did his best, except the villain who cut that coupling half through. They've told you about it?"

Jim nodded slowly. "Who could have done such a miserable and wicked thing?" he asked. "Not one of the white employees."

"It don't bear thinking about," said Phineas sharply. "No one can even guess who was the rascal. Leave the matter to the police; they're making quiet enquiries. But there's to be a testimonial, Jim, a presentation one evening at the club, and a sing-song afterwards."

"What? More!" Jim groaned. "Let them take this testimonial as presented. I'll come along to the sing-song."

"And there's to be promotion for a certain young fellow we know," proceeded Phineas, ignoring his remarks utterly. "One of the bosses of a section down by Milaflores locks got his thumb jammed in a gear wheel a week back, and the chief has been looking round to replace him. You've been selected."

Jim's eyes enlarged and brightened at once. He was such a newcomer to the canal zone that promotion had seemed out of the question for a long time to come. He told himself many a time that he was content to work on as he was and wait like the rest for advancement.

"The wages are really good," he had said to Sadie, "and after I've paid everything there is quite a nice little sum over at the end of the week. I'm putting it by against a rainy day."

And here was promotion! By now he had learned the scale of wages and salaries that were paid all along the canal. Such matters were laid down definitely, and were decidedly on the liberal side. With a flush of joy he realized that, as chief of a section, he would be in receipt of just double the amount he had had when working the rock drill.

"And of course there'll be compensation for the accident, just the same as in the case of any other employee," added Phineas, trying to appear as if he had not noticed the tears of joy which had risen to Jim's eyes. For who is there of his age, imbued with the same keenness, with greater responsibilities on his young shoulders than falls to the lot of the average lad, who would not have gulped a little and felt unmanned by such glorious news? Consider the circumstances of our hero's life for some little time past. It had been a struggle against what had at times seemed like persistent bad fortune. First his father ruined, then the whole family compelled to leave their home and drift on the Caribbean. The loss of his father and then of his brother had come like final blows which, as it were, drove the lessons of his misfortunes home to Jim. And there was Sadie, at once a comfort and an anxiety. Jim alone stood between her and charity.

"There'll be compensation for the accident," continued Phineas, "and reward from the Commissioners for saving that train of passenger cars. You've got to remember that it is cheaper any day to smash up a spoil train than it is to wreck one carrying people. One costs a heap more to erect than the other. So there you saved America a nice little sum. I needn't say that if the people aboard had been killed, compensation would have amounted to a big figure. So the Commission has received powers from Washington to pay over 500 dollars. I rather think that'll make a nice little nest egg against the day you get married."

Phineas roared with laughter as he caught a glimpse of Jim's face after those last words. Indignation and contempt were written on the flushed features. Then our hero joined in the merriment. "Gee! If there ever was a lucky dog, it's me!" he cried. "Just fancy getting a reward for such a job! As for the nest egg and marrying, I've better things to do with that money. I'll invest it, so that Sadie shall have something if I'm unlucky enough next time not to escape under similar circumstances. Bein' married can wait till this canal's finished. Guess I've enough to do here. I'm going to stay right here till the works are opened and I've sailed in a ship from Pacific to Atlantic."

Phineas smiled, and, leaning across, gripped his young friend's hand and shook it hard. Open admiration for the pluck which our hero had displayed, now on more than one occasion, was transparent in the eyes of this American official. But there was more. Jim had caught that strange infection which seemed to have taken the place of the deadly yellow fever. It was like that pestilence, too, in this, that it was wonderfully catching, wonderfully quick to spread, and inflicted itself upon all and sundry, once they had settled down in the zone. But there the simile between this infection and that of the loathsome yellow fever ended. That keenness for the work, that determination to relax no energy, but to see what many thought a hopeless undertaking safely and surely accomplished, had, in the few months since he came to the canal zone, fastened itself upon Jim, till there was none more eager all along the line between the Pacific and the Atlantic.

"Yes," he repeated, "I'll stay right here till the canal's opened. By then that nest egg ought to be of respectable proportions."

A week later there was a vast gathering at the clubhouse, when one of the chief officials of the canal works presented Jim with a fine gold watch and chain to the accompaniment of thunderous applause from the assembled employees. At the same time the reward sent or sanctioned by the Government at Washington was handed over to him. A merry concert followed, and then the meeting broke up. It was to be Jim's last evening in the neighbourhood of Gatun.

"Of course you'll have to live in one of the hotels at Ancon," said Phineas, when discussing the matter, "for it is too long a journey from there to this part to make every day. It would interfere with your work. You can come along weekends, and welcome. Sadie'll stop right here; I won't hear of her leaving."

The arrangement fell in with our hero's wishes, for there was no doubt but that his sister was in excellent hands. She had taken a liking to Phineas's housekeeper, and was happy amongst her playmates at the Commission school close at hand. Jim left her, therefore, in the care of his friend, and was soon established in his quarters in a vast Commission hotel at Ancon, within easy distance of Milaflores, the part where he was to be chief of a section of workers. He found that the latter were composed for the most part of Italians, though there were a few other European nationalities, as well as some negroes.

"You'll have plans given you and so get to know what the work is," said his immediate superior. "Of course what we're doing here is getting out foundations for the two tiers of double locks. You'll have a couple of steam diggers to operate, besides a concrete mill; for we're putting tons of concrete into our foundations. A young chap like you don't want to drive. Though it's as well to remember that foreigners same as these ain't got the same spirit that our men have. They don't care so much for the building of the canal as for the dollars they earn, but if you take them the right way you can get a power of work out of them."

The advice given was, as Jim found, excellent, and with his sunny nature and his own obvious preference for hard work, in place of idleness, he soon became popular with his section, and conducted it for some weeks to the satisfaction of those above him. Nor did he find the work less interesting. The huge concrete mill was, in itself, enough to rivet attention, though there was a sameness about its movements which was apt to become monotonous when compared with the varied, lifelike motions of the steam diggers. Rubble and cement were loaded into its enormous hopper by the gangs of workmen, and ever there was a mass of semi-fluid concrete issuing from the far side, ready mixed for the foundations of the locks which, when the hour arrives, will carry the biggest ships the world is capable of building. On Saturday afternoon, when the whistles blew earlier than on weekdays, Jim would return to his hotel, wash and change, and take the first available car down the tracks to Gatun. A concert at the club was usually arranged for Saturday night, while on Sunday he went to the nearest church with Phineas and Sadie, and then returned in the evening to Ancon.

"Strange that we should never be able to get any information about that runaway spoil train," said Phineas, on one of the occasions when Jim went over

167

to Gatun. "There's never been a word about it. The police have failed to fathom what is at this day still a mystery. But there's a rascal at work somewhere. There's been a severe fire down Colon way, sleepers near pitched a passenger train from the rails opposite the dam there, while one night, when the works were deserted, someone took the brakes off a hundred-ton steam digger, and sent her running down the tracks. She smashed herself to pieces, besides wrecking a dozen cars."

The news was serious, in fact, and pointed unmistakably to a criminal somewhere on the canal, someone with a grudge against the undertaking, or against the officials. It made Jim think instantly of Jaime de Oteros, though why he could not imagine. But he was soon to know; little time was to pass before he was to come face to face with the miscreant.

CHAPTER XV

Jaime de Oteros forms Plans

If ever there were a rascal it was Jaime de Oteros, the Spaniard, who, if his past history were but fully known, had left his own native country, now many years ago, a fugitive from justice. Armed with sufficient money to obtain an entrance into the United States of America, he had quickly re-embarked upon the course he had been following, and with the gang he had contrived to gather about him had committed many burglaries. Then, the police being hot on his track, he had left the country, and had begun operations again in southern America.

"That is our information about the man," said the police major, as he was discussing the matter with Phineas and Jim one Saturday evening, when the latter was over at Gatun for the usual weekend stay. "The rascal knew that the police in New York State were making anxious search for him, and with his usual astuteness—for the man is astute without a doubt, and is, indeed, well educated—he slipped away before the net closed round him. Later we hear of him at various ports along the Mexican Gulf, and then in the canal zone. Tom brings us news of great importance."

The big negro stood before them, looking magnificent in his police uniform, and with an air of authority about him which was entirely new, and which caused Jim to struggle hard to hide his mirth; for he knew Tom so well. Severity did not match well with the huge negro's jolly nature.

"I'se seed dis scum ob a man," he declared to them all, rolling his eyes. "Yo tink Tom make one big mistake. Not 'tall; noding of de sort. Me sartin sure. Him come cut ob a house in Colon. Same man, but different. No beard, face clean shaved; but scowl all de same. Tom know de blackguard when he see um."

"But," said Phineas, "if you knew him why did you not arrest him? There is a warrant out for his apprehension."

"And me try. but dat Spaniard dog quick, quicker'n Tom. Him slip back into de house and clear out ob de back door. Not dere two second later," declared the negro. "And not dere agin when me and Sam go some hours after. Not come all de time dat we hide up and watch. Him vanish into thin air."

It was a pretty figure of speech for the negro, and brought a huge smile to his jolly countenance. "Vanish right slick away into de mist," he added, as if to give more weight to his words.

"And has not been seen by anyone else, before or since," said the Major, his face become very serious. "But I believe Tom is right. Who else could be the author of these many affairs along the line of canal works?"

He looked closely at Phineas, and from him turned to Jim and then to Tom. There was indecision on all the faces, though in the hearts of each one there was not the smallest doubt that Jaime de Oteros was the instigator, even if he did not actually carry out the work. The matter was serious, very serious, without a doubt.

"It isn't as if there were one isolated case," said the Major. "There have been many, and though so far the running away of spoil trains, the upsetting of wagons, and so forth has not resulted in the killing of our employees, it will do so, perhaps, next time, if we do not take steps to put an end to such matters. The difficulty is to know where to begin. We have men engaged in watching every mile of the track, but they do not all know this ruffian, though we have circulated his photograph; besides, he has altered his appearance. He is the most elusive criminal I have ever had dealings with, and at the same time one of the boldest. But a feeling of revenge cannot alone cause him to stay on here in the canal zone, and risk arrest."

If only the Major could have known it, there was a good deal more than the desire to pay off an old score to keep Jaime de Oteros in that locality. The Spaniard had now put in at many a port along that part of the world, and had discovered that the canal zone offered finer opportunities to a man such as he was than any other place.

"Just because there's always money in plenty there," he told the four companions he now had, for he had gathered two recruits to take the place of those who had been lost on the launch. "It is like this, mates. Here, on the canal, nearly every soul is at work during the hours of daylight, and though the police have little to do, and therefore plenty of time to watch for people such as us, yet the fact that there is so little crime in the zone puts them off their guard. I'm tired of playing off that score. Reckon I'm near even with the lot of them; but there's still a little to do. There's that young fellow who ran the engine aboard the launch, and who was the first to come upon our gang and split it up. He's got to suffer."

He looked round at the ruffians assembled about him, and read approval in their eyes.

"A grudge is a grudge," said one of them fiercely, dropping his hand to the weapon he carried in his belt. "Where I came from an injury done was never paid for till a knife thrust had been given. This young fellow must suffer. How? What is the plan?"

Jaime shrugged his shoulders expressively, and shook his head. "That's for the future," he said quickly. "I'm thinking it out. I've an idea, a fine idea."

Into his eyes there came a savage flash which boded ill for our hero, while the brows contracted and the lips slipped back from his sharp teeth. At that moment Jaime de Oteros, in place of the polished, smooth-spoken man he could pretend so well to be, was actually himself, a villain who knew not the name of conscience, who would stop at nothing, whose savage disposition was capable of carrying out any atrocity. Then he smiled suddenly at his comrades, a crafty smile which was meant to convey a great deal.

"Let it rest for the moment, this idea of mine," he said. "What we've got to talk about is this cash. There's money due within a day or two, money for the payment of the hands engaged on the canal. Well, we've made one haul already; we can make another, and then clear for good. This zone will be too hot to hold us once the work's finished. Now, let me hear the report. A good general never enters upon an engagement before he has made full arrangements to get clear off in case of things going wrong. Well, things will go wrong here—not for us, but for the officials. They'll be real mad, and will do all they know to follow. Let me hear what has happened."

There was a snivel of delight on the face of the rascal who had formerly spoken, and who now responded to his chief's invitation.

"I was to see what sort of a boat there was ready to put out from Colon," he said. "I found one that was rather likely. The old pirate she belongs to has been here all his life, and what he don't know of the surroundings ain't worth knowing. He's ready to clear from the harbour, with two of his sons and two others he'll hire, the instant we want him to do so. Reckon it'll be nigh about sundown when the time for moving comes."

Jaime nodded curtly. "About that," he agreed, "Well?"

"This old pirate likes fishing. He'll watch for a fire signal way up over Gatun, and then he'll clear right off with his boat. Of course he'll do it secretly, but not too secretly. People'll be allowed to catch a glimpse of men getting aboard, and of the boat putting out. She'll disappear."

"Ah!" Jaime rubbed his hands together, and then began to roll a cigarette with the nimblest of fingers. A smile broke out over his face, and for the moment the man looked almost handsome. "She'll disappear," he giggled. "Yes, where? I begin to follow the move."

"Where? That's for the police to decide. Ef they was to ask me at the time I couldn't place a guess. But that old pirate knows a cove, quite handy to Colon, where, once a man's lowered his topsail, he can lay hid with his boat from all save those who care to come right into the cove. Our man says he'll do a bit of fishing. He'll pass his time with that and sleeping, while the police steam right on, searching for the boat that left Colon so secretly. Ef they ain't bamboozled, wall, call me a Dutchman."

There was a roar of merriment from the five ruffians. They lay back in their chairs, and closed their eyes, as if thereby to help themselves to imagine the spectacle of the Commission Police racing across the sea on a wild-goose chase. Indeed it was one of the enjoyments of their particular thieving profession to set the police at naught, and make them look foolish by their own astuteness. And here was an astute plan.

"It licks creation," laughed Jaime, bringing a fist down with a crash on to the table, and exposing a hand burned brown by the sun, and on the fingers of which more than one ring glittered. "This old man of yours will fool them nicely for us, and while the police are away on the sea, we shall cut off in a different direction. That brings us to the second report. You see I have to be very careful. Time was when I saw to all these matters myself; but hereabouts I'm known, and badly wanted. In spite of shaving off my beard I might easily be recognized, as by that nigger. Gee! Ef he comes up agin me again I'll give him reasons to mind his manners. Now, what about the horses?"

He turned to another of his comrades, to the second of the two new recruits he had gathered to his band, and looked inquisitively at him. The man was ready with his answer, and blurted it out eagerly, like a schoolboy who longs to make his own voice heard before all others.

"Horses," said the fellow, a dusky South American, whose swarthy features were deeply lined and pitted. "Trust me to pick the right sort when they're wanted. You told me to seek mounts strong enough to carry us across a rough country, and fix a rate to be paid for 'em. I went a little better. There ain't many cattle in this place, so that one hasn't to look far. But along over there," and he jerked his head over his left shoulder, "there's a biggish farm, where there's a dozen mounts. We'll want six, I guess, five for ourselves, and one for the dollars."

"Seven," corrected Jaime suddenly. "Seven, my comrade."

All looked at him curiously. Their chief was not wont to make mistakes, but here it looked as if he were miscalculating. However, Jaime smiled serenely back at them. "Seven horses without doubt," he said quietly, blowing a cloud of smoke from his lips, and cutting it asunder with a wave of his ringed fingers. "Precisely that number."

"I don't follow; six is the figure I put it at," came the answer. "Unless——" and at the thought the rascal's face lit up with glee, "unless you reckon the dollars'll be too many for one bag."

But the leader of the band shook his head, and smiled ambiguously. "Seven horses will be required," he said slowly. "Tell us more of the business. You arranged the payment?"

"I fixed the business in a different manner. I scouted round a little, and soon found that, at nighttime, there were but one man and a woman about the place. The stables are well away from the house, and easy to get at. I fixed that there wouldn't be any payment."

There was a cunning expression about his face as he looked round at his comrades, while the lines about his eyes were sunken deeper. Jaime rewarded him with a loud "Bravo!" "You begin well with us, comrade," he said eagerly. "The report is a good one. But one little matter occurs to me: this farm is near the works, eh? It is connected by telephone?"

The other rascal at once relieved him of the doubt. "It lies packed away in a hollow, just on the edge of the zone," he said. "The folks ain't never seen a telephone."

"Then that matter is agreed upon. We can now begin to decide what each one of us is to do. I'll tell you right now what I had intended. To call away attention from the place where the money's banked we decided to cause an upset pretty adjacent. Well, now, the Culebra cutting seemed to be the most likely spot of all. I've been thinking and planning. A ruction there could be heard way up and down the line, and would set people running. The point was, how to cause that ruction."

There was more than passing interest on the faces of his followers. In their opinion this leader of theirs was a fine fellow, a cunning man, one whom it was an honour to follow. They awaited the details of his plan with eagerness, not to say anxiety.

"And how did you fix it?" asked one of the men, proceeding to light his cigarette by means of the candle burning before him. "Another train let loose? A shot under the wheels of a passenger coach? A dozen diggers sent scuttling?" There was a snigger on his face, quickly copied by the others. Jaime showed his pleasure by smiling broadly. After all, it was one of his pleasures in life to have the praise and high opinion of his following. He pulled at his cigarette thoughtfully, and then proceeded with his plan.

"We've played too many of those games already," he said, with a short laugh. "The officials of the canal are always on the lookout. But the plan I fastened on to would have taken their breath away, if it didn't manage to deprive some of them of the same for good and always. I'd been watching those rock drills, and the powder men laying their shots. It seemed to me that once the shots were wired, and connected to the firing cables, a man had only to get to the firing-point and operate the igniter. I got asking questions. I've done a bit on electricity works before now, and I soon saw that the thing was possible. With a little luck I could fire their shots for them."

The faces about him showed doubt and a lack of comprehension, for Jaime was far more intelligent than any of the other members of his rascally band. "What was the object of firing those shots?" they asked themselves. But their leader soon explained the matter.

"It is like this," he said suavely, as if describing an everyday matter: "the shots are laid ready for firing, and when the works are cleared the man who operates the igniter gets to work and explodes them, one by one or in batches, according to the wiring. Well, now, if the place is cleared of workers, there's no damage done, though rocks and dirt fly out in all directions. But if there was an accident—if, for instance, I happened to meddle with the igniter before the works were cleared—there'd be a tremendous ruction, and that's what we're wanting."

The diabolical nature of his suggestion dawned only slowly upon the minds of his following; but when it did so, when they fully comprehended his meaning, their faces flushed with enthusiasm. Each of the five had worked on the canal, and had seen those dynamite shots fired. Tons of earth and rock spouted in all directions. That they had witnessed. To remain in the neighbourhood meant certain death for many, injury for not a few, and a commotion which the officials and workers had so far never experienced. There was joy on their faces. They banged the table with their fists, and stretched across to grasp the rascally palm of their leader; but Jaime silenced them with uplifted hand.

"It sounded right, I grant," he said between the puffs of smoke; "but there was a fly in the ointment. The igniter is kept under lock and key. The place is guarded. These canny Americans know that those shots mean danger, and they don't run risks. If I tried the game, the chances are I should be disturbed or taken in the act of trying. So I wiped it out; I started in to think out another plan, something noisy, something that would draw all officials to the spot, away from the place where the money is lying. And at last I fixed it. One of you men will change places with a hand at Pedro Miguel, where they're building in their foundations for one of the big locks at the end of the Culebra cutting. You'll work with the rest till the whistles go at sundown, and then, when the coast is clear, you'll sneak back to the workings. I'll give you the rest of the plan later on; but you'll be the one to create a most almighty ruction, you'll be the one to draw off every official, and while they're busy we others'll get to work at the money. It'll be eight o'clock before we can meet at this farm, and an hour later will take us into the bush. Next morning we'll be right away in the swamps, with friends about us, while the police will be following the old fellow, who will put to sea the previous evening."

They sat in silence for a while, Jaime regarding each one of his band in turn, scrutinizing their faces closely, as if seeking for something in particular. Then he fastened upon one of them, and stretched across to grip his hand.

"Juan is a brave man," he said impressively; "he will take the post of which I have spoken. To him falls the honour of creating such a trouble that those who go for the dollars may be able to take them easily. It is a post worth the having."

The rascal greedily accepted it He was one of Jaime's old hands, and had complete confidence in his chief. Moreover, he had now helped him in so many risky operations that fear did not enter into his calculations. Why should it, indeed, seeing that all others would be in ignorance? The plot was being hatched in secrecy. None would know that anything was to happen until the moment arrived. The hard-working officials of the canal would be unable to recover from their astonishment before he and his friends were gone. Juan drank deeply from the cup before him, and replenished the vessel from a stone jar standing on the table.

"It is settled; whatever the plan, it is accomplished," he said with the greatest assurance.

"Then we have merely to arrange the parts for the others. Miguel sees to the horses. Our friend Alfonso, who made the arrangement with the boatman, will be with Miguel, and will light a flare above Gatun at seven in the evening, or sooner if he discovers that there is a commotion. The two will then go to the farm, take the horses, and ride towards Ancon. There is a spot at the bottom of a rocky hill, where the road sweeps sharply round into the valley. My friends, we have all been there before. It is there that we will meet when the work is finished. Pedro and myself will take the money, then Pedro will carry it to the horses. But I ought to have said that Alfonso and Miguel will not ride towards Ancon with all the horses. They will leave three at the back of Gatun, at a spot we can arrange upon. There Pedro will take the money and load it on one of the horses. He will wait for me; I shall come, and then we will ride to the place of meeting."

There were inquisitive glances thrown at the man by his comrades. The question of the seventh horse again occurred to them. Jaime smiled when he remarked their curiosity, and busily employed himself in rolling a cigarette. It pleased him to watch his comrades as they endeavoured to fathom his purpose.

"You ride to join Pedro after a while then?" queried the rascal Juan. "What keeps you? Ah, I see it! A private grudge—that young fellow."

Jaime nodded easily, and smiled openly upon them all. "I have still some work to accomplish," he said slowly. "You would not ask me to leave this place allowing something to remain unfinished? Think for a moment. We were comfortable and content here till that young dog pried into our secrets. And what resulted? Three of us were arrested, and should have been hanged perhaps by now had we not broken out of prison. Two of our comrades were followed, and, though they were not killed, we have had news that they were badly wounded. In addition, our game here was spoiled for the time being. The officials locked their money up tighter than ever, so that we had to move elsewhere in order to earn a living. But that is all changed now; we are getting even with the fellows. Already we have caused them much trouble, and now we will skin them of every dollar, damage their works, and give this young dog such a lesson that he will never interfere again. Good! It is fine to feel that the day of reckoning has come at last. Juan, pass the bottle. With plans like these to act upon a man requires a fillip."

Far into the night they sat discussing their rascally movements, and the following day found all but Jaime abroad and active. That very afternoon, in fact, Alfonso brought them information that a ship had come into Colon bearing specie for the officials, money with which to pay America's army of workmen.

"I watched it unloaded," said the rascal, glee on his face. "There were boxes of silver and a huge mass of notes; for of course wages are paid in paper. All the better for us, my friends. Paper is easy to carry, and is still valuable. They can publish the numbers of the stolen notes as much as they like, but still we can get value for them."

"And the destination of these boxes?" asked Jaime anxiously.

Alfonso told him with pride. He had followed the consignment, and had seen it deposited at the door of one of the official offices. He had seen it carried in, and drew a plan of the building.

"Then to-night," said Jaime, pulling at the inevitable cigarette. "Juan has already gone across to Pedro Miguel. And you—you have made full arrangements with the boatman?"

"Full and complete; there will be no hitch to-night," cried Alfonso, banging the table.

A stranger happening to take rail at Colon on this day would have been utterly astounded had he been informed that there was to be a commotion that very evening. For the trip along the whole length of the Panama Railway would have shown him armies of men and officials engaged methodically with their work. The busy scene of smoking steam diggers, of rock drills, and hustling spoil trains would have resolved itself finally, when his eye was at last accustomed to the vastness of it all, into a scene of order and method, into a gigantic undertaking which occupied the wits and strength of all whom he saw. He would at last have appreciated the fact that those vast works at Gatun, and between it and Limon Bay, had a direct connection with that enormous cutting which occupied the time of such an army of delvers at Culebra, though twenty odd miles separated the two, and that throughout the length of the Panama zone, stretching from north to south of the isthmus, the work undertaken by any one man had some special relation to that appointed to another. Moreover, that, in spite of distances, in spite of the fact that the undertaking seemed to be progressing piecemeal at widely separated intervals, yet each and every part was a portion of the whole, a necessary portion, where the work in hand was conducted with a hustle and method truly American, and with a swing which augured for success. But of commotion there was not a sign. That traveller could not possibly have guessed that the evening had a disaster in store for the people who worked beneath his eye.

It was precisely half-past five on this special evening when a terrible explosion shook every one of the wooden buildings at Ancon, and caused the verandas at Gorgona to shake as if they would tumble. A vast flame seemed to leap into the air, there came a thunderous report, that went echoing down the Chagres valley, and then dust and debris obscured the sky in the direction of Pedro Miguel. The serene face of this portion of the zone, lit a second or so before by a wonderful moon, was obscured as if by the work of a volcano.

Instantly men poured out from the Commission hotels, and stood in the street of Ancon and the nearest settlement, asking what had happened.

"Guess it's the dynamite store gone off suddenly," cried one, his hands deep in his pockets, a pipe in his mouth. "Hope none of the boys ain't hurt, nor the works neither. It's been a bad blow-up anyway."

It was an hour later before details filtered through, then, all along the line, it was learned that an attempt had been made to wreck the foundation of the lock at Pedro Miguel.

"Another of them anarchistic attempts," growled one of the men. "Guess this is too almighty queer fer anything. Here's spoil trains been sent runnin' down from the cut, and the same with diggers. Sleepers and suchlike laid on the rails in order to throw passenger trains off the metals, fires, and what not. This is the limit."

"It's one of the most serious difficulties we have had to face, boys," said one of the canal officials, coming upon the group of men at that moment. "I've just come along from the dock at Pedro Miguel, and there isn't a doubt that some rascal endeavoured to blow the whole place to pieces. It's Jim Partington's section, and he'd left everything safe and sound. There wasn't a rock drill working there, and hasn't been this three weeks past. Consequently there weren't any dynamite shots; but a man was seen creeping down that way soon after sundown. Guess he'd fixed to place his bomb right in the trench where the foundations are being laid; but something went wrong with it. He was blown to pieces; there were only scraps of him to be found."

There was a grunt of satisfaction at the news; the men felt that such a fate was only just retribution.

"But what damage has been done, boss?" asked one of the men anxiously, as if the success of the canal depended on the answer.

"None; in fact the explosion seems to have helped us. Young Jim Partington tells me he was making a requisition for a rock drill this coming week, as there was a heap of stuff to break down before the diggers could get at it. Well, he's saved the trouble. That explosion brought tons of stuff away, and now there's hardly need for a rock drill. Of course you've got to remember that it's dark 'way over there, and a man can't fix exactly what may have happened. But we made a quick, and, I believe, thorough survey of the place, and I should say that I've told you everything. This blessed cur who has been worrying us these weeks past has come by his deserts at last."

There was, in fact, not the smallest doubt that the rascally plot of Jaime and his followers had failed at the very beginning. Juan, who had accepted the post of honour, had disappeared from the scene swiftly and terribly. He had been hoist by his own petard, and, as the official had stated, there was little left to show that he had actually existed.

But still there was Jaime to reckon with, Jaime de Oteros and his fellows, and the reader need feel little surprise when he hears that, later on in the evening, there was another disturbance. It was discovered that the pay offices had been burgled, and that a vast sum of money had been removed. Then came an urgent telephone message to Ancon. The instrument at the club rang loudly and continuously, causing one of the men to go to it instantly. Jim, who had just returned from an inspection of his section, where the explosion had taken place, sat at a table near at hand, and, though there was no reason why the telephone should be calling him more than any other, he watched his comrade and listened.

"What's that? Say, who are you?" he heard the man demand. Then he suddenly looked over his shoulder, and if ever a man bore a startled expression it was this one. "Say, Jim, there," he called out, "they're ringing you from Gatun. It's Phineas Barton; there's trouble down there as well."

Jim was beside him in a moment, the receiver to his ear; and at once he recognized Phineas's voice, but strangely altered.

"Yes?" he asked as coolly as he could, though something set his heart thumping. "It's Jim at this end."

"Then come right along without waitin'. We've trouble down this end. Bring a shooter; I'll tell you about it when you arrive. The Police Major is here waiting."

It was serious news, whatever it was, for Phineas's voice proved it. Jim crammed his hat on to his head, raced back to his quarters and snatched a mackintosh, a revolver, and a spare shirt, and then ran down to the railway. He found a motor inspection car awaiting him, with a couple of policemen in it, one of whom was Tomkins.

"You kin get along with it," said the latter curtly, addressing the driver. "And we ain't nervous, so let her go as fast as you're able. Jim, there's a regular upset from end to end of the zone, and I'm beginning to get through with it. That explosion was a blind, meant to occupy our attention while those rascals, for there's more than one of 'em, robbed the pay office. But that ain't all. They were up to some other sort of mischief down Gatun way, and the Major 'phoned through to us to come along that second. We were to bring you, too; so it seems that you've something to do with the business."

Let the reader imagine how Jim fretted upon that quick journey. He wondered why he should have been called, and how the matter could specially interest him. A thousand ideas flashed through his busy mind, and were banished as unsatisfactory. It was not until the motor raced into Gatun, and he caught a glimpse of Phineas's face, that he realized that the matter must be particularly serious. His friend took him by the hand and held it.

"Jim," he said, and his voice broke ever so little, "those scoundrels deserve hanging. We were right in thinking that Jaime de Oteros had to do with the business, and I guess he'd made up his mind to get even with you for finding the gang and getting it broken. He settled to blow up your section, then he

179

broke into the pay office, and last of all, to pay you out properly, the ruffian slank down to my quarters. Sadie was indoors, of course——"

Jim staggered backwards. He had never even thought of Sadie in connection with this disaster. The fear that she had been injured, perhaps killed, caused his cheek to pale even beneath the deep tan with which it was covered.

"Get on," he said a moment later, pulling himself together with an effort. "Sadie was indoors. Yes. That villain——"

"That villain had fixed to abduct her. We were all outside, watchin' for another explosion. This Jaime, or one of his men, slipped in at the back, seized the girl, and got clear off with her. Lad, it's a real bad business."

Jim held to the rails of the station. His head swam; he felt giddy, while the beating of his heart was almost painful. He was utterly unmanned for the moment. He, Jim Partington, who had faced so many dangers smiling, was utterly prostrated by the news imparted to him. Then, like the brave fellow he was, he threw off the feeling of weakness with a sharp shrug of his shoulders, and in a moment became his old self, cool and self-possessed, as he asked shrewd questions shortly and sharply.

"You will follow, of course?" he asked the Major.

"You can guess so. This time nothing shall turn me back."

"Then I can come?"

"Glad indeed to have you, my boy. We'll move the instant we get information. I've men making enquiries down at the port, while your negro, Sam, has gone off with a lantern. Better start on the right track than start early. Let's get in and have some supper."

It was one of the most anxious meals Jim had ever attended. He was eager to set out in search of his sister, but realized all the time that a wrong start might be productive of great delay and failure.

"But Sam will hit their marks if anyone can," he told himself. "Then I'll follow wherever the tracks lead. Sadie shall not stay in that man's hands an instant longer than I can help it. And if I catch that Jaime and his fellows——!"

His fingers came together; his two hands were clenched beneath the table. At that precise moment good-natured Jim felt that he was capable of anything.

CHAPTER XVI

The Major forms his Parties

Never before, perhaps, had the telephone system in the Panama Canal zone been so busily employed as on the night of Sadie's abduction. The bell of the instrument in Phineas's quarters seemed to ring without cessation, while the Police Major had his ear glued to the receiver by the ten minutes together.

"A crafty set of dogs," he declared, after one of these long conversations with his office at Colon. "They laid their plans most elaborately, and made every preparation to throw dust in our eyes. That explosion way over at Pedro Miguel wasn't the only little bit of by-play. It seems that they engaged a boatman to steal away from Colon this evening, and give us the impression that they were aboard; but that huge negro Tom put a spoke in their wheel. He happened to be in Colon, and reported to the office at once that he had seen a fire signal up by Gatun, way behind this house."

"And guessed it was meant for someone down by the sea?" asked Phineas, rising from his seat at the receipt of such important information. "Major, this Jim and his servants have done good service to our people here. I'm glad that Tom has shown himself such an excellent constable."

"He's one of the exceptions one finds amongst big men," declared the Major. "He's sharp, as sharp as a needle, for all his smiles and easy-going manner. He spotted this flare way back behind us, and looked well about him. He reported, a matter of two hours ago, that a boat had put off with some four men in her. Two of the crew at least he knew to be loafers about the streets of Colon, and one was the owner, a man of bad repute. Still, the fourth might have been one of the rascals we are after. So I sent out a steam launch, and her report has just reached me.'

"Well?" demanded Phineas shortly, while Jim leaned forward anxiously. "It wasn't one of the rascals; it was a blind, as you've intimated."

The Police Major nodded promptly. "Number two of the schemes of those rascals has failed. My people have just returned, and the sergeant has 'phoned me the news. He overhauled this boat and went aboard her. The fourth individual was another well-known character from Colon, while the owner of the craft, thinking perhaps that he would get into trouble, and hoping to set matters right for himself, admitted that he had arranged to slip off when a fire signal was lighted. The sergeant left him out there to go where he liked, and steamed back as fast as his engine would carry him. This time the pursuit will hardly be by way of the Atlantic."

"But perhaps by way of Panama, on to the Pacific," suggested Phineas.

"Or into the bush; that's where I imagine they may have gone," said Jim. "It seems to me that we have every reason to suspect that that is the course they will have followed."

His two companions in the room looked steadily at him. Before now they had known our hero to give common-sense solutions when there was a difficulty, and all through, since the moment when they had first known him, he had proved himself to be possessed of a level head, of that sharpness and shrewdness for which the American is notorious. It was therefore with a feeling of interest that they waited for him to speak.

"Every reason to think they've gone into the bush," repeated the Major. "I own that I have thought of the matter; but then, we all know the bush. It isn't everyone who would willingly make a journey through it; for fever frightens them, and besides, once you get a little distance from the zone, there are natives. There aren't many men who can tell us much about the latter. Of course it's part of my business to have found out something; and I have ascertained that while some are friendly enough, there are others who could not be trusted. They would kill a white man for the clothes he stood up in. Then why do you consider that they have gone by way of the bush?"

Jim stood up and walked the room backwards and forwards. Nerves were not things that he had much acquaintance with, but the reader can well excuse him if on this occasion he was fidgety. In fact, it was as much as he could do to keep quiet. He longed to rush off and make some sort of effort. It was only his solid good sense that restrained him, the good sense that showed him clearly how a false start, pursuit along a wrong line, might throw the game entirely into the hands of the miscreants who had abducted Sadie. It was for her sake that he stayed in the room, fidgeting at the delay, but waiting, waiting for some definite information to show him where the tracks of the fugitives led. And in his own mind he had traced those tracks.

"It seems clear to me, though of course I may be entirely wrong," he said as he paced the room. "But those fellows have been proved to have had dealing with the natives. The last time we chatted about the matter you, Major, told us that you had certain information that they had been selling guns, powder, and spirit to the natives along the coast. Then see how those fellows we chased across the lagoon made friends with the inhabitants of that part. It's perfectly plain that they had been trading over there. That being the case, and perhaps because the police have been careful to watch the various launches down at Port Limon, these men decided not to fly by way of the ocean. They thought that the bush offered better chances; but their destination is the same. They are making for those parts where we did our fighting, and once they have joined that tribe they imagine they will be safe."

The argument seemed to be clear enough, and for a while the Major stood by the telephone thinking deeply. And the more Jim's suggestions filtered through his mind, the more sure did he feel that there was something substantial about them. At length he almost took it for granted that the course outlined by our hero was actually the one which the miscreants were following. Then the question arose: how could the police best deal with the matter?

"See here, Jim," he said, after a while. "I believe you've just hit the right nail on the head. Let us suppose that these men have gone by the way of the bush, with the idea of joining hands with that tribe. What course do you advise for those who follow?"

Jim gave his answer promptly. In fact, as the others admitted, there could be little doubt as to the procedure to be adopted; but all depended on one particular.

"How many men will you employ?" asked Jim.

"As many as are wanted. A dozen of my own men for certain, and I can get a draft from the force of marines who are garrisoning the canal."

"Then I say that we ought to go in two parties. I with others will take horses and push on through the bush, where Sam will be able to lead us; the second party should make round by sea, cross the lagoon, and join hands with us there. We shall, in that way, be able to take them between us, and if one party is attacked first of all, it has the knowledge that the other will come to support it."

The Major at once went to the telephone, and rang up his office. The plan suggested seemed to him to be one of such common sense that it needed little argument to convince him. Therefore, within ten minutes, the officials down at Colon were making preparations.

"Meanwhile, those who are to follow by way of the bush had better be making preparations," said Phineas, who was nothing if not practical. "What have you to say, Major?"

"Just this, that I shall support you in every way. I shall command the party which goes by sea, and Jim here had better take the other. Tom and Sam can go with him, as well as Tomkins and four or five other constables. You see, we can't send many round that way, for horses are scarce hereabouts. Theirs must be in every sense a cutting-out expedition. I take it that Jim made his suggestion with that in view. What he wants to do is to rescue his sister. After that he will assist us if possible, once he has made sure the girl is in safety."

"Then let us set to work with food and other things," cried Phineas. "Look here, Jim, I can see that you're just fidgeting. Come along with me; it'll settle you a little to have something to do."

They went off to the kitchen promptly, and with Ching to help them quickly filled a sack with eatables. Meanwhile the Major again had recourse to the telephone, had detailed the four men who were to accompany Jim, and had asked for rations, arms, and ammunition.

"Not forgetting quinine," he told Jim and Phineas when they returned. "If you'll take my advice you'll make every man of the expedition, white or black, swallow two grains daily, just as a precaution. You can't be too careful, especially if it happens to rain, as is probable."

It was wonderful how quickly all their preparations were completed; so much so that when, an hour later, the diminutive Sam returned, Jim and his whole party were collected at Phineas's quarters. The four policemen had come up with ten horses all ready saddled and bridled.

"And we're lucky to have them," declared the Major. "I'm giving you ten mounts, so that, although there will be only nine of you, you will have a beast to carry blankets and ammunition. The men will carry their own rations, which will last for almost a week. By then you will have to fend for yourselves if you do not happen to reach us; but you should manage that. The spot where our action took place is barely forty miles distant. Of course, when you rescue the girl, you will put her on the spare horse. Now let us interview Sam."

The little fellow was ushered into the room, still carrying his lantern. Sam's face was sternly set, while his whole expression showed eagerness and determination. Indeed the little negro would have done anything for Sadie and for our hero. He put the lantern down on the floor and pulled off the sack which covered his shoulders.

"Got um!" he cried jubilantly. "Dem fellers tink dey fool de lot ob us nicely; but Sam tink otherwise. He get on de track ob one ob de men at once, just as once before. Any fool able to follow; Sam manage him blindfold. Him take Sadie way along at the back of Gatun, den him come to a spot where horses waitin'. Dere are three. Sam count 'em. Dey ride along towards Ancon, and me run all de way, followin'. Dere dey meet two oders, and strike right off for de bush. I come back runnin'; time we was after dem scum."

They gave the little fellow meat and drink instantly, for he was exhausted after his efforts. Then the whole party mounted, Phineas riding beside Jim, and just as the light was breaking they cantered over the edge of the canal zone and plunged into the bush.

"Sam'll go ahead," said Jim promptly, reining back his mount. "Tomkins and I will ride next; then, some twenty yards behind us, Tom and Ching, with two of the constables. Phineas, you take the rear with the last of the police, and ride within twenty yards of the main party. By dividing up like that we stand a better chance in case they try to surprise us. Now, Sam, we want to get ahead as fast as possible. The moon went down early last night, and though it will have helped those rascals at the beginning, they will have been forced to camp after a time. If, as I imagine, they believe that we are not likely to follow through the bush, in fact that they have covered their trail, and sent us off after that boat, they are not likely to push along very fast. That will be our opportunity; by making the pace we may come up with them."

Sam was like a dog as he followed. There was not the smallest doubt that the little fellow was gifted with the most wonderful power of observation, and with it that of deduction. For now that the sun was up, and the light strong, he led the party at a trot, never even requiring to climb out of his saddle. Dressed in tattered garments, which were still drenched with the rain that had fallen upon him during the previous night, the diminutive negro looked wonderfully woebegone. but that was from behind. One must not always judge by the condition of a man's garments; for seen from the front the little fellow was evidently very much alive. That same intent expression was on his face, while his piercing eyes were glued to the track. It was half an hour later when he threw up his hand and slid from his saddle.

"Camp here, dem scum," he announced as Jim rode up. "Four ob de rascal, and missie. Yo not tink so? Den see here; dem's her footmarks."

The most unbelieving person would have been convinced, for the ground bore undoubted witness to what had happened. It was thickly marked by horses, while near at hand the animals had been tied to the branch of a tree hanging close to the earth. A little camp had been formed within a few yards, and in and amongst the bootmarks of Jaime de Oteros and his fellows were the smaller shoe impressions of Sadie. Jim glowered upon them; his lips came firmly together, and with the impetuosity of youth, which brooks no restraint, he set his party in motion again. But when another two hours had passed Sam declared that the fugitives were still far ahead.

"Yo watch de hollows de horses make," he said to Jim, inviting him to join him on the ground. "It rain hard for ten minutes two hours ago, yo remember."

Our hero had not failed to recollect the fact. It was one of those little cloudbursts so often experienced in the neighbourhood. A sharp, heavy shower had fallen, and then the clouds had cleared away as if by magic, leaving a fine sky, with the sun floating in it.

"But how can you say from that shower that they are still far ahead?" he asked the little negro.

Sam screwed up his eyes before he answered, and then bent over one of the hoof impressions.

"Dere's water here, in de hole," he said. "Suppose no hole, den no water. Run 'way along de ground. Ebery one of dese marks here when dat shower come, and de water fill um. Yo not tink dat? Den look here; dis horse go close under a tree, where de sun not manage to reach. What now do you tink?"

Jim was wonderfully troubled. He had often read and heard of the ways of trackers, and had imagined the art not so difficult; but here was a poser. Jim showed him the hoofmarks of one of the beasts ridden by the fugitives, pointing out that they lay beneath the shadow of a tree, and asked him wherein lay evidence that the fugitives were far ahead. It was a conundrum; he shook his head impatiently.

"Read it for me, Sam," he said, "and quick about it. How far behind them do you reckon we are?"

"Tree, four hour p'raps. I tell like dis; dese marks here two hour ago, when de rain fall. Dat sartin'; but yo look at de water in de holes. Where de sun able to reach it it almost gone, sucked up into de sky. Dat take little time, longer dan two hour. Under de tree de holes full to de top, 'cos dey dere like de oders when de rain fall, and de sun not able to reach 'em. Dose men travelling quick."

"Then so will we. Forward," commanded Jim.

"Better go slow and sure than fast and knock up the horses," cautioned Phineas, riding up beside him. "Jim, if you'll take my advice, you'll set a steady pace, and keep going at it for the hour together; then give the animals a rest for ten minutes. In the end we'll cover the ground quicker than those rascals, supposing them to be riding on direct without halting."

It was undoubtedly good advice, and our hero took it. He found it hard to curb his impatience, for he was eager to rescue Sadie from such wretches. But he was sensible enough to recognize good advice when it was given, and promptly issued his orders.

"See here, Tomkins," he called out. "You come along with the main party. I'll go ahead with Sam, and one of your men can take your place. Then, in case there's need to change our plans, I shall be right at the head and able to stop the party."

They pushed on after that at a steady pace, covering ground which for the most part was only thinly studded with bush, and stretched out flat and level before them; but some five miles ahead a range of hills and broken ground cropped up before them, hiding the country beyond.

"Perhaps we shall be able to catch a sight of those rascals from the top," thought Jim, as he rode along in a brown study. "In any case there's much to be thankful for. That rainstorm has softened the ground and made it easy to follow; a little more this afternoon, or when the night falls, would give us a fine line for to-morrow."

Some two hours later they emerged at the top of the hilly ground, still on the tracks of the fugitives, and at a sign from Sam dropped from their horses.

"Stop here," he said at once, raising a warning hand. "Not show up above de skyline, else p'raps dem scum see us. Yo wait little while for me to squint all round; but not t'ink I be able to see um. De bush down dere very dense."

It was precisely as he had said, for as Jim laid himself flat in a tangled mass of brier on the summit of the ridge, and wormed his way forward till he was able to obtain a clear view beyond, he saw that the country down below was green with jungle. A vast sea of waving treetops lay below him, broken only here and there where rocky ground effectively opposed the irresistible march of creepers and verdure. The sight was, in fact, most beautiful, for the leaves shimmered and displayed a thousand different shades of green beneath the sun's rays, while, far off to the left, there came the gleam and scintillation of light falling on water.

"De lagoon," declared Sam without hesitation, tossing a finger to the front. "Not able to see de entrance, ob course, 'cos it too far away, and trees hide um; and not able to see where de riber lie for de same reason. But dat de lagoon. Sam stake him hat on it."

"And those men we are after?" asked Jim, his eyes searching every foot of the huge green vista.

"Dey down dar somewhere. Not see um wid all dose trees; but dere fo' sure. To-morrow we come up with them."

Our hero lay for a while gazing all round and thinking deeply. The sight of the lagoon shimmering and flashing beneath the sun had reminded him of those natives with whom the two rascals they had formerly followed had struck up an acquaintance. Jim remembered that it was more than a simple acquaintance, for it had since been proved that Jaime de Oteros and his gang of evildoers had for long carried on an illicit trade in guns and spirit with the tribe in that neighbourhood. Obviously they were making in that direction to join hands with them, and, once there, how was Sadie to be recovered?

"It will be harder than I imagined," he told himself despondently. "Once these men reach the natives with their prisoner, nothing but a battle royal and the defeat of the tribe can save her. If only I were near enough to come upon them before they could reach their friends."

Again he lay silent and thinking, till Sam looked at his young master wondering. "Not good lie here and stare," he said. "Dat not de way to save de missie. S'pose we make right way down de hill and get into the jungle. Dey down dere, I say. To-morrow dey come up wid the black men we fight wid way ober by de lagoon."

"And once there Sadie is almost lost to us," cried Jim, a tone of bitterness in his voice. "See here, Sam, I'm going to make a big effort. Tell me, can those fellows travel once the night falls? Can they push on towards those natives?"

"Dat not easy," came the answer. "Sam not tink dey try to do so. For why? I tell yo. What fo' need hurry when dey tink no one follow? Back away near de canal dey ride fast, 'cos p'rhaps someone discober where dey gone, and follow quick; but dey seen no one to-day. Dat I sure ob, 'cos dere tracks have never stopped fo' once; so dey t'ink dey got heaps ob time and all de jungle to demselves. Why den hurry, and bash de head against a tree in de darkness? Dat not good enough fo' anyone; dat all tommy nonsense."

"Then I shall do it."

Jim stretched his head farther from between the brambles and stared down into the jungle beneath, as if he were trying to penetrate it to the tree roots. As for Sam, the little fellow started, and looked queerly at his master, as if he half thought that anxiety and excitement had unhinged his mind; but Jim returned his gaze coolly, and once more repeated the statement.

"Then I shall do it," he said. "Listen here, Sam, and tell me what you think of the idea. You admit that these men will camp for to-night, satisfied that they are not followed, and that they can easily reach their native friends to-morrow. Once there, you can see that Sadie will be surrounded, and that rescue will be almost impossible. Well now, I'm going to push along through that jungle as quickly as horses can take me, and as quickly as the undergrowth will allow. This evening, the instant night falls, I shall go on on foot, taking the lantern. There's not much danger of the light being seen with all those trees about, and there is a good chance of being able to come up with the fugitives. If I do, I'll snatch my sister away, and return towards our party, who will mount and ride at the first dawn."

The little negro gasped as he heard the plan outlined. It was not that the danger of such an attempt staggered him; it was the shrewdness of the suggestion. He pinched himself as punishment for not having produced it himself, and turned upon his master with a flash in his eye which showed his pleasure.

"By lummy, dat fine!" he cried. "Dat de only way to do um. S'pose dem scum camp as I say—I shore dey do it. But s'pose dey don't, and ride right on, den no harm done; but if dey camp, den yo have de one chance of savin' missie. Ob course I had to go with yo; yo not able to follow de trail widout Sam. And Tom extry strong, and able to creep along right well, in spite of his size; besides, he able to carry missie once we have managed to rescue her. Den Ching know de ways ob de jungle; he mighty fine fighter. Him——"

Jim stopped the garrulous little fellow with a movement of his hand. Suddenly his finger shot out from the brambles, and he pointed towards the huge sea of waving palms and forest trees, all thickly clad in green. But it was not the jungle to which he drew Sam's attention; it was a wide patch of yellowish-white that cropped up amidst the green some miles away, direct in the line of the lagoon.

"Watch that spot," he ordered curtly. "I saw something moving, but the distance is too great for me. What do you see?"

Eagerly he awaited the answer, but it was more than a minute before the negro ventured to open his mouth. He plucked Jim by the sleeve and drew him backward, sliding through the briers himself as if he were a snake.

"Dat extry lucky," he suddenly whispered, when they had withdrawn from the skyline, and as if he were afraid someone beyond would overhear him. "Dat special fortunate, I tell yo. Fo' down dere on dat patch am de mens we follow. Yo see de little game, eh? Not see um? Den I gib yo dere reason. Dem scum now well away from de canal, and ride hard all de while. Dey say to demselbes: 'Stop little bit here, let de hosses hab a rest while watch de hill. If police follow, den sure to come by de way of de tracks we leab. Good! We see um come ober de hill. If dey come, we mount and push along; if not, take him easy, ride 'way on a little, and den sleep."

"Then we will take good care not to show ourselves; but advance we must," cried Jim. "See here, Sam, find a way over for us where we can pass without anyone being able to see us. If necessary I'll push on with a small party afoot and leave the horses to come later; but I'd rather take the whole lot on their mounts, because then we shall be able to get nearer to those ruffians. Look around and choose a likely spot."

He crept back to the party, while the negro stole off along the ridge, keeping well away from the skyline. In ten minutes he was back with them, his face shining under the sun, a hopeful smile on his lips.

"Come 'long, and lead de hosses," he whispered. "Sam make along de side ob de hill and find a place where we can slip to de bottom; but not ride. Ground very rough and full ob stones and holes."

They followed him in silence, each man leading his own horse, while the huge Tom led also the beast which carried their blankets and ammunition. And a very business-like party they looked as they filed away amongst the bushes; for each one carried a rifle slung across his shoulders, the muzzle sticking up well above his head, while a pouch attached to the belt about his waist was filled with cartridges. Khaki clothing was chiefly worn, for since the British introduced the colour many nations have adopted it for their uniforms. Water bottles were slung to the belts, and every member of the band was provided with a revolver.

"Best take 'em," said the Major, just before the expedition started. "I grant that a rifle is useful most anywhere; but there are times when it is apt to get into the way, and in case such a time should turn up you'd better carry shooters."

"Halt! Not come too fast," said Sam suddenly, when he and Jim had arrived at a rocky crevice which broke its way into the side of the hill. "Plenty hole-and-corner 'way in here, and mind yo go very careful. Yo Chinaboy, don't yo smile as if yo was clever'n anyone; yo hab a bad fall if yo not extry cautious."

A grim smile lit the usually saturnine face of Tomkins, the surly policeman; and indeed anyone could have been excused for merriment. For Sam's importance, his high-flown language, to which we cannot here venture to give outlet, and the quick way in which he flashed round upon the harmless Chinaman, was most amusing. However, Tom quickly silenced the little fellow.

"Yo leab dis Chinaboy alone," he cried, looking fiercely at Sam, but showing his teeth in a grinning smile for all that. "Yo look to yoself, little man. If dere holes way in dere, p'raps yo fall into one; den lost fo' good. No Sam to be found. All de boys call out hooray! Yo get along, young feller."

That set Tomkins grinning more than ever. To do the man but common justice, he was an excellent fellow at heart, though his taciturnity and the shortness and crispness of his remarks made people consider him to be surly. No one saw the humour of the thing sooner than he did, and no one was more ready to smile. He turned upon the two negroes a scowl which would have scared them, had they not been accustomed to the constable,

"See here, you two sons of guns," he cried, "there'll be something bad happenin' ef we have more of your lip. Get in at it; we ain't here to listen to darkies chatterin' as if they was monkeys."

Sam glowered upon the man, and looked as if he would be glad to do him an injury; but Tom gave vent to a roar, and, dragging his horses after him, stood to his full height within a foot of Tomkins. It looked for a moment as if there was to be a fracas, for the two men, white and black, glared at one another furiously; but no one could expect the jovial Tom to wear such an expression for long. He burst out laughing, and, swinging round, placed himself side by side with Tomkins.

"Oh, yo heard dat?" he called out. "He tink us like monkeys. Den yo say, Massa Jim, who de most handsomest, Tom or Tomkins."

But Jim was in no mood for jesting. He sent the huge Tom to the rear with an impatient movement of his hand, and then bade Sam push forward. A moment later he was following, holding his horse by the bridle. For the next half-hour silence again settled down upon the party, though in place of the sound of their voices there came the slither of hoofs on rocks, the crash of boulders falling, and now and again a sudden exclamation as a man just saved his animal from falling; for the gully which Sam had found and selected was rough, to say the least of it. Probably in the wet weather it was nothing but a watercourse. Now it displayed huge holes where the rains had washed the soil away, while every few feet the members of the party had to negotiate boulders, sometimes causing their animals to squeeze round them, and at others having to urge them over the obstruction. Finally they all arrived at the bottom, where they were thickly surrounded by jungle.

"Forward," said Jim at once, seeing the whole party mounted. "I suppose the first thing is to get back on the track, and then ride for that yellowish-white patch where we saw figures moving. Perhaps we'll get there before those rascals leave; if not, we can but follow."

Some three hours later, after making but slow progress through a jungle which was very dense in parts, and after having crossed a stream, the bed of which was soft and boggy, they came to the rocky part where no vegetation had succeeded in growing. It was almost dark then, and experience told them that within a few minutes it would be impossible to see more than a foot or two before them; for in jungle countries, even under a brilliant moon, the shadows beneath the trees are of the densest. No light can penetrate those thick masses of leaves and the thousands of gaily flowered creepers which cling to the branches. Here and there, perhaps, where the leaves give back from one another, or where a veteran of the forest has fallen to the ground, some few rays will filter through, making the trunks beneath look strangely ghostly, but for the most part there is dense darkness, the kind of darkness which one can almost feel.

"Here we camp for the night," said Jim, slipping from his saddle. "Tomkins, I am going ahead with the two negroes and the Chinaman. I leave Mr. Barton in charge of the whole party remaining; but of course, if there is fighting, you will handle your men. See here, I'm going to try to come up to the camp those fellows will have formed and snatch away their prisoner. Whatever happens, ride at the first streak of light and follow our tracks; we'll take good care to make them clear and open. Tom shall blaze the trees as we pass."

Some fifteen minutes later, having meanwhile partaken of a hurried meal, Jim, with Sam and Tom and Ching, slipped away from the little camp where their friends were lying. For a minute, perhaps, the gleam of the lamp that Sam carried remained visible; then the jungle swallowed it effectually, so that presently our hero had disappeared entirely. He was gone on an expedition which might bring success or failure, and which in any case meant danger for him and his little party.

CHAPTER XVII

On the Track of Miscreants

To those who have had no experience of the jungle, who happen never to have passed a night in such tropical forests as those which clothe the ground about the Isthmus of Panama, the deadly silence that pervades everything is perhaps the most noticeable feature of all. It is almost terrifying in its intensity, and with dense darkness to help it is apt to awe even the boldest. And when, as happens so often, that silence is suddenly and most unexpectedly broken by the call of some prowling wild beast, when a sharp hissing sound and a rustling amongst the fallen leaves near at hand tells of a creeping snake, then indeed the nerves tingle, the novice feels a strange sensation about the roots of his hair, while perspiration gathers thickly on his forehead. Yes, the bravest are awed. Even the old hand, the experienced hunter, holds his breath and halts to listen, his senses all alert, ready to defend his life against danger.

So it was with Jim and his friends. One only was accustomed to the jungle; and for a while, after diving into its darkness, they were overawed by its deathly silence at one moment, and at another moment by the weird calls which came to their ears. The lamplight shining on Tom's face demonstrated the fact that he was trying to smile; but it was an uneasy and an unnatural movement.

"By de poker," he gasped, "but not like dis at all! De leaves whisper murder. De branches ob de trees call out and say: 'Take care'. Tom all ob a shiber."

"He, he, he! Yo not like him, dis forest," grinned Ching, though, to tell the truth, the Chinaman's slanting eyes were moving restlessly from side to side, in a manner which denoted fear. "Yo hold de hand ob dis Chinaboy; den feel braver. No harm come when Ching near. Yo come along wid me, Tom."

His bantering tones caused the huge negro to change his smile for a scowl. He stretched out a hand and slowly doubled up the fingers, as much as to say that he could with pleasure take the Chinaman in one hand and crush the life out of him. He began to exclaim, but Jim cut him short. Our hero brushed the sweat from his forehead, and swung round upon the two.

"Silence, you babies!" he exclaimed. "A sound travels far in the jungle, and who can say how near we are to those villains we are searching for? Silence! Follow in single file, and take care that you do not tread on fallen branches and twigs. I have often heard it stated that the snap of a broken twig can be heard as plainly as the report of a pistol. Guess it's true, too."

"But dere no fear jest now, Massa Jim," interrupted Sam, his little eyes twinkling in the light of the lamp which dangled from his finger. "Still, all de same, dat lubber ob a Tom better take care and keep him mouth shut. Him never can speak soft; him shout and bawl. Him a great, big, hulkin' bull, I reckon."

That brought the big negro to the point of explosion. After all, it was an event of every day for these three faithful fellows, who had clung so well to Jim, to banter one another, and for that bantering to turn mostly against Tom. It was the fate of the ponderous fellow often to be the butt of his comrades, to provide them with a ready cause for wit at his expense, and always with the certainty that Tom would swallow the bait and lash himself into a pretended fit of anger, in which he threatened terrible things, gesticulated, and roared, and often enough shook his huge fists and bared his fine white teeth in a manner which would have disturbed the courage of a bold man, but which, with Ching and Sam, who knew him so well, or with our hero, merely resulted in roars of laughter and in further banter. However, this was not the time for such fun and frolic, and Jim put a stop to the noise promptly.

"Come," he said; "guess we've got Sadie to think about. That's better than badgering one another."

At once there came a serious look across the faces of his followers. Their eyes shone more brightly, while Tom gave vent to an exclamation, striking himself across his broad chest at the same moment. "I's ought ter be kicked," he said indignantly. "Yo see, Tom not say anoder word till missie found. But den, ha! yo take care, Tom smash dem rascals. Knock 'em all into cocked hat; make jelly and jam ob dem."

All his pretended ferocity was turned upon the rascals who had abducted Sadie; and to look at him as he spoke there was no doubt, remembering the huge negro's prowess in former scuffles, that he would be as good as his word. But Sam was already moving ahead, and Jim fell in immediately behind him. With the Chinaman as third man, and Tom bringing up the rear, the party pressed on as rapidly as possible through the forest. Nor did Sam seem to find any difficulty in holding to the track. His sharp eyes were bent for ever on the ground, while his lamp swung this way and that, lighting the hoofmarks made by the horses of Jaime de Oteros's party. And as they went, Tom, armed with a heavy knife, blazed the trees to the left, to afford a guide to those who were to follow. It was half an hour before the silence amongst them was broken; then Sam came to a sudden stop, and drew Jim towards him.

"Dey get off de hosses here," he whispered. "Jungle growing so low, dey couldn't sit in the saddle any longer. Now, yo watch extry close, and I show yo what happen. Here one, two, three, yes four ob de scum. Four ob de villain, sah, and here am anoder mark. Dat missie; yo see how small it am? Den I's sure dat missie. She walk between de rascal; two go in front, each leading a hoss. No; one ob dem hab two hosses. Den missie; she not hab a hoss. Den two oder blackguard, one wid two hosses."

It seemed clear enough to Sam, though for Jim the reading of these elusive signs was a somewhat different matter; but by dint of following Sam's indicating finger, and with the help of a little imagination, he was able to make out the various signs. Indeed, once the whole had been shown him he began to wonder how it was that he himself had failed to light upon them at once. However, a couple of hundred yards farther on, when they came to a halt once more, he was again at as much of a loss as before, and was glad to have Sam's help to read what the ground beneath the jungle had written upon it.

"Six hosses," he said. "One for each of the four men, one for Sadie, and a spare."

"For de swag," suggested Sam. "Dey's robbed de people ober at Ancon."

Jim remembered the fact, though till that moment he had lost sight of it; for all his interest was, very naturally, centred in Sadie. In his eyes that was the maximum offence Jaime and his rascals had committed.

"We'd best go very quietly now," he whispered to his companions. "If they have dismounted, as the marks show, and if the jungle continues to get thicker, as we can tell for ourselves is the case, why, guess they'll soon come to a halt and camp. That'll be our chance."

"Halt any time," answered Sam, stopping for a moment and facing round with brightly shining eyes. "Dey camp when dey find de right spot. Not care to lie out here in de jungle. Dat not do; p'raps some beast come along and gib trouble. Dey wait till dey find an open place, den spread de blanket, boil de kettle, eat, and sleep. Sam know; him libed in a jungle country before now."

He was filled with assurance, fortunately for Jim and his comrades, for otherwise there was no doubt that without a guide they would have lost the track and themselves many times before this. Seeing the difficulty of making a straight path through this trackless forest, it became evident to Jim before long that Jaime and his comrades, like Sam, must have had experience of the jungle. Indeed, had he but been aware of it, the ruffian who commanded the rascally band was an excellent leader in more ways than one. Putting aside his vindictive and cruel nature, which seemed natural to him, the man was exceedingly clever and cunning, as he had proved to the police of many a port along the Gulf of Mexico. But he was as accustomed to the wilds as to a city, and had indeed during the past two years found that safety, complete security from arrest in fact, lay in the jungle. He had made himself at home in it, had discovered the ways of trackers, and, thanks to his own hardiness, had so far defied fever. He was, then, just the man to lead a band across the isthmus, and the straight line which his trail had held all along showed that no novice was at the head of affairs. But in one particular he failed. Jaime had been too successful; he had for so long successfully hoodwinked the police, and had robbed with such little interference, owing to his wonderful astuteness, that he had become too sure of himself, and, as a natural consequence, had become careless. At this very moment he imagined that no one was in pursuit. He had waited on that open patch of ground where Jim's comrades were at this moment encamped, and had kept a watch on the top of the ridge. The fact that he had seen no one crossing it had convinced him that all was well, that the scheme of the boatman who was to put to sea from Colon had again put the police on a false track. And at once he had neglected further precautions.

"We'll jest run ahead through the jungle," he told his followers, "till we've put a good belt of it between us and the ridge. Then guess we'll take a fine sleep, and so be fresh by the time we come to the end of the journey. Gee! What a commotion there'll have been 'way down by Ancon! That explosion fairly shook the whole isthmus; but why Juan never came along is more than I can say, onless he was captured."

"Or blown sky-high with his bomb," ventured one of his fellows.

"Blown up by his own bomb! Don't you think it," came from Jaime. "Juan is too clever by half to do a thing like that. Most like he found himself cornered, and unable to come to our meeting place; so he's lying hid up somewhere, and when he gets the chance will make across to join us. See here, boys, we'll take a fine rest when we get to those natives. We'll lie up for a month, till things get blown over a little, and until people have begun to forget that dollar notes were taken; then we'll get aboard the launch, steam out from the lagoon, and take one of the passing traders. There won't be no difficulty about that. Guess we're armed, and the folks aboard the traders don't carry a weapon. Once we've got a boat, we'll sail to the nearest port, tranship to New Orleans, and from there to France. Paris will take every dollar we have, even though the numbers of the bills have been published. In six months' time we shall have enough to make a tidy sum for each of us when the stuff's divided."

He led his little following through the forest till they arrived at an open, rocky space, where the blackened ground showed that a fire had been made on a former occasion. Indeed it was a spot which Jaime knew well, for he had travelled this route many times now. Here saddles were taken from the horses, while the beasts were given a drink at a tiny stream which trickled from the rocks; then they were tethered to long ropes, which would allow them to graze. Sadie was not treated unkindly. Indeed, hardened villain though he was, Jaime had some pity for the child. He had her placed near the fire, and saw to it himself that food and drink were given her.

"You'd best get settled down in one of the blankets and take a sleep," he advised. "I ain't goin' to put any ropes on you, and I'll tell you why. If you were to try to make off into the jungle, you'd just get lost, and there's wild things in the forest that would scare the life out of you; so be sensible, and take a sleep."

Sadie was, in fact, far too frightened by her surroundings to venture to move. To speak the truth, the trying scenes through which she had passed had practically unnerved her, though the child had plenty of courage; but she was a sensible child too, and saw the futility of attempting escape at this moment.

As to Jim and his little band, they had no idea where the party they were in pursuit of had camped, if, indeed, they had camped at all. They pressed on slowly through the jungle, Sam leading with the lantern, and Tom bringing up the rear, slashing a tree every few paces as he passed. It was perhaps an hour later before the little negro came to a sudden halt, and lifted his head in the air.

"Smell hosses!" he whispered, snuffing at the breeze for all the world as if he were a dog. "Sartin sure I smell hosses!"

Promptly his hand went to the lamp and extinguished it. Jim heard the catch click to, and found himself in utter darkness. But though he held his head erect, and sniffed with all his power, he could detect nothing but the strong, aromatic scent of some tropical creeper clinging to the trees near at hand, and supporting from the finest tendrils some magnificent blossoms.

"Horses? You're sure?" he asked.

"Sartin sure," came the confidant whisper. "Listen to dat!"

Through the silence of the forest there came of a sudden a dull cough, and then a loud neigh. It was followed by a second, and then, faintly to Jim's ears, but with startling loudness to Sam's, there came the sound of stamping.

"I'se tell yo all about it," whispered the little negro. "One ob de hosses restless; de flies trouble him. He cough fust ob all, den he neigh. Now he stampin'. Dat all simple, simple as A B C. But him very close; too close. S'pose dem scum hab seen de lantern."

They crouched in the jungle in death-like silence for the space of ten minutes, fearful lest what Sam had suggested were the case; but though they listened there came no other sound than the stamp of the restless horse which had first attracted their attention—that and an occasional cough from the same animal.

As to Sam's statement that he could smell horses, a statement which must have been true, and which had undoubtedly saved Jim and his party from blundering into the enemy's camp, our hero could not even now detect the characteristic smell. Nor could Ching nor Tom.

"But dem dere all de same," whispered Sam, chuckling at the recollection of his own sharpness, "and precious near too. What yo do, sah? Wait here and listen."

"No; I shall creep forward at once. We'll all go, for if we were to divide we might never find one another. Wasn't there a moon when we started?"

Sam took his young master by the sleeve and pulled his arm towards the right, to a spot where the trees gave back from one another, and a long ghostly stream of pure white light broke in from above and bathed the tree trunks.

"What dat say?" he asked. "Yo can see fo' yoself dat dere's a moon; but down here dark as a ditch, black as de hat. Out in de open splendid light; see to read if yo like to."

"Then we may be able to see them. Lead along, Sam; clear the ground before you as much as you can."

They set forward again, this time on hands and knees, and slowly, inch by inch, approached the clearing where Jaime had made his camp. Not that they could see it yet; but Sam proclaimed the fact that they were nearer with his usual assurance.

"Tell dat by the sniff ob de hosses," he said shortly; "anyone can say dat fo' sure. In ten minute yo see dese scum, and den know what to do."

True enough, that number of minutes brought the whole party to the edge of the jungle, though as to their knowing how to act, that was a very different matter. Jim stared out into the open, and saw there five figures, huddled within a few feet of one another, wrapped from head to foot in blankets. Farther away were the horses, half-hidden in the shadow cast by the far edge of the jungle, while to one side was a pile of bags and kit, amongst which were the saddles. And little by little, as the scene unfolded itself to our hero, and from gazing at the whole he was able to concentrate his attention on each individual item, he was able to decide which of the five figures was that of his sister.

"She lies to this side of what has been a fire," he told himself, "while those rascals are on the far side. That is in our favour at any rate; but to reach her will be a bother. How's it to be done?"

Once more his eyes passed round the clearing. They went from the figure of Sadie to those of the band of ruffians, and from the latter to their saddles and other possessions. Then they passed to the horses, and so round the edge of the clearing till he found himself leaning far out from the undergrowth and staring into the faces of his own followers. There was Sam's, his eyes twinkling as ever in the moonlight, every feature denoting eagerness, while the broad line across the forehead, and beneath the tattered peak of his dirty cap, seemed to show that he, too, was puzzling his brains as to how to act. And there was Ching's Oriental countenance next to Sam's, the slant-like eyes gazing upon the scene as if it were one of the most ordinary, as if he could see nothing before him to arouse unusual interest, nothing to disturb his accustomed equanimity. The man was actually toying with the end of his pigtail, as if he could find nothing better to do. But who could really read those features? Not Jim, nor Sam, nor Tom; not even a European accustomed to China and its natives. The face was inscrutable those blank, immobile features hid a mind which, for all its seeming somnolence, was working fiercely, relentlessly, and shrewdly to provide a solution for this difficulty. For Ching was possessed of a doglike faithfulness; he would gladly have given his life for that of "the missie" or for that of his master. And Tom—what did his expression show? The thick lips were moving as Jim looked, while the alæ of his wide nostrils were dilated widely, pulsating as if with excitement. The usually merry, childish face was set with an expression so severe that our hero was astonished. It brought a gulp to his throat as he suddenly realized to the full what he had known now for so long, that these three men were such true comrades. Then back went his eyes to the figure of his sister.

"I'll risk it," he whispered to himself. "I'll creep out there and bring her back with me. But supposing they awake, supposing Jaime or one of the others suddenly sits up and lets drive with a shooter?"

His hand dropped to the butt of his own weapon, and for a while he crouched in silence. Across his mind there flashed a scheme which might help. There were the horses; he could send Sam or Ching across to them and cut them adrift. He could make it appear that an attack was to take place from that quarter. Then he banished the idea just as swiftly.

"Wouldn't do," he told himself; "they'd sit there in the centre and shoot. They would still be close to Sadie, and could hit anyone who attempted to reach her. It's got to be done in some other manner."

He did not forget that Jaime and his comrades had already a reputation as marksmen. Now that he and his fellows had actually reached the gang, and were so near to success, Jim swore that he would not ruin everything by acting hastily. Better, far better, sit there for a while than act on the spur of the moment and lose his own life and that of his helpers in place of effecting a rescue. It was Ching who came forward with a cunning suggestion.

"Not move now, Massa Jim," he whispered. "Dey not dead fast asleepee. Yo waitee little while, den creep in, and Ching come along wid yo. We go round to de top side ob de clearing, and creep along de hollow. All open here; but dere, shut in; keep away de bullet."

Jim stared in the direction indicated, and made out by the shadows that a hollow ran across the rocky ground from the northern side, till it actually reached the edge of the tiny camp which harboured the sleepers. In fact, though he was ignorant of it at the moment, this was the watercourse which, beginning still farther to the north, at the foot of some rough rocks, carried a stream right across to the southern side of the clearing. Instantly he decided to follow the advice given.

"See here," he said, calling his three comrades round about him till their heads were as close as possible. "Ching has given good advice. I shall go across to the far side in the course of an hour. That should be giving them long enough to get dead sleepy."

"Dey sleep like pig den," agreed Ching. "Not wakee so easy."

"Then I shall creep along that channel, and Ching with me. You two, Tom and Sam, will lie just here, where you can see everything, and will be ready to shoot if there's trouble. But I hope there won't be that; we ought to be able to retire up that gully without disturbing the gang. If they do rouse, we shall still have a good chance, for the sides of the channel will protect and hide us. So bear this in mind, even if they suddenly get up, don't shoot unless you see that they have discovered us in the gully. Then pepper them for all you are worth."

"Golly," exclaimed Tom, his eyes wide open with amazement, "dat a real fine business! But what yo do supposin' dey discober yo?"

"I shall creep back along the watercourse or gully, whatever it happens to be, while Ching will fire at the ruffians. Then we will all come along here. Don't forget that, once we are hidden in the jungle, silence is most required. A noise would bring bullets."

The three heads nodded vigorously, while muttered exclamations came from the negroes. Then Sam asked a question.

"Yo and Ching creep along way ober dere. Dat right," he said. "Yo wake de missie, and go back extry quick. Dat right also. What Ching do?"

Jim was ready with his answer, and flashed it at them. "Ching goes for a special reason," he said. "I happen to have had a report from the police major before I left Gatun. You will remember that a huge number of American notes were stolen. They were tied in bundles, and wrapped in waterproof paper, then the bundles were locked in boxes. Jaime and his villains broke the boxes and carried away the bundles. If those two objects out there are not the very ones we are talking of, why, call me a donkey."

Out went his finger and he pointed to the piled-up saddles and other articles which the gang had brought with them in their flight. The moon fell clearly on them all, giving every item a sharp outline; but it fell darkly on two of them, for the simple reason that they were covered in black material. Without doubt the bundles were those containing the notes filched from the Commission offices, notes which Jaime and his rascals hoped to convert into silver dollars one of these days, and so procure a fortune. Tom gasped, Sam's eyes looked as though they would fall from his head, while the Chinaman gave vent to a sniggering giggle.

"Yo am velly cleber, Mass Jim," said Tom simply. "Dem bundles de swag fo' sure, and, by lummy! me see what yo up to. Yo goin'——"

"Ching is going right now to bring 'em along with us," declared Jim in an excited whisper. "If we can take Sadie from 'em, why we'll rob the rascals of their booty also, I guess. And, gee! won't they be mad when they discover what's happened. But, boys, see here. Our job is to get away and leave them none the wiser. We want to clear off through the forest back to our people, for you may be sure that Jaime and his men will be mad when they learn how they've been fooled. So silence is important, and you'll see to it."

As if by common consent they ceased whispering to one another, and for the better part of an hour lay still in the jungle, only their heads protruding. And during all that time not one of the blanketed figures lying in the open moved so much as an inch, though there was an occasional snort or a gentle stamping from the horses.

"Guess it's time," said Jim suddenly. "Those fellows haven't moved an eyelash since we watched, and there's not a doubt but that they're properly wearied and worn out by all that they've been doin'. Tom and Sam, you know what's wanted. Give us a whistle as we come back, and then be ready to make off through the forest."

They wasted no more words. Jim went off at once on hands and knees, and, discarding the shelter of the undergrowth, made his way just within the margin of the clearing. After him came Ching, his pigtail gathered into a round coil beneath the billycock hat that he always insisted on wearing, and which, indeed, has for long been a favourite with the Chinaman. Otherwise the man was dressed in his native costume; for here, again, the wily Chinee shows his astuteness. Indeed, John Chinaman has proved to himself that his own clothing is infinitely more comfortable than European when he is located in a hot climate, and he adheres to it rigidly. Not a sound did the man make as he crept along, while Jim could not have been accused of want of caution. He carefully set aside all sticks and stones, and all fallen leaves, and never moved unless he were sure that the path was clear before him. All the time, too, he kept swinging his eyes round to the centre of the clearing. It seemed ages before he and his companion reached the northern side; but at last they were at the point where their attempt at rescue was to begin in earnest. At their feet lay a pool of water, and from it a gully some four feet deep ran right out into the open.

"Couldn't be better," whispered Jim. "We can get along on hands and knees, or wade through the water; but I hope there's little of the latter, as the splashing might be heard. Don't forget, Ching; once I have my sister, you snatch the bundles."

He waited to see the Chinaman nod, and then at once pressed on into the gully. Within a few seconds he had an agreeable surprise. Only a tiny stream was trickling down the very centre, insufficient, in fact, to cause any splashing, though the size of the gully itself, its smoothly worn walls showing so clearly in the moonlight, demonstrated the fact that when the rains fell, and the wet season was in progress, a torrent went gushing along the channel. But now it was almost empty, while the moon rays, falling obliquely upon one bank, cast a shadow more than halfway across the gully.

"Step along here," whispered Jim, pulling the Chinaman on to the side which lay in the shadow. "And one more warning. Supposing those men suddenly wake, and look around for us. Just lie as still as a mouse until you are sure they have spotted us in this channel. Then it'll be time for shooters."

Once more the Chinaman nodded, and the moonlight falling on his face at that moment showed our hero, if he had had any doubts, that here he had a most excellent ally. For the same expressionless features gazed at him. There was not so much as the smallest trace of fear or excitement about Ching, the Chinaman.

"Forward!" Jim whispered the word, and promptly proceeded along the edge of the channel. Bending low, so that he was altogether hidden, he halted every ten paces, to glance across at the motionless figures of the robbers; but there was not a movement from them till he was within some fifteen feet of his sister. Then, suddenly, one of the figures rolled over. A moment later the man was sitting up, still swathed in his blanket. He leaned his weight on one hand, and cast his eyes in a wide circle round the clearing. A horse stamped heavily, and coughed, and at the sound the man slowly shook the blanket from him. Jim watched as he dropped the covering and climbed sleepily to his feet. The fellow gazed at the moon, and then, as if the soft, silvery light had affected him peculiarly, stretched out his arms widely, rose on his toes, and yawned loudly. At that a second figure moved. The man rolled over; then, to Jim's relief, he snuggled down into his blanket, as anyone does who has been disturbed, and who desires to rest further. In a moment he was as motionless as formerly.

"Gee! Jaime of all people," said Jim suddenly, beneath his breath. "That's bad for our business. I thought I recognized the rascal."

His hand went to his revolver, for he was tempted to use it; then he sank still lower into the gully. For Jaime it was who had risen; the rascally leader of the band stretched himself and yawned again in the moonlight. He drew something from a pocket, and, to his disgust, Jim saw that he was rolling a cigarette. Indeed the Spaniard was never awake but he was smoking. The habit had grown upon him so that now once his fingers were idle they always slipped into his pocket. It was a marvel to watch how nimbly they plucked the shreds of leaf, how they rolled the whole to a correct length and thickness, and how rapidly a cigarette was completed. In less than a minute now there was one between his lips. Jaime stepped slowly across to the blackened ashes of the fire, stirred them with his foot, and selected a brand from the very centre. It did not even glow red, but he managed to obtain a light from it. Then a horse coughed suddenly, and once more Jaime swung round.

"Flies at them," Jim heard him declare. "Nothing more; there's no one but ourselves hereabouts."

He strolled to and fro for some ten minutes, while Jim's impatience grew almost unbearable; then he stood regarding the bundled blanket beneath which Sadie was sleeping. A moment later he stepped across to the two parcels which contained the stolen notes, and a gleam of triumph swept across his bearded features.

"Riches!" he growled. "The finest haul we have ever made. If things go on like this America'll find it'll cost her a heap more to build that canal than she looked for. Helloo! That horse again. It's flies for sure."

The same beast stamped again, and whinnied. Jim could see its legs moving. It swayed to one side, and bumped into the next animal, causing the latter to kick and squeal angrily, while the one who had caused the commotion responded with a savage bite which caused the other poor beast to squeal again still louder. The noise and commotion set Jaime off in their direction. Jim watched him as he sauntered down towards the horses, and waited till he had reached them.

"Ready?" he asked, swinging swiftly round upon the Chinaman. "Then forward. Seize the bundles; I will take Sadie."

In an instant he had crept from the gully, and with Ching close behind him slid at once towards his sister.

CHAPTER XVIII

Rescue by Moonlight

"Golly! Him must be mad! Yo see him? Yo see de master come out ob de hollow den? By de poker, but him scared right clean off him head. Sam, I tells yo him mad. Him blind; him eberyting yo like to think ob."

The huge negro Tom gripped at the ground on which he lay with his strong fingers, and writhed beneath the covering of undergrowth. His staring eyes passed from the crawling figure of Jim to that of the Chinaman, and then slid away to regard the horses on the far side of the clearing. Back they came to Sam's face, as he lay beside him, and there they rested eagerly, as if seeking some consolation. But the little negro was just as scared as Tom. He, too, had watched the figure of Jaime de Oteros rise from its blanket, he had kept his eyes on the robber chief as he stretched and yawned beneath the moon, and more than once Sam's hand had slid down to his revolver. Then he had stared at the man as he strolled away towards the horses.

"Now," he told himself, "am the time for Massa Jim." And then a second later: "No. Not do now. Dat scum turn and see um; then not hab time to creep away. Hab to rush, and dat spoil eberyting. Yo stop still and shut yo ugly mouth," he exclaimed, turning angrily upon his comrade. For the over eager and less crafty Tom was grunting and groaning as if he were in pain, and Sam was fearful that the sounds might betray them. "Yo lie still dere and wait till yo's told to speak," he commanded. "Little bit more, and yo wake ebery one of de rascal; den see Massa Jim cut to pieces. Fine dat, eh? yo great big silly."

Tom nearly exploded with anxiety for his young master and indignation at Sam's words. He stifled his groans with difficulty, and, so as to hold himself in as it were, and keep control over his feelings, he dug his fingers deep into the ground, and tugged heavily. Meanwhile Jim had not been idle. With an eye always on the horses, and the figure strolling round them, he stepped briskly across from the gully, his back bent double, his figure close to the ground. It seemed an age before he reached the blanketed figure which he believed to be Sadie, though as a matter of fact only a few seconds had passed. He was in the act of stretching out his hand to touch her when Ching suddenly arrested the movement.

"No, no, no," he whispered urgently. "Not missie; look at de boot."

Jim did so, and the sight staggered him. He went pale for the instant; for the boot was large, and bore a spur at the heel. It obviously belonged to one of the miscreants, and distance had deceived him as to the size of this figure. Hurriedly he looked at the others. One turned, the one nearest to him, rolled over on its side, and then suddenly sat up. The blanket fell back from the head and shoulders, and then, to his delight, there was Sadie, her long hair streaming about her shoulders.

"Sadie, Sadie," he whispered ever so gently, and to his surprise, instead of showing astonishment, his sister merely smiled at him, shook off the remainder of the blanket and stood up. "Come," whispered Jim. "Come with me."

He beckoned to her, and, stepping swiftly across to where she stood, took her by the arm. Within a minute he was hurrying her into the gully which had allowed him and the Chinaman to approach so close to the group without danger of being seen.

THE RESCUE OF SADIE

"Jim, I knew you'd come," whispered Sadie bravely, clinging to her brother as if he alone stood between her and the miscreants who had taken her from Gatun. "Ever since that horrid Spaniard came to Mr. Phineas's quarters and forced me to accompany him, I guessed that you would follow and rescue me. But, oh——"

She was beginning to sob, now that the greatest part of the danger seemed to have passed. Her voice trembled; but Jim silenced her firmly and kindly.

"Hush!" he said. "Not a sound, lest they hear us. Guess we've friends close at hand, and in a little while we shall be with them. Stop here a moment; we must wait for Ching."

He peeped out of the gully and watched the Chinaman bending over the bundles that contained the precious notes which Jaime and his comrades had stolen. Then he found it hard to repress a shout of warning; for the figure which he had taken for that of Sadie, the man wearing the boot with the spurred heel moved. Then the man sat up suddenly, and rubbed his eyes. A moment later he was regarding the Chinaman's back, endeavouring, no doubt, in his half-awake state, to determine who it could be. As for Ching, he seemed to have forgotten all about the gang of desperadoes. Jim could have kicked him for being so irritatingly slow, and to all appearances careless; but he could not read the thoughts passing through the Chinaman's brain, nor guess what it was that delayed him. A moment later, however, he became aware of the fact that if his follower were to carry out the orders given him he must bear away from the enemy's camp more than had been arranged for. For the two dark-coloured bundles were wound about with rope, through which a chain had been passed, and the latter had been locked to an iron bar passing across the top of a form of pack saddle. As Jim looked he saw Ching whip out a knife, and deliberately set to work to sever the strands of rope. But by then the man behind him was fully awake. He started to his feet with an exclamation, that caused Ching to swing round on the instant. A second later a shot rang out, and our hero saw his follower stagger backwards and tumble across the bundles.

"Stay here; don't move an inch," he commanded Sadie. "I'm going back to help him."

But whatever help he could have given would have been useless to the Chinaman by the time Jim could have arrived; for the rascal who had fired followed up his attack by rushing towards the fallen Chinaman. Jim saw him bend down swiftly, and then, just as swiftly, he went reeling to one side; for Ching had risen. Like a greyhound set loose he sprang upon his enemy, and the moon shining down upon the whole scene flashed upon something in his hand. Ching had used his formidable knife. The Chinaman, it appeared later, when he was able to give his tale, had merely feigned to be hit. He had waited for the man to come closer, and then had stabbed him. Now he finished the work he had begun with a swiftness which was appalling. He was close to his man in an instant, showing an agility of which Jim had never suspected him capable before, and quick as a flash the knife went home, sending the robber thudding to the ground.

"Back! Run!" shouted Jim, for there was now no need to keep silent. "Back here, and let us get to cover quick!"

"I coming, allee lighty," came the laconic answer. Ching swung the two bundles across his shoulder, bearing the pack saddle with them, and ran swiftly across to the channel; but as he ran the two remaining figures beside the blackened ashes of the fire sprang to their feet, and shots rang out loudly. There came a loud thud as one of the bullets struck the pack saddle, then Ching was out of range.

"Allee lighty, Massa Jim," he sang out coolly. "Ching here; him follow."

And our hero waited for no further information. He took his sister by the arm and hurried her along the gully.

"Bend low," he urged her as they came to the end. "Then run into the jungle; I shall be just behind you."

In a moment or two they were speeding across the open, across the rocky ground which intervened between themselves and the forest, and with a gasp of relief Jim felt that the branches and leaves had closed over them.

"You there?" he demanded of the Chinaman.

"Allee lighty, massa," came the laconic repetition.

"Then lead the way; you know it."

He gripped Ching by the end of his pigtail, for the Chinaman handed him that article promptly, realizing, perhaps, that it was well suited for the purpose; then, holding Sadie with the other hand, he followed close on Ching's heels. In that order they came within a few minutes to the spot where Tom and Sam were lying.

"Missie! De Lord be praised!" exclaimed the former with a sob of relief, taking the child in his arms in his delight at her deliverance. Then he swung her up on to his shoulder in preparation for the flight which must now commence. As for Sam, though none the less demonstrative where Sadie was concerned, he knew well enough that the safety of the party depended in no small measure on him.

"Massa Jim," he called gently. "Dis way; yo come 'long o' Sam. Him hab de lantern all ready lighted, and hidden way ober here. Yo come right 'way at once, before dem debil see yo. Dey makin' dickens of a hullabaloo."

Jaime and his comrades were indeed creating an abundance of noise, and for a while amused themselves by blazing away with their weapons into the forest. And, as fortune would have it, the leader of the gang went within an ace of being slain by one of his own following; for it will be remembered that a fit of restlessness had caused Jamie de Oteros to rise from his blanket and go down towards the horses. The crack of his comrade's revolver had set him running back towards the camp, and it was at that critical moment that a second follower, springing to his feet, and as yet not fully awake, nor alive to the circumstances of the matter, took him for an enemy and fired point-blank at him. With a shout Jaime reached the man, and floored him without hesitation; but being unable to trace at the moment what had actually happened, or where those who had intruded in the camp had disappeared, he joined his fellows in firing wildly in every direction. Then, with an angry shout, he stopped the fusillade.

"This won't help us," he exclaimed. "Let us decide what has happened. Ah, Pedro is killed! Strange, he often had an idea that a man would stab him. I saw a man dressed as a Chinaman strike at him."

"It was a Chinaman," declared Miguel. "I saw him distinctly. I fired direct at him, but the bullet drilled a hole through the pack saddle."

"Pack saddle, man! Pack saddle!" shouted Jaime, a horrible suspicion crossing his mind. "What do you mean?"

Miguel felt frightened for the first time for many a day. Jaime glowered at him and toyed with his revolver, as if he would willingly shoot him if his answer were not satisfactory; then he blurted out the truth. "Why, the pack saddle with the two bundles of notes chained to it," he said sullenly. "The Chinaman stole them."

"And you let him go free! Gurr!"

Jaime stamped in his anger. He kicked the ground as if it had done him some injury. Then he stepped across to the spot where the five figures had been stretched when Jim and his friends first looked into the clearing.

"The girl?" he demanded. "She has gone too? With the Chinaman?"

"With another man. I just caught a glimpse of him; he was standing in the centre of the hollow that carries the stream."

Slowly the matter dawned on Jaime in its true light. He came to see that this attack was not what he had at first suspected—a sudden raid made by natives living in the forest, a raid led by some stray Chinaman, who had taken service with them. It was an organized raid, an attack made by those men from Colon. In a flash he realized that his carefully laid schemes had come to naught, that his track through the forest had been discovered, and that already his enemies were about him. The thought sent the blood flying from his swarthy face till the skin looked ashen grey and lifeless. He growled out violent exclamations beneath his breath, and for a while paced to and fro restlessly. Then—for custom is so strong that few can resist it—the fingers of his right hand dived into his pocket, and within a moment he was rolling a cigarette.

"I see this," he said at last, when the weed was lighted, and he had puffed some clouds of smoke into the air; "the men who just now took the girl away, and stole our money, were not strong enough to capture our whole party. We were but four, so that we may argue that their numbers were no greater. It follows that if we get on their track and pursue we may find ourselves the stronger party, and so may retake our possessions. I will tell you something. I feared some sort of trouble, and before we set out on this journey I forwarded a warning to our friends the natives. I asked them to come towards the zone, so as to meet us. They will not be far away; to-morrow we may meet them. Then they will pick up the tracks of these rascals and follow. To-morrow will be soon enough, for none but a native can pass through the forest swiftly in the darkness. Besides, these men who attacked us will be tired; and, also, they have the girl with them."

In the course of a life which had been evilly spent almost from the beginning Jaime de Oteros had met with much good fortune. On this occasion he seemed to be in luck's way as much as ever. For those two shots fired in the clearing had reached the ears of the party of natives waiting his arrival, and to his huge relief they put in an appearance within some twenty minutes of Jim's retreat into the jungle.

"Get the lamps lighted at once," commanded Jaime, beckoning the native chief to come to him, and addressing him as if he—Jaime himself—were king of the race. "Now, my friend, let us have the best trackers, and put them on the trail of these people. There must be no delay; take care of that. I'll give fifty guns, with powder and bullets, if we retake the girl and the booty these rascals stole from us."

The promise of such a rich reward caused the chiefs eyes to dilate, and at once he set his men to accomplish the task before them. Within the space of a few minutes the sharp eyes of the natives had discovered the track made by Jim and Ching as they escaped with Sadie. Swiftly it was learned that two others were of the party—one a small man, and a second of abnormal proportions. Then the chase began in earnest, Jaime and his comrades following the party, while three of the natives came behind with the horses. So rapidly, in fact, did the trackers amongst the tribe who had come to Jaime's help pick up the trail left by our hero, that but a couple of miles separated the two parties. Indeed, within half an hour of Jim's entering camp, and being greeted by Phineas and the others, Tomkins reported that he had seen a lamp swinging in the forest. Sam declared within the minute that he could hear men moving, while hardly had the words left his lips when a number of men burst into the moonlit opening. There came at once a sharp fusillade, while bullets spluttered about the heads of Jim and his comrades. Then Tomkins shouted, and without a second's hesitation threw himself face downward on the ground, and jerked his rifle into position.

"Get down close, every mother's son of you," he called out, while the lock of his weapon clicked sharply. The butt came to his shoulder, his cheek fell upon it, and then a stream of flame issued from the muzzle. Nor were his comrades slow to follow his example. Before the enemy were halfway towards them all the members of the party save Jim and Sadie were using their rifles.

"They'll never face a fire like that," called out our hero, standing to his full height and watching the horde of natives rushing forward. "Keep peppering them. I will look for some spot where we can get shelter."

He took his sister with him, and clambered towards the centre of the rocky elevation which cropped up in the middle of the clearing; then he shouted again.

"Mr. Phineas," he called out.

"Aye, aye,' came back the cheerful answer. "We drove 'em off easy. Guess they've left a few kicking the dust down there."

Jim had, in fact, seen the swarm of natives, with three white men amongst them, suddenly turn tail and run, and his watchful eye had also observed the figures lying prone not far from the edge of the forest. But he had some intelligence of his own to communicate, and shouted back to Phineas.

"Bring the whole party right away up here," he said. "There are boulders hereabouts which will shelter us and help to keep off their bullets. Make a run for it; bring all our baggage."

He left Sadie in a large hollow on the summit of the eminence, and returned to his comrades. By then bullets were coming thick from the depths of the jungle, and here and there queer little jets of dust spurted up from the ground, while there was a strange whistling in the air. But our hero had been under fire before, and took not the smallest notice of the missiles. He reached the camping ground which he and his friends had been occupying but a short while before, and at once snatched up the two black bundles which contained the store of notes which Jaime and his rascals had stolen. Then, waiting to see that the others were already running up the hill, he followed swiftly, the huge Tom bearing a case of ammunition just before him. Two minutes later all were under cover.

"What now?" said Phineas, wiping the sweat from his forehead. "I never did come across such a fellow as you are, Jim. Always getting into scrapes, and dragging your friends into them with you. But what now? Here we are under cover, and I ain't so sorry. But there must have been fifty of those natives down below, as well as the three white men. Jaime and his crew, I suppose?"

"Jaime for sure, and sorry he'll be that he ventured to follow," answered Jim curtly. "I tell you straight, that fellow has been no end of a bother to me. And now, to add to all the mischief he's done, he deliberately fires at Sadie. Luckily the bullet just missed her. But there you are! I say he'll live to be sorry. I'll teach him a lesson this time that he won't forget."

They were big words, spoken in a moment of intense vexation; but big words for all that, as Jim was the first to acknowledge when his temper had cooled a little. Here was his slender little party surrounded, and the enemy were by no means to be laughed at; for Jaime and his comrades had been busy on those occasions when they had been away from the Panama zone. They had done a big trade in rifles, or, rather, in obsolete muzzle loaders, with which almost every one of the natives accompanying them was armed; while the latter began to prove already that, obsolete though their weapons might be, they could at that range make fine practice with them. Indeed, every second now a ball struck the boulders behind which Jim and his friends were crouching, while before many minutes had passed the shots came from almost the entire circle of jungle. The party who had come to rescue Sadie was, in fact, practically surrounded.

"Which don't say as they're goin' to take us," growled Tomkins, who was endowed with splendid pluck. "Now that we've got this shelter, and each man has selected a spot from which to fire, I guess we'll give a good account of ourselves. But what are the orders?"

He appealed as if by custom to our hero, and Jim answered promptly.

"We lie just as we are," he said. "I see that each one has taken up a position, and the only alteration I can suggest is that the four policemen separate and place themselves between the others. They are used to rows more than we are, and will be able to give advice. For the rest, reckon we'll sit tight."

"Sit tight!" echoed Phineas, somewhat at a loss.

"Just lie as we are, and never give them a shot back unless a man exposes himself. When'll the moon go down?"

It was a question of some importance, and our hero breathed more freely when he heard that the morning would come and still find the moon in the sky.

"Then we shall have light right through," he said in tones of relief. "Don't forget; not a shot unless you see a man. Just lie still under cover. Ching, guess you could manage to light a fire and get some grub cooking."

The Chinaman smiled on them all. Cooking, after all, was his forte, not fighting, though he was no laggard where that was concerned, having already shown that he possessed courage. He rose from his prone position, re-arranged his pigtail, and set about the preparation of a meal for the whole party with just the same calmness and method as he was wont to employ in Phineas's kitchen. Within five minutes he had collected sufficient driftwood to make a fire, and had laid it at the bottom of a little hollow. In double that time he had a billy slung over the flames, so that very soon a most appetizing steam pervaded the place. Then he wagged his head in a manner all his own and declared that the meal was ready.

"And we for it," said Jim, rising from the position he had taken beside Tomkins. "See here, Ching. Dish out an allowance for each man, and bring it to him. It won't do to leave our stations. We'll grub right where we lie, and so be ready."

It was a wise precaution to take, for none could say when the enemy would attempt a second rush. Meanwhile bullets streamed from the jungle, now from this point, and then from that, a splash of flame lighting up the dense shadows for an instant. But of late the firing had become far less rapid, while the characteristic crack of the Mausers which Jaime and his rascals employed had ceased altogether.

"Simply showing that they are otherwise engaged," said Jim, discussing the affair with Phineas and Tomkins. "They are, no doubt, hunting for a likely spot from which to make a charge; and to my mind there's one spot above all others which they are likely to select. Look away over here. This rocky eminence runs on into the jungle, so that a band dashing out there would not have to come uphill. It's level ground all the way. Again, it happens to be a shorter cut from the jungle, and will give us less time to put in our shots. That's my opinion."

Tomkins surveyed his surroundings in silence for some little while, as he ate his steaming rations methodically and unconsciously. He showed not the smallest trace of alarm, though he must have known, better perhaps than any of the others, how desperate were the fortunes of the party. But the man had such a reputation for brusqueness and straight speaking that Jim felt sure that if he disagreed with what he had just expressed as his opinion, Tomkins would promptly say so, and that with the utmost bluntness.

"Guess you'd better make a change in the posts we're filling," he said at last. "Ef there's a rush, it'll come from 'way over there where you've been pointin'.

That bein' so, better fix it to pour in a fire that'll choke 'em. There won't be too much time, and it'll want to be magazines, and shooters to follow if they get within distance. Pity we couldn't place a mine to blow 'em to blazes, or have a gun to shoot direct at the varmint. But guess our rifles'll make hay with 'em; the boys here'll make them niggers sit up lively."

He relapsed into a moody silence, and went on eating his meal, his eyes roving along the edge of the jungle; but he was ready as soon as Jim called him. Our hero placed the four police behind a mass of boulders facing the part from which attack was feared, and then stationed Tom and Sam and Ching behind them.

"You'll just lie here with Mr. Phineas," he said, "and if there's a rush you will be ready to come to the help of the one who's most attacked. You can see that the policemen are three yards good from one another, so that it may well happen that one will be more pressed than his comrades. For the rest, you'll keep an eye all round, and look after Sadie."

Very quietly the men moved into their positions, crouching low as they went, so that the enemy might not see them. Then, each man having selected a niche through which he could fire, and Jim also having discovered one for himself in their centre, all lay absolutely still, awaiting developments.

"Look out for trouble, boys," sang out our hero a good half-hour later. "Their bullets are beginning to come along again, and I should say that we guessed right when we decided their rush would come from over in this direction. Do you hear that? A Mauser for sure, and there's another and another. That shows where the leaders are."

Tomkins, who lay next him, gave vent to a hoarse chuckle. "That 'ere Jaime thinks he's a fine dog, he do," he called back. "See what trouble he took to throw us off the scent from the beginning. Now he's manœuvring a rush, and telling us just where we may expect it because he must go and blaze with his own rifle. Ah! That was a man; I saw him come from the jungle direct before us. Gee! The game's beginning."

The words had hardly left his lips when a couple of dark figures leaped from the cover, brandishing weapons over their heads. An instant later twenty dusky natives had joined them, while in their centre were the figures of three white men plainly distinguishable under the moonlight. There came a loud shout across the clearing; then, as if shot from the same gun, every one of the figures bounded towards the spot where Jim and his friends were lying.

"Magazines," growled Tomkins, dropping his cheek on to the butt of his weapon. "Let 'em have it."

"Fire!" shouted Jim.

Bang! His own rifle was the first to discharge a missile; but the others followed swiftly, and within the minute five men were engaged in sending a shower of bullets at the enemy. Never before had Jim worked so energetically. No sooner was the trigger pressed than his hand gripped the bolt and threw it open. Click! The empty case flew back over his shoulder, while another rose from the magazine as if by magic to replace it. Bang! He pushed the lever home, and down went his eye to the sights so quickly that it never seemed to have left them. As for the enemy, they came forward at an astounding pace, without pause or hesitation. In spite of the number which fell out of their ranks and went crashing to the ground, the remainder came on steadily. Then a second party followed, as if to reinforce their comrades. Phineas gave a shout instantly. "Get along into the firing line, boys," he called to Ching and Sam and Tom. "I'll stop back here and make sure that none are trying to come from behind. Then I'll join you."

"You can go now, Mr. Phineas," came in a quiet voice from close beside him, and, looking down, he saw Sadie, her cheeks pale perhaps, but her eyes and her lips steady. "Go," she said. "I will watch behind you, and will call if there is need."

Phineas gripped her hand promptly, and ran forward. By then his own little party had joined Jim's, and were aiding them with their rifles. Indeed the rattle of the weapons was deafening, while anyone could see that the enemy were suffering. But the natives hardly seemed to know what fear was, while Jaime and his fellow robbers showed splendid pluck. Nothing stopped them. They leaped over the bodies of their fallen comrades, and came racing forward, their eyes blazing, their weapons brandished over their heads. In an incredibly short space of time they were within ten yards of the spot where the defenders lay.

"Time for revolvers," shouted Jim. "Up on your feet—revolvers and clubbed rifles!"

The scene which followed was almost too rapid for description, for the leaders of the attacking party threw themselves on Jim and his men with a ferocity and a quickness which were appalling. Revolvers snapped on every hand, while two of the policemen clubbed their rifles and dealt swinging blows. It was left to the huge Tom to relieve the situation. Rifle in hand, he sprang over the intervening boulders and launched himself upon the attackers with a howl of rage. His huge mouth was opened wide, displaying a set of formidable teeth, while his muscular arms swept the rifle round in huge circles, laying the enemy low for all the world as if it were a scythe. Then he pursued his old and favourite tactics. He hurled the weapon at one of the white men, and, leaping forward, gripped Jaime round the waist. The rascal was whirling in the air in a second, and within the space of three had been thrown into the centre of his supporters.

"Bravo, Tom, bravo!" shouted Jim, rushing to join him, with Ching and Sam close at hand.

The enemy were more terrified by Tom's presence and appearance than by all the bullets. They turned as Jim came forward and fled for their lives, dragging Jaime with them. A minute later the defenders were behind their boulders once more, breathing heavily, while the fusillade of musket balls had again opened from the fringe of the jungle. Still the enemy were not beaten. As the dawn came they showed at the edge of the forest, and with shouts of triumph announced that they had received reinforcements. Indeed, within a few minutes Jim saw that at least a hundred men were crouching just within the shadow. Then there came another shock, which set his heart palpitating.

"More of the varmint," suddenly announced Tomkins, swinging round and pointing to a spot behind the party, where, up till now, they had seen no enemy. "Gee, if there ain't two hundred against us!"

He dashed across the hollow, threw himself on his face, and levelled his rifle. But he never pulled the trigger: Jim stopped him peremptorily. A single figure suddenly pushed to the front of this second mob of natives, and advanced a few paces bearing a white flag. He waved it and shouted. Then, followed by his men, he came running towards Jim and his fellows.

CHAPTER XIX

Jim Meets with a Surprise

It was an exciting and an anxious moment for Jim and his comrades as they saw the strangers bounding towards them, and for one brief instant our hero hesitated, wondering whether he ought to respect the white flag which the leader of this new band bore. He had already arrested Tomkins's intention of firing on them, and now peremptorily restrained the others.

"Stop!" he shouted. "Not a shot. I believe they are friends. Why, as I live, if that isn't a white man at their head!"

But the light just now was not so good as it had been. The moon was waning, and the dawn half broken. In consequence, though the party anxiously watching the strangers from the rocky eminence could make out their numbers, and each individual member of the band, they could distinguish nothing more than that. Phineas drew in a deep breath. He had learned to trust Jim's judgment, but on this occasion he feared greatly that he was making a gigantic error.

"Gee!" he cried in anxious tones. "Supposing they are enemies like the rest. They will cut us to pieces. Get ready to shoot, you men."

"By de poker, but if dey not friends, den Tom talk to them same as he talk wid de oders," growled the negro. "But me tink Massa Jim right; Massa Jim neber make mistake."

It was like the huge fellow to support his young master, of whom he had an absurdly high opinion; but Sam and Ching were just as emphatic.

"Not need fear rumpus any longer," said the former, dropping the butt of his weapon to the ground. "Massa Jim know what him talking about. No flies on him anyway."

"He, he, he! Velly nice for dis party," lisped the Chinaman. "A minute ago me tink soon hab ebelyting ober. Soon be chopped to little pieces, same as Ching chop de meat for de stew. But now ebelyting jolly. Yo see precious soon. Ching knowee well dat dat a white man. Him seen him before; him know de movement of him legs. Him and Ching great friends some time ago."

Could it be true? Even Jim, as he anxiously watched the approaching band, and with no little doubt as to their friendly intentions, could not fail to observe that the leader, who in the dim light had the appearance of being a white man, certainly walked in a manner with which he was familiar. The swift fling of the legs reminded him of someone; but whom? Where had he known that someone? That was the question. Less than a minute later he was staggering backwards as if someone had struck him a heavy blow. As for the strangers, there was now no doubt that a white man led them. A tall, thin young man, with somewhat cadaverous cast of countenance, halted within ten paces of the party, still waving his white banner, and gave vent to a cry of astonishment, a cry which Jim echoed. Then Sadie, half-hidden behind the men of her party, pushed her way resolutely through them, ran forward, and gazed at the man. In an instant she had thrown herself upon him.

"Jim!" she screamed; "it's George, George come back to life! George alive, when we thought he was dead in the jungle."

"IT'S GEORGE, GEORGE COME BACK TO LIFE!"

The meeting staggered our hero. He could hardly believe that it could be his brother, he whom they had lost in the jungle now so long ago. Even the strong grip which George gave him failed to convince.

"How's it happened?" demanded Jim. "We settled that you were dead, that the fever had killed you, and that you had fallen in some hollow in the jungle. Who are all these men here? How is it that you have turned up right away at the very instant when help is wanted? My head is all of a whirl: I guess I'm getting silly."

"Then you needn't blame yourself," came George's answer. "Reckon you'd be a strange fellow if you weren't a little bit overcome by my turning up after you'd given me over for dead. But, see here, Jim; I'm your own brother George right enough, though how it comes that I am still alive and kicking is a long story. As to how I arrived here on time, that's much simpler. The natives I have been living with are at daggers drawn with a tribe over by the lagoon, and have been greatly troubled because some beggarly European rascals have been selling guns and powder to them. For three months past I've been a kind of king amongst them, and of course I've taken steps to have that other tribe watched. Well, we heard that an expedition was coming this way. We shadowed the natives through the forest, and then heard a shot. Later we followed again, and then there was heavy firing. I made out your party from the edge of the jungle, and I reckoned that I would help. Of course I couldn't tell who was in the right. I only knew that the natives who are enemies of ours were attacking a small party, and so I decided to help the weaker side. Here we are, seventy of us in all, and quite sufficient to make short work of those fellows. Now tell me all about the bother."

As rapidly as possible Jim told him how Jaime and his rascally comrades had abducted Sadie, and how he had followed.

"It's a precious long yarn, like yours," he laughed, gripping George's hand for the twentieth time, for even now he found it hard to believe that this good news was actually and really true. "But, to begin with, I took a job on the Panama Canal."

"Won a job is truer, I guess," interrupted Phineas, who was beaming on our young hero and his long-lost brother. "Won a job on the Panama Canal, sir. Let me tell you that this young Jim of yours has done mighty well since you took it into your head to clear off into the jungle. To begin with, he started right off for New York; for he had to find a job somewhere. Then there was a collision. The ship foundered, and I was left aboard her when the crew took to the boats. Jim there swam out and saved me. Give you my word, the risk he ran makes my hair stand on end even nowadays. Of course I was grateful. After all, life's pleasant to a man working on the canal; there's a real interest in it. I offered to get our young friend a job, and house his sister. That's how the business started. He won the job, siree; won it outright and by as fine a show of grit as ever you could come across."

George's sallow, fever-haunted face brightened at the words: he stretched forward a hand to grip his brother's, and then to take that of Phineas.

"It's the one thing that has troubled me ever since I was lost in the forest," he said feelingly. "There was always Sadie, and what had happened to her. I knew that Jim and the boys would stick to her and support her; but the willingness to do so doesn't make it always possible. Guess I owe you a lot, Mr. Phineas, and Jim's my own brother. I always knew he had grit."

"See here." burst in Phineas, who seemed to have suddenly found a loose tongue, "you don't owe me a cent's worth. I'll get ahead with this yarn, for this young Jim ain't likely to give it all. And ef I wasn't to tell every word, there's Tom and Sam and Ching would soon see that the news reached you. Eh, boys?"

In the fading moonlight Tom gave an expansive, seven-foot grin, and wagged his head. Sam's little eyes twinkled brightly, while the Chinaman undid his pigtail, and coiled it again, glancing from one to the other. "If you not guess dat Mass Jim play de game, den you velly stupid, sah," he said. "But you know him from de days when we were all on de salvage boat. Massa Jim a demon to work, and never know what it am to fear."

"Listen to this," went on Phineas, wagging a finger at the three, to silence them. "There were a number of Spaniards aboard the boat that foundered. They fought for the boats, and Jim and Tom had a stand-up fight with them, supporting the captain and crew thoroughly. Well, Jim here knocked a rascal down, who, it turned out, was one of a gang of ruffians who had been infesting ports along the Gulf of Mexico, and who of late had been carrying on their evil practices on the canal zone. This rascal was brought back to Colon with the others, and the gang began operations again. But this particular man imagined he had a grudge against Jim. He deliberately fired at him one night when in my quarters. Of course we followed, that is, Jim and his boys did. They tracked the fellow to a house where the gang were situated, and as a result, when the police arrived, three of the gang were taken, though not until Jim had nearly lost his life. Two got away, and the police followed right away along the coast, across a lagoon to the jungle 'way ahead of us. There was a fight between themselves and the native tribe these rascals had taken refuge with, while the two men were killed or severely wounded. Back comes Jim, takes on a special job on the works, and then gets mixed up with the remainder of the gang. They play all sorts of tricks, and finally rob the Commission offices, and, as a special mark of their hatred to Jim, abduct Sadie. There we are, siree. Right down to the present moment. Jim and the boys went off this very evening, crept up to the gang, and brought away the girl and the plunder. You've seen what followed."

The sallow face of the man who had so suddenly joined the party lit up again, while he regarded his brother in a manner somewhat different from that he had been accustomed to aboard the salvage boat. For then Jim had appeared as only a boy to George. But now it was as a man that his brother found him, a young, strenuous, self-possessed man, who, without a shadow of doubt, had been winning the golden opinion of those with whom he had come in contact. In place of being stranded by his past misfortunes, and finding life a struggle, George had now learned that Jim was prospering, that he had won a lucrative job on the canal works, and later, when Phineas was able to speak further with him, that there were many amongst the officials who predicted that our hero would rise high, and would, when he was a little older, fill a position of responsibility.

"And so you rescued Sadie, and took their plunder from them!" gasped George. "That's a good beginning, and those bodies lying out there show that your party has done well in the attack. Now let me give a little further information. Guess those rascals you followed across the lagoon were wounded only, for our tribe have had certain news that two white men were with their enemies. Guess they've come along with this second party, and have now joined hands with the men you tracked to this spot. Who's leader here?"

Phineas jerked his head in Jim's direction, while Tomkins, who had stood near at hand all the while, grinned ever so little.

"Young, ain't he?" he asked, in his usually blunt manner. "But there ain't no flies on him, siree. He's shown us how to move, has Mister Jim."

"Then what do you propose? Stay here and build up a barricade of stones, or attack the enemy boldly?" asked George.

Jim did not answer for the moment. He knew that even now that his party had been so well reinforced it was smaller in numbers than the enemy. To march out across the open would certainly lead to great loss, for most of the natives with Jaime and his ruffians were armed with firelocks. On the other hand, there was not much to be gained by staying in their present position, for that would carry them no nearer to safety. Unless——

To the surprise of all he suddenly struck his thigh with the palm of his hand, and gave a shout of triumph. He was in the very act of telling those who stood around what plan he suggested, when a rifle snapped from the forest, and a bullet whistled just overhead. Then a storm of balls came swishing out over the open, and were followed by the appearance of the enemy. They swarmed from the shadows, massed in one corner, and then, to the thunderous beat of native drums came racing forward.

"Back to your places," shouted Jim. "Fire as soon as you are in position. George, how many of your men are armed with guns?"

"Thirty at the most; they trust to spears and a long curling knife."

"One more question; did those rascals see you join us?"

"Certain to have done so," answered George. "But whether they have a correct idea of our numbers is an altogether different matter."

"Then line up all the men without guns at the back of the firing party. When I give the word, lead them out against the enemy; we must drive them back whatever happens."

The ten minutes which followed were full of movement, and were, in fact, more than strenuous; for Jaime was desperate. He was furious to have been worsted so easily, and, reviewing the whole affair, it made him tremble with rage when he recollected that all his carefully made plans had come to naught. The greatest blow of all was that the treasure which he had stolen had been taken from him, and that by four men alone, simply because he himself had relaxed his usual caution. It was therefore with shouts of rage that he led the enemy. Dashing forward at the head of some hundred and fifty of them, he urged them on in spite of the bullets which hissed through their ranks. He himself seemed to bear a charmed life; for though Tomkins made more than one effort, he failed signally to bring the robber chief to the ground. Always his bullet struck the man on one or other side, or him who was following.

"Thunder!" shouted the policeman at last, angry at his want of success. "That's the fifth time I've drawn a bead on him and missed. See if I don't do it this time. It's the only thing that'll save us."

He leant his cheek against the butt of his rifle with more than usual care, and pulled steadily on his trigger. Then he jerked the weapon backward with an exclamation of disgust, and rapidly pushed a charge of cartridges into his emptied magazine; for Jaime was still untouched. The bullet intended for him had struck one of his white followers, and those who watched saw the man pitch forward with arms and legs outspread, and come with a thud to the ground. Nor did he move a muscle afterwards. By then Jaime and those with him were within twenty yards of the eminence.

"Ready?" asked Jim, placing himself beside George at the head of his natives, while the ever-watchful Tom came sidling up to him, his rifle gripped in his enormous hands. "Then charge!"

George shouted. A man amongst the natives blew on a horn, while another beat a drum. Then some forty of them launched themselves past the firing line, and fell upon the charging enemy furiously. At once it became evident that the fight was to be one to a finish. The men who had followed George had without doubt the greatest hatred for those others, and for that reason fought with a ferocity which was terrible. Shouts of consternation came from the enemy at their sudden appearance. Men in rear turned and fled, while those in the van came to a halt. Jaime turned and beckoned to them. In the short space at his disposal he threatened his followers. Then he and those with him were overwhelmed. In one brief minute the rush of Jaime and his supporters was converted into a mad retreat, with a band of dusky men in rear of them slashing and cutting desperately. As for Jim and George, they were carried forward by the natives, and, with the lusty Tom beside them, thrust their way far in amongst the flying enemy, striking right and left with their rifles. Nor was Tom satisfied with that. The negro was possessed of enormous strength, and nothing could resist him. He dashed far beyond his comrades, discarding his rifle. His ponderous fists shot out in every direction, flooring the enemy; then, catching sight of Jaime struggling amidst the natives, and possessed, it seemed, with the same terror which had suddenly assailed them, Tom leapt at him, covering the ground in enormous bounds, and easily clearing a path before him. In a trice he was level with the robber, and though the latter turned and endeavoured to bring a weapon to bear on the negro, the gallant Tom was too quick for him. He had him by the collar in an instant, the fingers of his right hand encircled the back of the neck, causing the wretch to drop his revolver and shriek. Then, just as had happened earlier on, the man was swung like a bale into the air, and was whirled above the heads of the others.

"By de poker, but dis time yo not get 'way!" bellowed Tom, mad with excitement. "Yo not get back to dem scum to lead dem against Missie Sadie. See here, me break yo neck if yo move. Me crush ebery bone in yo body. Yo hear dat? Den keep quiet or me pound yo to a jelly."

The miserable fellow was not able to move so much as a finger, so firmly did Tom grip him; and if he imagined that his comrades would help him, he was much mistaken. For they were terrified, and fled back to the forest with George's men hanging on behind them. Indeed, in five minutes there was not a trace of the enemy, save the numerous bodies which lay in the open. There was only Jaime de Oteros, a prisoner now, cringing at the feet of our hero, and looking askance at the panting men about him.

"Now, sah," said Tom, drawing in a deep breath, "not want dis scum any longer. Suppose we hang um straight off and so save heap ob trouble."

"Tie him up fast, and set a watch over him," commanded Jim promptly. "Now George, I'm ready to give you my plan for the future. I was about to do so when the enemy charged. But, first, are they likely to leave us?"

George shook his head promptly, then exchanged a few words with one of the natives who was evidently of some importance. "They will stay there in the forest," he said at last. "They have the great advantage of possessing rifles, and guess they still far outnumber us. So they'll lie there in hiding, and pepper us whenever we show a finger. If we go out to attack them, they will break up and move away; but if we attempt to make for Colon, they will hang on our flanks and kill us little by little."

"Then we'll keep them hanging about in the forest. See here, George," said our hero eagerly. "This party of mine was to be merely a sort of cutting-out expedition. We rode hard in order to come up with this ruffian Jaime, and rescue Sadie. The main party was to steam to the lagoon, and there attack the natives. They were then to endeavour to join hands with us. Seems to me we have an excellent chance of a combined movement. We stay here, and make pretence that we dare not move. Meanwhile you send off a couple or more men to our other party. When could they reach us?"

"To-morrow morning, perhaps a little earlier. Gee, this is a good plan! The head of the lagoon is only a bare twenty miles from us. My men could reach the spot by late this afternoon. Your other party would march right off, and, allowing for the difficulties of getting through the jungle, could be here even earlier than I said. It's a fine move; fine, and will be just the thing to put an end to this matter."

"And your men could start at once, and leave without the enemy being the wiser?"

Once more George appealed to the native chief, and presently returned to his brother. "They shall go at once. We will send two parties, consisting of three men each. They will slip away from this spot without anyone seeing them, and will each bear the same message. They will march back with your people, and will crawl in here to let us know of their arrival."

Jim called Phineas and Tomkins to him, and discussed the plan with them for a few moments. Then, as all agreed with it, George nodded to the native. Almost instantly six men stood forward from amongst the seated throng, their eyes shining in the sunlight, for by now broad day was upon them. A few guttural words were spoken, then, one by one, the natives wormed their way from the eminence. Jim could hardly have believed it possible that men could leave the spot without watching eyes discovering them; but he had never watched such natives as these before, nor seen how it was possible to take advantage of hollows and boulders.

"Gone!" said George, at length, giving vent to a sigh of satisfaction. "Now I suppose we can settle down to the ordinary life of those who are besieged?"

"Which reminds one of breakfast. Ching!" shouted our hero. "Breakfast for our party, and slippy with it," he commanded, when the Chinaman had put in an appearance. "I suppose your natives will fend for themselves, George?"

"They are almost vegetarians," came the answer, "and each man carries sufficient with him to appease a hearty appetite and to slake his thirst. That's the best of their diet. It supplies food and drink at the same moment. And talking of vegetarians reminds me of myself; you remember I was down with fever?"

"And dived overboard when delirious," Jim nodded.

"And swam like a maniac till I reached the jungle. Well, I must have raced through it for a couple of miles or more before I came to a stop. At last I dropped down in the very middle of a camp formed by these natives. I was dead beat, raving with fever, and as weak as a child. By all accounts, too, guess I had hardly a shred of clothing left on me, and my skin was torn by brambles. By good luck, anyway, I had stumbled amongst natives who had met white men before, and had no particular dislike for them. In fact, they have an absurdly high idea of them. They treated me like a brother. They looked upon me from the first as if I were a great chief, and fed me with fruits taken in the forest. And it seems that fever is not unknown amongst them. You see, they don't inhabit the swamp lands, so they do not often come in contact with malaria. Guess they ain't acclimatized to fever the same as other natives who live on the lagoons; in consequence they get attacks whenever they come down to the water, and have learned how to treat their patients. I mended slowly. For weeks I couldn't walk, and had to be carried on a form of stretcher; but I shook off the fever. Life became altogether more pleasant, and though, of course, I was longing to get back to settled parts, so as to rejoin you and Sadie, yet, while I was tied by weakness, I admit that I found life pleasant, and kinder hosts I could not have wished for. At last I was about strong enough to travel, and had already arranged for an escort to take me to Colon when this affair turned up. Gee! It's the strangest thing that ever happened. To think that in place of discovering you in New York, or somewhere in the States, you should have run up against me out in this jungle!"

They chatted for long over their breakfast, Jim learning every detail of his brother's life, while George gathered a good deal of what had happened at Colon. But from Phineas he heard fuller particulars.

226

"You can't expect the lad to talk about himself," he told George. "It's dead against his modest nature. But he's done fine. He's shown real grit from the beginning, and alongside of it a determination to get on and a common sense that was bound to win advancement. He's earning good wages. Jim is well enough off at this moment to offer you a home, and can support you till you also are earning wages. Mark this too: if we come out of this soundly, and Jim gets back to Colon with those dollars, the Commission will have heaps of praise and thanks to give. Shouldn't wonder if it resulted in further advancement. I know he's young; but guess that don't matter. America's a go-ahead country. She don't reckon a man to be a Solomon just because he's old and wears hair on his face, no more than she reckons that a youngster without a line on his lip is clear out of sense. She judges a man by what he does, and gives her favours without thought of years and appearance. Well, here's Jim young enough we'll allow; but he's done things. His name's known better than the Police Major's from end to end of the canal works. He's come out trumps on every occasion, and if he wins home now I say it'll be a triumph."

Let the reader imagine George's amazement at all he heard, for he had always looked upon Jim as too young for serious consideration. And here he was, a man in effect, though hardly come to that station in point of years; but a man for all that, and already occupying a fine position. It afforded food for thought, and for long George sat sucking the stem of the pipe which Tomkins had generously loaned to him. And all the while bullets flickered from the jungle; they clipped corners from the boulders, smashed heavily against trees on the far side of the clearing, or sent spurts of dust into the sunlit air. It was an occupation, in fact, to watch the result of the enemies' efforts, and to speculate on the effect of the next shot. But it was an occupation also which was apt to become monotonous. Men fell asleep, in spite of the bullets, and only wakened now and again when the thumping of a native drum warned of a possible rush; but though the enemy massed at times, and seemed on the point of charging, they never actually came into the open. They contented themselves with more or less continuous firing.

"Which don't hurt a fly, and only makes a chap hungry," said Tomkins, as he lay on his back in the shelter cast by a boulder. "But guess we shall want to be careful once the darkness comes. If there's a bright moon it'll be right enough; if not, there'll be ructions."

The hours dragged by slowly, and at length evening arrived. Jim looked overhead anxiously, and noted that thick banks of clouds were floating in the sky, while the moon would not rise for two hours.

"It'll be dark in an hour," he said, stretching himself beside Phineas and his brother. "I've been talking to Tomkins, and he agrees with me that the most dangerous time will be before the moon rises, which means that the enemy may attack immediately night comes. Have either of you a suggestion to offer?"

"Just this," answered George. "As soon as it is sufficiently dark we'll send my fellows into the jungle across there. They'll be back within five minutes with as much firewood as we want. Then we'll lay a pile some twenty yards from our position, and so all round this eminence. Once in position we'll set fire to them, and the glow should last till the moon helps us."

The scheme found approval with Jim and Phineas at once, so that, as soon as it was dark enough, George sent a dozen of his natives creeping into the forest. They were back within a few minutes, and at once others helped them to place the wood they had brought in piles all round the eminence. The last match was being lighted when the silence of the forest was suddenly broken by the beating of a drum. And then a horde of natives launched themselves into the clearing.

CHAPTER XX

Success to the Panama Canal

Even in the machinery shops at Gorgona Jim had never listened to such a din as came from the charging enemy as they burst from the cover of the forest; for a dozen native drums were being thumped, horns were sounded, while each individual shouted and shrieked at the pitch of his lungs. It seemed, indeed, as if Jaime's followers imagined that the racket would scare the defenders and help them towards victory. The giant Tom, standing over the captive, saw his eyes scintillate, while Jaime half rose to his feet; but in a moment he was cowering again. Not because Tom scowled at him, and stretched forth a hand, but because the native placed to guard him flourished his long knife before the prisoner's face.

"So, yo know what to expect if yo try to escape," said Tom. "I leave yo wid dis friend while I go to teach those scum manners. Yo move one little piece, and see how nicely he cut yo to tiny bits."

He indicated the native with a wave of his hand, then went off to the firing line, swinging his rifle as if it were a toy and weighed but a few ounces. Meanwhile the defenders had opened fire upon the enemy.

"Steady does it, boys," sang out Tomkins, who was a tower of strength to Jim and his friends. "Use your magazines, but see that every shot tells. It don't do to fire and miss every time. Let each bullet find its man. It'll bring them to a halt sooner than anything."

But there are limits to the powers of such a small force as Jim commanded; for though George's natives who were armed with guns blazed at the enemy, it was clear that they missed their aim more often than not. Then, too, the light was tricky. The flickering flames cast by the circle of fires served to show the figures of the enemy; but here and there were black shadows, and the rifles had to catch their men as they raced across the lighted parts. In consequence the host of attackers soon approached the eminence on which the defenders had taken their stand. They were abreast of the fires in two minutes, and, at a shout from Jim, George prepared to launch his second party of natives at them.

"Wait till they have almost reached us," cried Jim; "then let them go. Call to the others who are firing with their guns to join in the charge. This time every man will have to be employed."

The situation was indeed very critical, for the enemy had advanced in full strength, while the fitful light had helped them. In the space of a few seconds the leaders were within a yard of the boulders behind which Tomkins and his party were lying, and rifle practice was no longer possible. George shouted. His natives gave vent to a hoarse bellow, while the man with the drum thumped it madly. Then some seventy black figures leaped over the boulders, and there began a hand-to-hand contest, the ferocity of which can hardly be described. The two bodies of men, attackers and attacked, swayed this way and that. Some of the enemy even managed to leap over the boulders and gain the inner circle, only to be shot down instantly by Jim and his friends. Then, when matters had become desperate, and the din was deafening, shouts were heard from a distance. Sam dashed up to Jim, his face working with excitement, his eyes blazing.

"Friends comin', sah," he bellowed. "I see dem run from de forest. Dey charging from behind; dey policemen."

Whoever they were, the rear ranks of the enemy quickly discovered their presence, and turned to face them. Then across the clearing there came the sound of cheering. A loud command rang out, and in a trice a strong body of men had hurled themselves against the enemy. Not a shot was fired; for to have done so would have been to have risked shooting Jim and his party. But long, gleaming bayonets were at the ends of the rifles, and the strange weapon played havoc with the natives. The shouts of those in rear reached their comrades in front, and caused them to turn away. Then, for some five minutes, the enemy were caught between two forces, George's natives using their knives with terrible purpose. A few moments later and those of the enemy who were left turned tail and fled to the forest, pursued by volleys.

Have you ever heard excited men cheer, men who had hardly expected to be alive at that moment? That is how Jim and his men cheered. They set the jungle ringing, they dashed out into the open and wrung the hands of the Police Major and his party, and then they sat down and roared at the antics of George's natives; for the latter were filled with triumph. Undoubtedly they had fought most bravely, and had proved the salvation of Jim and his tiny party; but in doing so they had gained their end. They had broken the power of the tribe which had threatened to molest them, and which had been so plentifully supplied with muskets by Jaime and his men. George's hosts had broken their power for evil, and had themselves now become possessed of the weapons; for the enemy had cast them to the ground as they fled.

"Gee! What a sight!" cried the Major, as he surveyed the scene, now that the moon had risen and lighted the clearing. "There's a heap of men killed, and I'm told that amongst them are four white men. But Jaime isn't there. The scoundrel who led the robbers, and caused all this trouble, has had his usual good fortune, and managed to get away."

Jim smiled, and winked in Tom's direction. Then he nodded to Ching, and at the signals the two fine fellows darted away to the back of the camp.

"Major," said our hero a moment later, as he saw Tom and Ching returning, "allow me, first of all, to present you with a prisoner. He is Tom's capture, and was snatched from the midst of his men. Allow me to introduce Jaime de Oteros."

His pluck evaporated, all his assurance gone, Jaime stood with Tom's grip on him as if he feared that the next moment would be his last. His knees knocked together, his lips trembled, while his shifty eyes looked askance at the negro.

"Dere you am, sah," cried Tom, lifting his prisoner by the arm as if he were a toy. "Dis am de scum dat cause all de trouble, dat dare to capture missie."

For a full minute the Major regarded Jaime; then he spoke quietly.

"Jim," he said, "it's you who should have the post of police superintendent, for this is a most important capture. Tom, too, has done finely; finely, I say. But in capturing this man you give us the opportunity of bringing him to his deserts, and so making absolutely sure that no other people shall be victimized. More than that, perhaps, you give the Commissioners a chance through him to recover the money he has stolen."

Jim signalled to Ching, and at once the Chinaman approached the party, his pigtail swinging out behind him. On his broad shoulders two black bundles were supported, and these he dumped upon the ground at the Major's feet without the smallest ceremony. Indeed he might have been handling merely a parcel of clothing.

"Why! What are these? Where's that description?"

The police officer dived into an inner pocket, but Jim saved him the trouble of referring to the description of the missing property. "See here, Major," he said, "Ching and I had a bit of fine fortune. When we crept into Jaime's camp to rescue my sister we brought away at the same moment these two packages. We knew the dollars stolen were wrapped in black waterproof paper, and we guessed clean off that these were they. Since then I have opened both in Mr. Phineas's presence. There ain't a doubt as to what they contain."

The Major could have hugged our hero. His delight was more than evident. The sight of the recovered treasure took his breath away, and sent him spluttering and coughing. Then he began to laugh. He rocked from side to side, holding his flanks, till the tears ran down his cheeks. And Tom joined in with him. The huge negro's face broadened, his mouth expanded till it was a veritable cavern, then he bellowed with laughing, shaking in every limb, and almost knocking the breath out of his prisoner's body.

"Gee! It do take eberyting, don't it, Major, sah?" he shouted, when at length he could control himself. "Here am dis scum dat cause all de trouble. Him ride off from de canal works tinking he made fools of all ob us. But he hab to reckon wid very wise people. Massa Jim dere to stand in him way, and yo too, sah, I reckon. See what happen. All him friends killed, and, lummy, dat a good t'ing for 'em. Missie am taken from de ruffian, and den, on top of all, he lose ebery one of de dollars. Oh, dat too sweet altogether! Him should be very happy now, for when him hanged he hab nothing to lose but him life, and dat ain't worth countin'."

The huge fellow went off into another loud guffaw till Jim stopped him. As for the Major, he had now become more serious. Warmly he congratulated Jim and his comrades on their prowess, while George came in for a particular friendly greeting.

"Guess there'll be shouts when we get back to the canal works," he said at length; "and the sooner we go the better. Are your party too tired to march in the morning?"

"They'd rather set out soon than stay here much longer," came the answer. "We've still some hours before morning, and if you and your men will settle matters here, and see to the burial of those who have been killed, my party will take a sleep, which will put them on nicely. It will be the first time many of us have closed our eyes since we parted from Colon."

A little while later a number of figures were snoring in their blankets, while the natives whom George had brought aided the Major's party. Wounded men were attended to. Palanquins were made for those amongst their number who were unable to walk; and fortunately there were only three in the Major's party, while Jim's had come through the ordeal scathless. As to the men who had suffered damage amongst George's natives, arrangements were made for them to stay in the clearing till their comrades returned. At an early hour on the following morning the whole party set out for Colon, a dozen of the police going by way of the lagoon, where they would pick up the long launch which had brought them, while the rest—Jim and the Major amongst the party—rode through the forest. About noon on the following day they reached the summit of a ridge overlooking Gatun, and at once cheered loudly.

"Ain't it a sight for sore eyes?" cried Phineas, his face shining in the sunlight. "You'd hardly expect to see men 'way over there, working as if time was pressing. But see 'em. Gangs at the dam, gangs on the railway, and hundreds hidden from sight in the valley, or 'way up at Culebra. And watch the smoke from the diggers, the locos, and the drillers! It's good to think that it's all American, and that things are going smoothly."

"Thanks to the fact that a rascal has been captured," ventured the Police Major. "Don't forget that, please. The best of energies may be brought to naught if there is a rascal secretly at work attempting to wreck matters. Things were getting to look bad when our prisoner made his last little effort. But Jim has seen to that. Say, lad, was it a section you were bossing?"

Our hero coloured and admitted the fact as if he ought to be ashamed of his advancement.

"Ah, well," went on the Major, smiling slyly, "guess there's other billets going! But there's Gatun: I'll send the sergeant along with Jaime to the station, and then we four will ride to Ancon. There I can report, and hand over the dollars."

Need the reader wonder that the return of the party caused a huge sensation? Indeed the excitement nearly caused a stoppage of work along the zone, a matter almost without precedent. For the hustle and perseverance of the white employees is something out of the ordinary. The fever to press on with an undertaking in which their own personal honour becomes, sooner or later, helplessly involved will hear of no delay, and thrusts aside all obstacles. But the news 'phoned up and down the zone was really too entrancing. Jim's name was soon on every man's lips, while even stolid officials cheered when they heard that the gang of robbers was destroyed, the leader captured, and the dollars recovered. Besides, Sadie was back again, and that caused the utmost satisfaction, her abduction having roused the anger of the workers. A week later found Jim promoted to a still more responsible position, while a reward in money was handed to him, and to his three trusty servants. With the help of Phineas and other people George obtained a post amongst the employees, and should you happen to call in at the isthmus, there you will find him and his brother, as eager as their comrades.

For strenuous work is the order of the day, and every day, along the fifty miles of works. Let Americans not forget it. Let those who can, pay a visit to their kith and kin slaving at the vast project their country has commenced on, and bear in mind that the spirit of dogged courage, of common sense and energy, which won advancement for the hero of this narrative, is possessed by one and all of the workers. For those others, the more numerous body, who for business reasons and others are unable to visit Panama or Colon, we say, let them obtain the fullest information as to the giant canal which is building there. The day is coming, is indeed getting very near at hand, when America will achieve a triumph, and when it will behove each and every citizen to know every detail, so that the boys and girls of the race, the future citizens of America, always eager for knowledge, may be told how the triumph was accomplished, how thousands laboured and slaved for years far from the sight of their fellows, and how by dint of superhuman effort, by astuteness and most praise-worthy perseverance, they brought their task to a successful termination. For ourselves we long for the day when we may board a steamer and voyage on her decks from the Atlantic up through the giant locks of Gatun to that vast lake which will extend to Obispo, and from thence steam through the cutting at Culebra, finally descending through the locks at Pedro Miguel and at Milaflores to Pacific level. We look forward to that great day, knowing that none will admire more than we shall the work which Jim and thousands of others will have helped to accomplish. As for Jim himself, we wish him all prosperity. He is a true American. Idleness he does not know, while a strenuous life attracts him. Our hero is made of the stuff which forces difficulty and danger aside cheerfully, and which points without hesitation the road to success.

The End

www.ingramcontent.com/pod-product-compliance
Lightning Source LLC
Chambersburg PA
CBHW060617290526
45793CB00001B/55